Forgotten Freedom
No More

Protecting Religious Liberty in Australia

Analysis and Perspectives

Edited with an Introduction by

Robert Forsyth and Peter Kurti

CONNOR COURT PUBLISHING PTY LTD
PO Box 7257
Redland Bay QLD 4165
sales@connorcourt.com
www.connorcourtpublishing.com.au

ISBN: 978-1-925826-80-7 (pbk.)

Cover design by Karla Pincott

Printed in Australia

Dedicated to Greg Lindsay, founder of the Centre for Independent Studies in 1976 and a determined defender of liberty in Australia.

CONTENTS

CONTRIBUTORS

Tanveer Ahmed is a psychiatrist and author.

James Allan is Garrick Professor of Law, TC Beirne School of Law, The University of Queensland.

Michael Bird is Academic Dean and Lecturer at Theology at Ridley College Melbourne, Victoria.

Benjamin J. Elton is Chief Minister of The Great Synagogue, Sydney, New South Wales.

Henry Ergas AO is an economist and columnist for *The Australian*.

Lorraine Finlay is a lecturer in the School of Law at Murdoch University and an adjunct senior lecturer at the University of Notre Dame (Sydney).

Robert Forsyth is a Senior Fellow in the Culture, Prosperity and Civil Society Program at The Centre for Independent Studies, and the former Anglican Bishop of South Sydney.

Peter Kurti is a Senior Research Fellow in the Culture, Prosperity and Civil Society Program at The Centre for Independent Studies.

Rocky Mimmo is Founder and Chairman of the Ambrose Centre for Religious Liberty

Paul Morrissey is the president of Campion College, Sydney, New South Wales.

Patrick Parkinson AM is the Academic Dean and Head of School for the TC Beirne School of Law, The University of Queensland and chair of Freedom for Faith.

Julian Porteous is the Catholic Archbishop of Hobart , Tasmania.

Michael Quinlan is a Professor of Law, Dean of the School of Law, Sydney at The University of Notre Dame Australia.

Augusto Zimmermann is Professor and Head of Law at Sheridan College in Perth, Western Australia and President of the Western Australian Legal Theory Association.

In the future days, which we seek to make secure, we look forward to a world founded upon four essential human freedoms. The first is freedom of speech and expression--everywhere in the world. The second is freedom of every person to worship God in his own way — everywhere in the world.

- Franklin D. Roosevelt, 1941 State Of The Union Address "The Four Freedoms" (6 January 1941)

We are a diversity of creatures, with a diversity of minds and emotions and imaginations and faiths. When we claim freedom of worship we claim room and respect for all.

- Robert Menzies, The Forgotten People and Other Studies in Democracy (Sydney: Angus & Robertson, 1943), 22-23.

[T]he two freedoms — freedom of expression and freedom of religion — are fundamental to the whole idea of democracy.

- H. V. 'Doc' Evatt, circa 1944, quoted In Brian Galligan, A Federal Republic : Australia's Constitutional System Of Government (Melbourne : Cambridge University Press, 1995), 98.

FOREWORD

I am delighted to be asked to write this forward. A book of this kind plays an important part in the public debate around religious freedom and its related freedoms — of speech and of assembly.

All three freedoms are acknowledged universal and fundamental human rights. However, Australia has no legislative enactment that enshrines these fundamental rights. Religious liberty in Australia is protected by way of exemptions within state-based discrimination laws or equal opportunity laws.

Freedom of speech *per se* is an implied constitutional right in the context of political speech. However, freedom of speech is also restricted to the extent that defamation laws may impact on speech in some cases. Further, some discrimination laws and race discrimination legislation can limit speech.

The freedom of assembly is subject to approval by authoritative bodies in the context of not unduly disrupting the free movement of others. This applies in particular around abortion clinic safety zones. Some regard — wrongly in my view — this restriction to be an affront to religious freedom.

The public debate on religious freedom has been brought into sharper focus largely, but not entirely, due to the legislative introduction of same-sex marriage. Albeit, it needs stating some of the concerns for religious freedom since the introduction of same-sex marriage may be more speculative — at this stage — than real.

A problem surrounding the issue is the lack of clarity as to the source and nature of religious liberty. Some believe it was the work of the Enlightenment that shone light on religious freedom. Others may believe the International Human Rights Instruments are responsible for discovering the principle of the freedom of religion and the manifestation of religion. But these beliefs are mistaken.

It is well established in human rights and natural law that many religious believers organise their lives around their beliefs. They conduct their daily affairs in accordance with their beliefs. Their religion informs their beliefs and conscience. Laws that require religious believers to act contrary to their beliefs are offensive and coercive.

It is therefore important to emphasise why religious freedom is vital for believers. Many people hold the sincere belief that it is wrong to offend their God by performing an act they believe is against their conscience, or the teachings of their faith or church leaders. In such cases, the state should not act as a coercive agent or instrument to make unlawful a sincere and genuinely-held belief that believers should not wrong their God.

The third century Christian writer known as Tertullian of Carthage coined the clearest expression why coercion is wrong and offensive and an insult to religious freedom.

Tertullian is reported as saying:

> It is only just and a privilege inherent in human nature that every person should be able to worship according to his own convictions; the religious practice of one person neither harms nor helps another. It is not part of religion to coerce religious practice, for it is by choice not coercion that we should be led to religion.

Tertullian, of course, was referring to the persecution by the Roman authorities of those turning to Christianity and away from the Roman gods and pagan worship. It was at a time when Christianity was slowly gaining converts from the Roman religion of paganism. To deter such converts, they were persecuted and driven out of towns. Tertullian's reference to "by choice not coercion" that people turned to religion is very apt in modern Australia.

However, note should be taken that we live in a secular country — no longer Christian — and of the reality that religious believers are in numerical decline. Much has changed. It is a justifiable concern that the voices for religious freedom protection do not overshoot the runway for fear that more damage than good may result. Reading media comments calling for stronger religious protection laws for believers is understandable and desirous, but it needs to be measured and considered.

Not every person or organisation that opposes additional religious protection laws is necessarily hostile or antagonistic towards religion. Many people simply do not accept the story about a heavenly God or a spiritual well-being. Many believe religion to be irrational and essentially based on superstition. It is not true to think all opponents of religious protection laws are anti-religious activists.

Such considerations are not examined in a vacuum. When Australia adopted the constitution in 1901, in the order of 90 per cent of the population anecdotally believed in a heavenly God... and perhaps also believed in hell and life after death. It is well to keep this in mind when religious believers — and I am one — campaign for better laws.

What is also true is that religious believers differ. Some Christian churches differ in their views. Some interpret the same message in the Bible differently. The Jewish religion is based on the Old Testament whereas Christians principally, although not entirely, rely on the New Testament. Islam has its own holy book, the Koran. Similarly do Hindu and Buddhists beliefs.

However, Tertullian's advocacy for "choice not coercion" rings true today, and offers a common ground to unite all religions on the principle that governments should not coerce religious believers on matters of sincere and deep beliefs.

The task for a government — irrespective of its political colour — seeking to strengthen religious protection laws, is nevertheless very difficult in coming up with a satisfactory Bill. It would necessarily and sensibly ask itself: If we are to give greater protection to religious believers, then which groups of believers do we target; and which of their teachings requires the protection? If it is not their teaching, then what practices? Secondly, apart from the group of believers, teachings or practices, what is the doctrine upon which they (religious believers) act upon or keep sacred?

The Morrison government has promised legislation to protect religious freedom. A draft Bill has been released and will be further amended before a final draft makes it before parliament.

In the meantime, public debate will be encouraged. This book is part of that public debate. The contributors are learned and informed, and

11

have given us different viewpoints and subject matters for readers to consider, including on the merits or otherwise of a religious freedom act of some sort.

Rocky Mimmo LLM
Founder and Chairman, Ambrose Centre for Religious Liberty

INTRODUCTION

Robert Forsyth and Peter Kurti

Until very recently, religious liberty was the forgotten freedom in Australia.

Although freedom of religion had little formal protection in Australian law, most people didn't know this; and the issue was rarely a subject of immediate cultural or political importance. The right of Australians to practice (in the full sense of term) their faith was a taken-for-granted feature of Australian democracy, and was considered part of Australia's inheritance of British traditions of unwritten rights and freedoms protected by custom and the common law. Given that the vast majority of Australian society was connected to a religious institution — or closely associated with someone who was — there was also little need practical need for formal protection of expression of religious belief.

Religious tolerance — which in practice, historically, often meant freedom from discrimination for being a Roman Catholic — also seemed to be a natural feature of the 'live and let live' egalitarianism characteristic of Australian life. The fair go ethos — which calls on fellow Australians to treat each other as equals and as they wish to be so treated — allowed religious freedom to exist without significant controversy. This was reinforced by the contemporary belief in Australia's future as a multicultural society that welcomed migrants with diverse (that is, non-Christian) religious beliefs.

However, religious freedom is the forgotten freedom no more. Its status and protection has become a contentious issue due to a constellation of social, legislative, and political factors that are exposing religious liberty to real and imminent challenges. Threats to religious freedom in Australia exist particularly due to the actions and inactions of Australian parliaments that have passed laws with major implications for the purpose and future of faith-based organisations. The challenges that now exist therefore pose major questions about the future of Australia as a free, tolerant, and robust liberal democracy committed to upholding the principles of civil society.

A Vulnerable Freedom

It will surely strike many people as odd, or exaggerated, to speak about threats to fundamental freedoms in a prosperous and peaceful nation such as modern Australia. The heart of the issue is that the fundamental right to religious freedom is vulnerable because it formally exists mostly as exemptions to the growing body of anti-discrimination laws introduced by federal and state legislatures since the 1970s.

There are only limited protections for religious freedom under Australian law. Section 116 of the Commonwealth Constitution — known as the establishment clause — constrains the federal parliament from restricting the open practice of religion as well as from making religion part of the law of the land. All other formal protection for freedom of religion is found in far-reaching human rights legislation that was originally designed to prevent discriminatory behaviour based on race, sexual, and gender orientation in the workplace and marketplace for goods and services. These laws also target discrimination on the basis of religion; however, most protections for religious liberty are expressed as mere exemptions and exceptions to anti-discrimination laws.

Religious bodies and organisations are not exempt as such from anti-discrimination law; it is rather that the law makes exceptions on certain terms. For example, the *NSW Anti-Discrimination Act* 1977 (section 56: 'Religious bodies') reads:

> Nothing in this Act affects:

14

(a) the ordination or appointment of priests, ministers of religion or members of any religious order,

(b) the training or education of persons seeking ordination or appointment as priests, ministers of religion or members of a religious order,

(c) the appointment of any other person in any capacity by a body established to propagate religion, or

(d) any other act or practice of a body established to propagate religion that conforms to the doctrines of that religion or is necessary to avoid injury to the religious susceptibilities of the adherents of that religion.

Notwithstanding such exemptions, the new threats to religious liberty arise from the way the scope of operation of anti-discrimination law has extended in recent years to cover more areas of society. This especially applies to the area of sexual behaviour and identity in which broad societal norms have undergone rapid and on the whole welcomed change in the past 50 years. However, the differences between many aspects of mainstream culture that have been modernised and become far more tolerant, and many religious bodies adhering to traditional faith-based views have become more acute, specifically in relation to anti-discrimination law. Aggressive secularism and progressive activism committed to getting rid of exemptions in name of 'diversity and inclusion' threaten the continual existence of those religious communities who find themselves recalcitrant minorities on questions about the nature and purpose of human sexuality especially.

Hence, regardless of the protections enshrined in legislation, freedom of religion is vulnerable to accusations of prejudice, bigotry and discrimination when the views and practices of religious believers conflict with secular norms. The very language of 'exemptions' has the unfortunate effect of suggesting there is an accepted norm from which some religious people and bodies are permitted to diverge and engage in what would otherwise be unlawful behaviour.

These provisions actually are mechanism that balance the right to non-discrimination with other fundamental human rights, such as freedom of religion and freedom of association, as recognised under international law (see next section). Such religious exceptions do not exist for the pejorative purpose of 'excluding' people, but rather to enable religious communities to exist and operate in accordance with their unique cultures and beliefs.[41]

Nevertheless, there is a growing constituency arguing actively for the elimination of religious anti-discrimination exemptions that allow, for example, a Catholic school to discriminate in order to hire teachers supportive of the Catholic traditions. The Australian Greens have long argued for the removal of all religious exemptions from anti-discrimination law.[1] There is no reason to think this pressure will not continue at the state and territory level.[2] This also appears to be the agenda of some LGTBI activists, such as the peak lobby group, Equality Australia (formerly Australian Marriage Equality), which has endorsed the repeal of religious exemptions in state and federal anti-discrimination law.[3]

For religious communities and institutions to continue to exist they need to have the power to select leaders and employees appropriate to the world view and practices of the community or organisation. And to teach members and raise their children in their particular understanding of human life. As the growth of antidiscrimination law and the winding back of exemptions threaten these very powers, so they threaten such bodies very existence.

---

1   This is analogous to the position of political parties that are freely able to maintain their institutional integrity and can refuse to employ persons who do not subscribe to a party's philosophies — without attracting legal claims of discrimination — because political belief or activity is not a protected category or attribute under federal anti-discrimination law. Moreover, under state anti-discrimination law regimes where discrimination on grounds of political belief or activity is illegal, political organisations are granted an exemption. Section 27 of the Victorian *Equal Opportunity Act 2010*, for example, provides that:

An employer may discriminate on the basis of political belief or activity in the offering of employment to another person as a ministerial adviser, member of staff of a political party, member of the electorate staff of any person or any similar employment.

What is Religious Freedom?

To fully appreciate exactly what is at stake in the current debate in relation to the role of religion as a legitimate part of Australian society, it is crucial that the right to religious freedom be properly defined and understood — and especially that it not be understood to simply mean creating the right to discriminate or be a bigot.

The standard, internationally agreed definitions of religious freedom form part of the key United Nations human rights declarations. The understanding of religious freedom promoted under international law reflects the way that liberal democratic nations — given the premium they placed on maximising individual freedom and a flourishing civil society — have sought to eliminate religious persecution by the state and/or its agents by protecting the religious rights and liberties of all citizens, of all denominations, on a basis of civil equality.

Article 18 of the Universal Declaration of Human Rights of 1948 states:

> Everyone has the right to freedom of thought, conscience and religion; this right includes freedom to change his religion or belief, and freedom, either alone or in community with others and in public or private, to manifest his religion or belief in teaching, practice, worship and observance.

Article 18 of the International Covenant on Civil and Political Rights of 1966 states:

> Everyone shall have the right to freedom of thought, conscience and religion. This right shall include freedom to have or to adopt a religion or belief of his choice, and freedom, either individually or in community with others and in public or private, to manifest his religion or belief in worship, observance, practice and teaching.

Two important aspects of religious freedom are clear in these definitions. First, religious freedom is not just a freedom to hold, or not to hold, certain religious beliefs. Importantly is it also the freedom to manifest such beliefs in behaviour and actions. Nor does religious freedom only involve freedom to worship or attend services in church, synagogue, mosque or temple. It involves freedom to live out the religion in daily life.

This reality can be overlooked if religion is, for example, too narrowly conceived in terms of protestant Christianity with its emphasis on belief. In contemporary multicultural Australia, this is more and more evident in the religious life of Hindus, Sheiks, Buddhists, Muslims and Jews — just to name a few religions that emphasise social practices as much as creedal beliefs.

Secondly, religious freedom is expressed in, and empowered by, community. This implies that religious freedom is not just individual freedom, but involves the freedom of communities and institutions to survive and be effective. The maintenance of religious community identity will involve the freedom of association within that community. The freedom of such religious institutions and communities to select and — where necessary — dismiss employees or members, is essential to the existence of such bodies. Otherwise they lose control of their identity and integrity.

This is why current anti-discrimination law exemptions matter — and why any effective removal of these exemptions would pose such a threat to religious freedom in Australia. Further, the maintenance of religious community will involve the ability to educate children and adults in the teachings, practices and moral values of the religion.

The Consequences of Marriage Equality

As a result of the new threats to the fundamental human right to religious liberty, and because of the apparent need for parliamentary action to create adequate legal protections, the issue is now the subject of a swirling cultural and political debate that will determine the place that religious freedom will hold in the civic firmament of 21st century Australia.

The current debate about religious freedom has been intensified as a consequence of the 2017 same-sex marriage plebiscite (postal vote) and the subsequent passing by the federal parliament of the *Marriage Amendment (Definition and Religious Freedoms) Bill 2017*.

During the campaign, 'No' supporters suggested that changing the definition of marriage would have adverse effects on the rights of parents to have the say over the moral teaching of their children, on religious bodies freedom to teach their doctrine of marriages, and would encourage the 'weaponized' use of anti-discrimination laws to attack the integrity of faith-based institutions.[4] Although raising concerns about the impact of legalising same-sex marriage on religious freedom was a controversial tactic, the leaders of both major parties at the time — Prime Minister Malcolm Turnbull and Leader of the Opposition Bill Shorten — expressed commitments as to the importance of religious freedom, even as they celebrated the victory of the 'Yes' case.

Yet when same-sex marriage was formally approved, attempts to introduce provisions into the amending legislation that would have given increased protection for those with a conscientious objection to same sex marriage were rejected.[5]

Instead, in November 2017 Prime Minister Turnbull referred the question to an inquiry, appointing an Expert Panel to examine whether Australian law adequately protects the human right to freedom of religion.

Speaking at the announcement of the terms of reference some days later, the Prime Minister reaffirmed the importance of dealing properly with the issue: "Australia is the most successful multicultural society in the world. Right at the heart of our success as a free society is freedom of religion."[6] Opposition Leader Shorten had also spoken equally enthusiastically about freedom of religion in parliament:

> The Labor Party believes in religious freedom, we understand it is central to our democracy and our society. It is a most important issue and one we must all treat with respect … Respect for sincerely held views of people of faith, respect for the rights of religious institutions to practise according to their own tenets is proper.[7]

Unfortunately, subsequent events — marked by delay and inaction — belied the sentiments and seeming bi-partisan support for religious freedom

The Wentworth Panic

Although the Expert Panel Religious Freedom Review (the Ruddock Report) was completed in May 2018 nothing was heard of it from the government until almost the end of the year. This was despite the fact that the panel had received no less than 15,620 submissions from individuals and organisations, something the then Prime Minister had described as "unprecedented."[8]

During the long delay, political events interceded and both inflamed and illustrated the issues at stake.

In October 2018 during the Wentworth by-election a selective leak of the recommendations of the Report appeared. A recommendation that religious schools' existing exemptions from anti-discrimination law concerning the sexual orientation of students and teachers should be limited was misleadingly presented as, in the words of the *Sydney Morning Herald* print edition[9] headline, "Secret Plan for Laws to Reject Gay Students and Teachers." In the moral panic which followed the urgent call for the immediate abolition of such exemptions altogether was made in order to protect gay and lesbian students and teachers from the danger of imminent expulsion. This was despite the fact that there was no evidence of any such expulsions and that the very same Labor Party so exercised over the exemptions had legislated for them only five years earlier.[10]

Nevertheless, the Morrison government was moved to commit to removing the exemption concerning sexual orientation of students, without releasing the full report. The whole matter ended in a stalemate when the government, then with a minority in the House of Representatives, failed to have amendments to a Labor/Greens bill adopted. In the words of one observer "The expulsion 'emergency' had all the marks of a beat-up of one part of the Australian community in order to win the votes of another part."[11] By pre-empting the report, the selective leak of the most emotive and damaging recommendation was designed poison the political well and make it much more difficult to address the issue of exemptions in a manner that would strengthen religious protections.

The Ruddock Review

The report of the Expert Panel and the government's response was finally released in mid-December 2018. Overall, the Ruddock Review turned out to be timid and narrow. Although the panel conceded that the change in law which had raised the need for the review had only been recently introduced, it deliberately took a limited historical evidence-based approach in seeking to "identify real-world examples of infringement on people's right to freedom of religion." It then unsurprisingly found (given that only five months had elapsed since the passage of same-sex marriage) that there was "absence of clear information that the current framework is causing real problems", and that "[t]he vast amount of public interest and contestability around these issues stands in clear contrast to the number of formal complaints."[12]

This approach was an inadequate basis for fulfilling the mandate "to examine and report whether Australian law . . . adequately protects the human right to freedom of religion." What the Panel ought also to have considered was the question in the light of future possibilities in a time of fast changing shifting social change as the gulf between the teaching of religious communities and the mainstream culture is growing wider, especially on sexual issues.

This divergence is taking place at a time when concerns to protect individual dignity from harm now clash with the expression of what was once orthodox religious teaching on behaviour. When 'dignity' is conceived as a person's worth in their chosen self-identity, and non-discrimination is aimed at avoiding status or dignity harm, then the mere existence of an apparent discrimination becomes problematic in itself — irrespective of whether or not there are many other opportunities to obtain the relevant service or employment.[13]

In the face of this, teachings and doctrines that were one accepted simply as sincere points of view in a diverse society are now taken as homophobic and harmful, and, if you are prominent enough, could well cost you your job. The Wentworth Panic — and the sacking in May 2019 of Israel Falou by Rugby Australia for publicly expressing his religious convictions — show how volatile and unstable the situation has become.

Unsurprisingly given its flawed findings about the problem, the Ruddock Review was equally timid and narrow in regards solutions. Its major recommendations were limited to the proposal for the development of a "Commonwealth Religious Discrimination Act directed at the provision of comprehensive protection against discrimination based on religious belief or activity, including the absence of religious belief."[14] It consciously avoided any recommendations on any fundamental reforms to improve religious freedom such as such as replacing the current framework of exceptions to anti-discrimination law with a general limitations clause, or developing a Religious Freedom Act.[15]

2019 Election

Nevertheless, the Morrison government's response was basically sympathetic to the report, accepting what it took to be its central conclusion, "that there is an opportunity to further protect, and better promote and balance, the right to freedom of religion under Australian law and in the public sphere."[16] It committed to implementing the less contentious recommendations (which mainly concerned clarifying and strengthening existing provisions) to seek to reach bipartisan support for a Religious Discrimination Bill. And in April 2019, it also sent the contentious recommendations around religious schools off to the Australian Law Reform Commission which is due to report a year later.

Although the Ruddock report did not recommend it, the government also committed to appointing a standalone Freedom of Religion Commissioner at the Australian Human Rights Commission. The Labor opposition remained uncommitted saying only that they would look at any legislation when it is released and that they were against discrimination in every form.[17]

Then came the 2019 federal election. Although contested by some,[18] there is good reason to believe that concerns over religious freedom played a significant role in the unexpected Coalition victory.[19] Given that religion played a political role not evident since the 1950s and 1960s battles over communism and the state-aid for religious schools, we might expect the newly re-elected Morrison government to, at a minimum, make good its promises to act on the Ruddock report. There are also indications that the Labor Party is now more open to action on the issue and to rebuilding trust with religiously concerned voters.[20]

Time will tell how seriously the issue is now treated by politicians newly awakened to its electoral implications. Generally, the role religion played in the election has been a wakeup call to political and media elites who don't take religion seriously and so do not think other people take it seriously either in what they like to falsely consider (or wish) to be a secular society.

The key lesson that should be learned from the political message sent by the 'Quiet Australians' is why protecting religious freedom should be of paramount concern for both religious and non-religious Australians alike, in the best interests of ensuring Australia remains a tolerant and harmonious polity. What this issue is really about how is how Australian society — as one of the oldest liberal democracies in the world — handles genuine diversity among its citizens. This is to assert that there are good reason why action should be taken — well beyond implementing the limited Ruddock report recommendation — so that the politicisation of religious concerns does not progress further — at the risk of undermining genuine tolerance and community harmony.[21]

This Book

As one of the co-editors Peter Kurti wrote in his 2017 book, *The Tyranny of Tolerance*, "democracy promotes the interests of all citizens, irrespective of their beliefs, allowing them to uphold and express their beliefs".[22] This is context in which The Centre for Independent Studies — one of the few, if only, secular organisations in Australia with a strong and proven track record of advocating for improved protection for religious freedom consistent with liberal democratic principles — has gathered a number of diverse analyses and perspectives on the importance of the issue today and what should be done about it.

Forgotten Freedom No More contains a wide range of contributions from writers sympathetic to promoting religious freedom in Australia. Each of the contributors agree on the importance and yet fragility of religious liberty in Australia, while approaching the issue from varied viewpoints and experience, even at times disagreeing with each other. Some offer a general analysis of the problem as they see it with suggested ways forward. Others bring a more personal perspective. For this reason, as well as asking for legal and academic contributors, we have also sought to hear from some who write from a particular religious, or in one case, non-religious point of view.

The objective is two-fold. The chapters in the first half of the book that employ an analytical lens are designed to illuminate and amplify the relevant issues in the hope that this will clarify the importance of the issues at stake for both policymakers and the wider public. Those chapters in the latter half that bring a personal perspective to bear are designed to broaden and inform the debate by exploring the 'lived experience' of the authors. As noted, not all are believers; but some who write from a religious point of view provide a valuable insight — especially for sceptical secular audiences — into the importance of religious freedom to allow deeply-held spiritual convictions to be 'lived out' and to animate individual identity across their social, professional, and civic spheres of action and purpose.

By demonstrating both the breadth and depth of concerns about religious liberty in Australia, the book is designed to make a contribution to the debate about protecting religious freedom that is greater than the sum of its parts. In these pages, policymakers will find cogent and compelling legal, philosophical, policy and personal arguments for why action should be taken to address what has emerged as an increasingly important political issue.

Almost all of the chapters grapple with the sources of current-day controversies. This begins with Henry Ergas's historical survey of the philosophical origins of the concept of religious freedom, the development of which in recent centuries in the West has allowed for tolerance and "mutual accommodation" of religious belief and practice. This occurred in recognition of the fundamental right for individuals to live according to "one's innermost convictions", and a vital need for the state to permit for religious disagreements within a free and civil society in order to keep the social peace. The contemporary relevance of these achievements lie in the tragic consequences of irreconcilable clashes between religious and other new rights. Ergas argues that when the law seeks to resolves such clashes there ought to be a strong presumption in favour of religious freedom, recognising the damage that is caused when individuals are obliged, by the coercive powers of the state, to act against their life-defining commitments.

The following chapter explores the origins of the threats to religious liberty. Augusto Zimmermann explains how tolerance in the classical liberal tradition of John Locke was based on the belief that competing religious views — even those considered false and absurd — should be tolerated as the free expression and debate of contesting ideas was central to the pursuit of truth. Post-modern dogmas that hold that truth is relative, and that such claims are mere instruments of power, justify efforts to circumscribe religious liberty and associated freedoms of thought and expression to achieve political objectives. Efforts to proscribe traditional freedoms in the name of promoting the 'new tolerance' of diversity, and which seek to protect the values and beliefs of certain groups from challenge by 'offensive' opinions and counter-views, are a perversion of the true concept of tolerance.

In his chapter, Julian Porteous, the Catholic Archbishop of Tasmania, catalogues threats to religious freedom including by recounting his own experience under his states' anti-discrimination regime. He argues that the change in the legal definition of marriage is a turning point in Australia, not only given the nature of change itself, but as a revelation that Christianity is fast becoming a minority religion. The Ruddock Report, alas, offers little way forward to deal with the new social realities that mean religious freedom is no longer a given for faith-based schools and social welfare agencies, whose religious tenets are increasingly clashing with the aggressive secular demands of activists and civil authorities under the law.

Paul Morrissey's contribution drill downs and focuses on the threat to religious liberty in the key area of education. With one-third of Australian children enrolled in religious-based schools, the freedom of these institutions to maintain their integrity became a political issue at the 2019 election. He argues that protecting the right of religious schools to freely act in accord with the teachings of their faith is crucial to their mission. This is not merely to propagate religious beliefs, but also to thereby impart moral instruction and cultivate the virtues that will equip students to contribute to the nation and fulfil their responsibilities as citizens in a free and democratic society. To fulfil this mission — and to preserve parental choice and educational diversity in Australian education — it is therefore reasonable for religious schools to have the right to control their enrolment and employment practices to ensure that students and staff support their ethos, or else these institutions will risk losing their *raison d'etre*.

Patrick Parkinson then brings the discussion of the cultural and legal threads of the threat to religious liberty to a point by making the case for greater legislative protections. He sets outs the need for, and the terms of, a Religious Freedom Act, which would resolve the issue by defending religious freedom as a positive right under Australian law.

The next two chapters — which close the *Analysis* section and open the *Perspectives* section — question the case for legislative action on religious freedom. Lorraine Findlay argues that too much has been said, and too little has been done to strengthen religious freedom. The best way forward would be not to introduce new legislation but to remove those laws that inappropriately trespass on those freedoms. Importantly — and entirely in keeping with the aims of this book — she also stresses the need for greater awareness of the importance of religious freedom as an asset for the nation, recognising that the best defence is a cultural presumption in its favour throughout the community.

James Allan provides an atheist's perspective drawn from the writings of David Hume. Recognising the benefits religion brings to society is too often overlooked, Allan's defence of religious freedom is thoroughly democratic: attempts to exclude religious convictions from the public square are simply a self-serving exercise in stacking the deck by secularists. He too counsels against statutory provisions, fearing unelected judges — no matter the will of the parliament — tend to favour 'equality' objectives over protection of fundamental freedoms when deciding between competing rights.

Michael Bird's chapter elaborates much more than an Anglican perspective on religious liberty. Without genuine legal protections, he foresees continued encroachment by government on religious freedom. The real danger is 'Civic Totalism' where the state and its apparatuses impose its progressive will and secular values upon religious communities. With Australia's success as a multicultural society depending on maintaining the right to be different without fear of sanctions, the application of the true principles of secularism is imperative to ensure that in a pluralistic society, religion is free from government interference, and government is likewise free from religious domination.

The next two chapters contribute non-Christian perspectives to the discussion in keeping with the multicultural realities of modern Australia. Benjamin Elton reminds us that for most of history in Australia and elsewhere, Jews have been a religious minority. This has made the Jewish community particularly thoughtful in matters of religious freedom, as these circumstances have deepened its understanding of its necessity, tempered by a careful realisation of its proper limits, without unreasonably limiting the rights of others. As Jews have negotiated the challenges of pre-modernity, modernity, and now post-modernity, they have sought to make a positive contribution to wider society and create an atmosphere disposed towards both religious freedom and social responsibility as citizens. How the Jewish experience underlines the need for certain humility in pressing claims for religious liberty — free of any demand for ascendency — is a powerful lesson for Christian faiths entering a new age when they too are likely to become a minority in a non-Christian land.

Tanveer Ahmed reminds us of the preciousness of religion freedom by providing a pessimistic account of its fortunes in the Islamic world. The concept exists scripturally within Islam and occurs in practice in limited corners. But the two key models in Islamic countries tend to be secular repressive ones and those with some version of an Islamic government. How the tensions within Islam concerning freedom, religious or otherwise, are resolved is an issue not only for Muslim nations but for the social cohesion of our own in relation to our minority Muslim communities.

The final chapter by Michael Quinlan also recognises the limits of legal and political solutions, which will be but temporary solutions in the absence of actions by Christian's today to improve the climate for religious freedom. Asserting that Christians are themselves partly to blame for the present problem, and taking inspiration from the example of the early Christians, he argues that long-term improvements depends on living more fully as Christians to convince more Australians of the worth of religion's contribution to Australian society, and thus the merits of protecting religious liberty.

The ramifications of the threats to religious liberty for Australian democracy — the elaboration of which it is hoped might help spur remedial parliamentary action — are the questions addressed by Peter Kurti in the Coda that forms the conclusion to this book. Kurti argues — as the various chapters show — that the application of anti-discrimination law, in combination with the rise of identity politics has, ironically, inflamed social divisions in a fashion that "has only made it harder, rather than easier, to accommodate difference in wider society." What is at stake over the issue of religious freedom is the wider health of Australian society in which dissent against orthodoxies is permissible. The routine deployment of arguments relying on claims of 'offence' and 'harm' are calculated to silence full and frank debate, and restrict not only religious liberty but the democratic right of all citizens to exercise freedom of thought, speech, and association. The triumph of such 'tyranny' practiced in the name of false name of 'tolerance' threatens to rewrite the famous aphorism coined by former Prime Minister John Howard, and to make this country unrecognisable to the one most wish to live in. For if the threats to religious and other fundamental liberties proceed unchecked, the impact on Australian society will be to render the anti-democratic values that divide Australians more important than the democratic virtues which have in the past — and should continue in the future —to unite us.

It is important to clarify that views expressed by the authors do not necessarily reflect the position of The Centre for the Independent Studies (CIS), where the co-editors of his book are employed. This is particularly the case where the views expressed — either directly or by inference — reflect the religious convictions of the contributor, particularly on sensitive questions of sexuality. As a secular organisation, the CIS is not concerned with questions of doctrine and theology, nor with the advancement of any particular faith-based position on any social or political issue. Our concerns are limited wholly to the appropriate protection of the right to religious liberty in a free society, whilst placing an equal and appropriate emphasis on respecting the democratic rights of others to disagree fully and frankly with religious views and values.

It also needs to be clearly stated that in no way is this book an exercise in wistful harking back to less tolerant and pluralistic times that saw the law (along with discriminatory cultural sanctions) used to enforce traditional sexual morality with punitive and persecutory effect. This extends to treating the most recent development in the story of LGTBI rights — the legalisation of same-sex marriage — as a settled question that has been placed beyond the remit of politics by the democratic decision of the Australian people and their parliamentary representatives. The important issues that are contemplated in this book solely concern the consequences of the status quo with specific respect to ensuring appropriate accommodation of the right to religious freedom within the legal system.

As noted, not all the chapters agree about what needs to be done to protect religious liberty in Australia. Two contributors — by two lawyers — are particularly concerned about legislative changes that might empower judges unfriendly to religious freedom and make a bad situation worse. One response might be that a looming fight with the judges over competing rights appears inevitable, and the better approach might be to reset the legislative terms of the legal contest, including over the wide struggle between parliament and the judiciary over the making of the law. The alternative strategy recommended is to repeal the root cause of the problems, the anti-discrimination laws that operate in all Australian jurisdictions — a herculean political task. The prospects of success are slim, and for not the least reason being that such a course would immediately identify the cause of religious freedom in the public and policymaker's mind with the pursuit of an unfettered right to be a bigot.

A right to exercise religious liberty is certainly needed because — as Patrick Parkinson argues persuasively in his pivotal chapter — Australian parliaments have already regulated and constrained religious freedom by creating a legislative framework that permits its exercise as mere and vulnerable legislative exemption to the rule of anti-discrimination law. In the wake of the legalisation of same-sex marriage, political realities, and the fundamental principles at stake, dictate that the federal parliament should fix what is broken in the Australian polity in respect of religious liberty by creating a positive right to exercise it. Here in lies the case for a Religious Freedom Act to create stronger legal protections — the liberal democratic dimensions of which are explored in the following sections.

The Liberal Case for Protecting Religious Freedom

The passage of same-sex marriage has certainly sparked heightened interest — as the chapters in this book demonstrate — in religious freedom issues. But it is vital to stress that this debate is not about revisiting that law. To reiterate and underline the central premise and point of this book, the future of Australia as a liberal democracy in a changing world is at stake in how this matter is dealt with by Australian parliamentarians and by the Australian people.

The issue of religious freedom is part of the wider issue of diversity in Australian society. That is why it is a pity, though perhaps inevitable, that the question of religious freedom has arisen in Australia in its present form partly in response to the extension of full civil rights, including the right to marry, to LGBTI people. This has led some commentators to treat the issue simply as a threat to diversity, rather than an aspect of it. For example, a long time LGBTI rights campaigner has stated that it is a fact that "the contemporary 'religious freedom' movement is not about protecting people of faith, but is actually about taking basic rights away from LGBTI people."[23] This is a serious misunderstanding.

Liberal democracies both value, and are built on, the right to freedom of thought, conscience and religion. Such freedom of belief, together with other freedoms of association, speech and the right to own property, is crucial to the health of our society and the flourishing of its people. There are benefits in allowing the freedom of such religious pluralism. It brings freedom of choice, the competition of different visions of the meaning and purpose of existence, and contributes to realisation of a truly civil society. This freedom is relatively new in human history. It is only in the past few hundred years that states or societies no longer enforce a limited range of religious options for its people. In many parts of the world today, such freedom to religious pluralism still effectively doesn't exist.

It therefore needs to be made very clear that supporting freedom of religion in a liberal democratic society does not require — or amount to — agreeing with religious truth. Even those who think all religions are false should still agree with them having appropriate freedom; just as liberal democracy respects and protects a plurality of political beliefs.

And important as the right to religious liberty is, it is also crucial to add that protecting it should not entail any kind of quasi-blasphemy laws that remove others' rights to criticise, deny or even ridicule any particular religious belief or practice, as long as it does not involve incitement to discrimination, hostility or violence.

Nor can religious freedom protection guarantee that religious points of view will necessarily be listened to, or religious leaders respected in public debate. These are matters properly outside the reach of law in liberal democracies.

The real question, however, is whether it is good to live in a society that values religious freedom irrespective of the truth of any particular religious claims.

Since religion is about the human pursuit of ultimate meaning and value, it is reasonable to argue that any erosion of religious liberty impedes that pursuit and so diminishes opportunities for human fulfilment. To respect a person's religious belief and behaviour involves more than just respecting their individual conscience, as it can include respecting their conviction that what they are acting on is a transcendent authority.[24] In respecting the rights of someone who thinks God forbids him or her to do something, liberal democracy does not recognise the reality of that transcendent authority, but only its possibility. In doing so, liberal democracy humbly allows the possibility of an authority outside of itself. Moreover, in general, religious freedom and pluralism enables religious communities to be other locations of authority in civil society other than the sovereign state and the needs or preferences of the individual.[25] This deepens and enriches society.[26]

This is to say that the liberal case for religious freedom rests on the protection of fundamental freedom of the individual citizen to pursue their conception of a 'good' life, on the freedom of religions to exist being in general beneficial for society as a whole,[27] and — most crucially of all — on the maintenance of the harmony and peacefulness of society in general.

Liberal democracy's accommodation of maximum religious pluralism — achieved through the state's neutrality on matters spiritual — was designed to eliminate political conflict over religion by creating freedom for all belief; and special favour and privileges for none. Arguably, the most important aspect of diversity in the historical evolution of Western society has been hard-won protections for diversity of faith of all kinds. By achieving civil equality for all individuals and religions — as was the aspiration behind the inclusion of section 116 in the Commonwealth Constitution — the aim of liberal democracy was to enable the community to live together peacefully despite their doctrinal and theological differences that, historically, had caused bitter social division and strife.[28]

Race, gender and sexual orientation are not the only forms of diversity — and protections of such diversity are of concern to our whole society. So too should protection of religious diversity be of importance to all, and not merely the preserve of religious adherents alone. The right to religious freedom is not the only fundamental human right. It cannot therefore be absolute, but exists alongside other rights. How different rights and freedom coexist is the big question facing our nation today.

The real test of religious freedom today is whether we will give space to those who have different views; even if those views may cause offence to some group, at some point, in any diverse, modern society. The bigger question is whether the civil compact — the equal protection of religious liberty for all — that has enabled liberal democracies to minimise religious conflict, will be broken in a manner that could risk religious groups having no recourse other than to politically mobilise around these issues; a result that will ultimately leave us as a more divided community.

A Religious Freedom Act

Given that religious freedom is clearly important and integral to liberal democracy, and that existing framework of protections are inadequate due to the changing political and social environment, there is a case for a new approach to protecting religious freedom.

A proposal worth considering therefore is that the federal parliament enact a religious freedom act that, in effect, seeks to clarify and codify common law concepts of religious freedom, as well as existing statutory anti-discrimination protections, into Australian statute law. As proposed by Freedom for Faith — a Christian legal think tank — such an act would directly address (without shifting the present balance of rights nor compromising public safety) the threats that anti-discrimination law poses to religious freedom.[29]

Such legislation would have an impact on state and territory anti-discrimination laws because of section 109 of the Commonwealth Constitution which says that "when a law of a State is inconsistent with a law of the Commonwealth, the latter shall prevail, and the former shall, to the extent of the inconsistency be invalid." This would mean that while the states and territories would keep their legislative powers, the federal law would place certain constraints upon the scope of, and application of, any laws they make; but only to the extent that their application in any given situation would be in breach of long-held protections for freedom of religion.

While there are good reasons to restrict the expansion of Federal powers over the States, the protection of religious freedom — to the extent any legislation is necessary — is legitimately a national matter warranting central government action.

Though some have called for the direct incorporation of provisions of the International Covenant on Civil and Political Rights in Australian law as a means of ensuring religious freedom, it should be noted that these rights and freedoms do not exist because of international covenants. Instead, they come from Australia's inheritance of the English tradition of unwritten rights and freedoms that are protected by custom and the common law. Any support found in the enunciation of the principle of freedom of religion in international law is in addition to — not the source of — such rights. As such, a federal religious freedom act would not increase freedoms; but guarantee such as exist and clarify their genuine limitations. It would not therefore be a 'mini bill of rights' but a modest action on strengthening religious freedom.

Given the present state of Australian society, there is a need for a federal act that will guarantee religious freedom into the future by legislating proper protections of existing rights to religious liberty, as opposed to creating specifically any new right or rights. Rather than permit anti-discrimination law to be used to eradicate differences between Australians by mandating uniformity of belief, thought, speech, and action, the federal parliament must establish a new law to protect religious freedom that will allow Australians to live together harmoniously despite their differences of belief, thought, speech, and action.

If this could be done in a way that neither increases nor diminishes existing common law freedoms, and is supported by a wide section of the community — and if, ideally, has the backing of both sides of politics — the matter would in effect be settled for decades. The achievement of such an outcome will require leadership, as well as a spirit of trust and compromise from the various sections in society that have a stake of one kind or another in the issue.

We are at a crucial moment in our history if we are to avoid religion becoming unduly politicised. How the issue is dealt with will be a test of Australia's political maturity.

The Morrison government's Religious Discrimination Bill

As this book was being finalised (in late August 2019), the Morrison government finally unveiled its proposed laws to better protect religious liberty. The chapters in the book remain as written in July 2019; this section brings subsequent developments up to date.

Attorney General Christian Porter announced that the government would implement the recommendations of the Ruddock Report and seek to enhance the statutory protection of the right to religious freedom in Australia by legislating a Religious Discrimination Act.

With some important exceptions, the exposure draft of the bill — which was released for public comment and is scheduled to be introduced into parliament in October 2019 — was generally received as a good start. Its chief feature is the extension of the standard federal anti-discrimination law framework to prohibit discrimination on the ground of religious belief or activity . Beyond legislating a new general protection against religious discrimination, the bill also seeks to address specific concerns that have animated the debate about threats to religious liberty.

This includes new provisions that — in the wake of the legalisation of same-sex marriage — would protect the rights of religious organisations to teach and uphold the traditional definition of marriage, by ensuring that the ability of people to express their religious beliefs in good faith is protected from the operation of federal and state anti-discrimination law. Designed to prevent a repeat of the 'Porteous case' that arose under Tasmanian anti-discrimination law, this would mean that a person cannot be found to have discriminated against anyone by making a statement expressing genuinely-held religious beliefs that are reasonably regarded to be in accordance with religious doctrines, tenets, beliefs or teachings. New provisions are also included in the bill to address the circumstances of the 'Folau case' by requiring businesses over $50m in size to prove that imposing restrictions on (or terminating the employment of) employees private religious activities is necessary to avoid unjustifiable financial hardships.[30]

The Attorney General flatly stated that the government's intention is not to create a "positive right to freedom of religion" and that the option of a Religious Freedom Act had been deliberately eschewed. Instead, the draft bill provides that — with respect to only federal anti-discrimination law — religious institutions such as schools and charities are permitted to engage in "legitimate differential treatment" and cannot be found to have discriminated when manifesting their religious beliefs by engaging in good faith conduct in accordance with their faith. Religious leaders — amid concerns about lack of consultation and the unwise decision of Catholic and other Christian groups to boycott the Attorney General's speech at the Great Synagogue in Sydney — rightly pointed out that the new laws would not override state anti-discrimination laws and thus did not address concerns about the vulnerability of the existing religious exemptions regimes.

The Attorney General also defended the government's decision to address religious liberty protections by adopting an approach that was "complementary" to existing state anti-discrimination laws. He asserted that a positive rights approach, by contrast, would open the way to judges making law regarding "sensitive public policy decisions" when forced to adjudicate competing rights.[31] This is sound in theory. But it also ignores the reality that judges are already empowered to make such decisions under the operation of anti-discrimination statutes. Moreover, the proposed laws will also require the courts to determine whether religious statements or conduct are sufficiently reasonable and in good faith — such as in cases determining whether religious schools can only hire teachers who support or agree to support their doctrines — in order to justify abridging the rights of others not to be discriminated against.[32]

Hence the debate will continue about the need for, and extent of, statutory guidance by parliament of the courts — the substantive question raised by the call for a Religious Freedom Act — particularly when the Australian Law Reform Commission is still to present its report (due April 2020) on the removal of religious exemptions from anti-discrimination laws. However, rather than legal philosophy *per se*, political realities have dictated and constrained the action the Morrison government is currently willing to take to protect religious liberty. As the conflicting responses to the draft bill by government MPs and Senators demonstrated, the federal Liberal Party is divided on the question of a positive rights approach to religious liberty.[33]

The government has taken a cautious line — so as not to inflame internal divisions, it seems — and has sided for the time with the position of the so-called 'modern Liberals' (many of whom drove the same-sex marriage debate within the Liberal Party) but based, as well, on broader political considerations.[34] The adoption of a traditional anti-discrimination approach and the reluctance to appear to be undermining state laws is probably motivated by an understandable desire not to risk proposing a bill that would be easily (but wrongly) portrayed as overturning the anti-discrimination legal architecture of the nation — and which would be sure to be falsely characterised by opponents as legislating for a 'right to be a bigot'.

The response by advocates of stronger legal protections for religious freedom at this point should be to understand that the Morrison government's actions have been pragmatic, and that these actions also need to be interpreted as measure of the fact that the political circumstances do not yet exist that can justify more far-reaching legislation. For the reality is that the legal, political and cultural threats to religious liberty in Australia have not as yet led to real and verifiable harms to religious freedom of sufficient scale that would clearly demonstrate the need for stronger parliamentary action.

Long may we hope that a culture of mutual respect for the religious freedoms of all citizens remains a defining characteristic of Australian democracy. But this also means that 'events' — as always — will determine the course of politics with respect to protecting religious liberty. The Morrison government's proposed legislation, and the limited protections offered to religious believers and organisations, are unfortunately unlikely to put an end to the issue. This is illustrated by the hostile response to the draft bill from 'diversity' activists opposed to 'religious exceptionalis'[35] and any additional so-called 'new privileges to people of faith.'[36]

The political realities of the contemporary social landscape mean the concerns and warnings contained in this book will remain relevant to an ongoing debate about religious freedom in this country. The arguments presented in *Forgotten Freedom No More* will therefore be of enduring importance, and will help guide and inform the debate for better protection of religious liberty when future political events dictate that the moment for greater parliamentary action has arrived.

Conclusion: Diversity in Difference

We hope this collection of essays is informative and helpful to readers of all kinds of backgrounds and beliefs. Each of the contributors brings to bear a distinct perspective on the issue of religious freedom. We also wish to acknowledge the very significant contribution that Dr

Jeremy Sammut, our former colleague at CIS, made to the editorial shaping of this collection before he moved on to yet greener pastures. Sammut's clarity about the key principles at stake ensured that the focus of the collection remained sharp.

Greater mutual understanding across cultural and social divides is important to help stimulate parliamentary action on religious freedom. This goes to the heart of our overall objective: to create the social, cultural and political environment that allows all citizens, irrespective of their faith, to exercise their fundamental freedoms of speech, thought, and conscience, and live harmoniously together in true diversity, despite their differences, and united in mutual respect for the rights of all.

This is to underline that there is much more to preserving religious freedom than the having the appropriate laws in place — as some of the contributions to this book rightly emphasise. Without being naïve about the forces of social change in Western societies which are leading to the new threats facing religious freedom today, we should not discount the contribution religious adherents can play in improving the situation as well. We cannot ignore the deleterious effect of the loss of respect for religious people and institutions brought about by their own failures and behaviours. In particular, the standing of religion itself has declined significantly in recent times due, amongst things, to the fear of religious extremist violence as well as the justified horror at revelations of child sex abuse in religious institutions. Even if it is operating at only a subtle level, the loss of trust and respect undercuts the motivation to take the protection of religious liberty seriously.

This is why the way religious people and institutions exercise their religious freedom matters. Integrity, respect for others and holding firm convictions with humility are called for. The words of the Apostle Paul to early Christians in Rome are a good guide to people of any religion in Australia today. "If it is possible, so far as it depends on you, live peaceably with all."

Chapter 1

RELIGIOUS FREEDOM'S HISTORY AND FUTURE?

Henry Ergas

If religious freedom was not a feature of the Australian colonies at the time of their birth, it was certainly part of the landscape by the time they were toddlers. There was, for sure, plenty of bitter sectarian conflict, then and in the years that followed, but the freedom of Australians to choose and practice their religion was never seriously threatened.

It may therefore seem odd that religious freedom should now figure prominently on the public agenda. Analysing the concept, some of the forces that have caused its recent prominence, and the approaches which might be adopted to it in the future, are the purposes of this essay.

What the term means: the concept of 'freedom'

A useful, but certainly not simple, place to start is by examining the constituent parts of the phrase 'religious freedom' itself.

Each of those parts is the subject of enormous debate in the scholarly literature. Without pretending to draw together the threads of that debate, it is clear that the concept of freedom involves three components: a subject or agent; an object, which is or can be among the subject's goals or intentions; and the presence or absence of constraints which might impede the agent from achieving or undertaking the object.

Freedom of the press, for example, involves the press itself as the subject; the reporting of news as the object; and the social, economic and legal factors that can affect the press' ability to investigate, analyse and disseminate news as the potential constraints. To say a country has a free press is to say that those factors that might act as constraints do not obstacle the press (the subject of the freedom) in reporting the news (the object of the freedom) to an extent that raises significant concerns.

In exactly the same way, 'religious freedom' implies that the factors which might prevent the practice of religion by those who want to do so are not, as a factual matter, serious impediments.

Obviously, the notion of 'impediments' involved in this approach to defining freedom can be as broad or narrow as the subject matter demands. For example, in considering whether people are free to make the best use of their talents, the potential constraints might well include socio-economic factors, such as the impact of family income on access to education; in contrast, freedom of the press and religious freedom are more commonly assessed with respect to legal constraints — that is, whether the coercive powers of the state are used to limit the exercise of religion.

In that sense, while the freedom to make the best use of one's talents is a form of positive freedom, freedom of the press and religious freedom primarily involve negative freedom, that is, freedom from coercion. That links them closely to the notion of individual autonomy, which means literally 'giving the law to oneself', and which, in the Kantian tradition, entails the ability to live under a law which one could rationally have chosen. If autonomy is, as Kant put it in the *Groundwork of the Metaphysics of Morals*, the foundation of "the dignity of human nature and of every rational nature," and respect for autonomy the "sole" and "supreme" principle of morals, then it follows, as Kant shows in *The Doctrine of Right*, that 'Right' is "the sum of conditions under which the choice of one can be united with the choice of the other in accordance with a universal law." Religious freedom would therefore occur where the law under which one exercised religion respected individual autonomy — which does not mean the absence of any regulation, but rather that regulation is limited to that needed to render each person's autonomy compatible with the autonomy of others.

However, at least in Western thought, there is a deeper duality that is highly relevant to understanding the concept of freedom, and relatedly that of autonomy. It is well known that our intellectual outlook reflects both Athens and Jerusalem: both the political and philosophical legacy of the Greeks and the worldview and orientation to life of the Jews. The first conceives of freedom as the absence of domination: to be free is to not be a slave, i.e. not subject to the will of a master. In the second, freedom is the predicate for responsibility: to be free is to be accountable to God for the exercise of one's will. As a result, the Western concept of freedom involves more than the scope to make a choice — it also entails bearing the burden of that choice, living with its consequences, shouldering its outcomes.

In that sense, the freedom our tradition prizes is not antinomian; on the contrary, it is to be answerable for one's choices, and most notably, for the decision of whether to live with integrity — that is, in a manner consistent with one's innermost convictions.

'Religion'

Mention of innermost convictions leads naturally to the question of religion, and here too, it is important to examine what the term means. It is obviously a complex concept, all the more so because the range of social practices it encompasses is bewilderingly wide; and grasping it is not made any easier by the fact that even its greatest students, such as Max Weber and Emile Durkheim, were far more concerned with analysis than with definition.

That said, if what we call 'religion' has a common core, it consists of three elements: the definition of a relation between the immanent and the transcendent; the specification of a systematic set of practices whose accomplishment is required to act as a bridge between them; and the designation of a 'faith community' whose members share that understanding of the sacred cosmos and collectively undertake the practices it mandates. In short, 'religion' is the combination of a systematic conception of a sacred cosmos and an equally systematic set of collective practices which — through ritual, worship and prayer — allow individuals to approach the sacred in everyday life.

In the modern world, the notion of religion is closely identified with belief; but that is a relatively recent — and potentially misleading — view, as the concept's development shows.

In effect, the word that is its closest equivalent in classical Greek, *thrēskeia*, referred primarily to the observance of ritual practices, rather than to a set of ideas. Equally, while the precise significance of the Latin term *religio* has been the subject of much scholarly controversy, we have it on the authority of the great philologist Émile Benveniste that Cicero was right in defining it as scrupulous care in, and meticulous attention to, the sacred rites.

These were, in other words, terms that referred to *pious behaviour* — in the sense of behaviour that gave the gods their due — and not to the ideas in the minds of the pious. Moreover, that emphasis on command, duty and observance, rather than thought or belief, was apparent in the language used in the lengthy interval that went from the rise of Christianity to the Reformation. During those centuries, the terms commonly used to describe what we would now call religion — say in Boccaccio's famous story of the three rings or Chaucer's 'The Squire's Tale' — were variants or derivatives of '*lex*,' that is, law. Islam, to give another example, was often referred to as the '*lex Saracenorum*': the law which guides how the Saracens live.

The stress was therefore on what was demanded or required of the faithful, which certainly encompassed the beliefs they should hold, but stretched far beyond them. If *religio* or its variants were used, that was likely to be a reference to a life consumed by devotion to the sacred, much as a '*religieux*' in contemporary French means a monk.

The rise of the word 'religion' itself, and the narrowing of the concept to give primary weight to belief, occurred as part of the far-reaching changes that are broadly associated with the Reformation. Perhaps the most obvious manifestation of the change lies in the titles of some of the Reformation's canonical works themselves. Calvin called his masterpiece *Institutio christianae religionis* (1536) — a 'course in Christian religion' — subtitling it as "containing virtually the sum of piety and all that needs to be known in the doctrine of salvation." Equally, Zwingli, in 1525, wrote *De vera et falsa religione Commentarius*, that is, lessons on true and false belief. In each case, the point was that doctrine not only mattered but was literally the vital concern.

That emphasis on doctrine was, to some extent, inherent in the fact of a religious revolution. But the underlying transformation goes much further than a mere focus on the credo. Perhaps most importantly, it involved a new-found stress on subjectivity, as the ascetic Protestant notion of grace was internalised in the seventeenth century and came gradually to be identified with the emerging concept of conscience, for example, in the 'ethical inwardness' of the Cambridge Platonists.

Inevitably, placing subjectivity at the core of the religious experience altered the epistemic status of what might loosely be called religious claims. Augustine in his influential polemic against the Manicheans, *On the Profit of Believing*, had distinguished three adjacent kinds of truth-claim: understanding, belief and opinion, summarizing them as follows: "What then we understand, we owe to reason; what we believe, to authority; what we have an opinion on, to error." Now, with subjectivity acquiring a core role, authority — which until then had given the truth-claims of religion a privileged status — lost its commanding position. In its place came the concept of belief as a form of personal commitment, akin to the idea of 'faith', with all of that word's connotations of trust.

There is, in the characterization of religion as involving commitments to life-defining beliefs, a crucial truth. Faith, as Paul Tillich famously put it, is "the state of being ultimately concerned," an "act of the total personality" which accepts an "unconditional demand" that promises "ultimate fulfillment" if it is respected, and threatens "the exclusion from such fulfillment through national extinction and individual catastrophe" if it is not. Accepting faith, and abiding by its requirements, is therefore as consequential a decision as one can imagine, laden with implications that reach from the present into the indefinable future.

But while the weight which the subjectivist outlook places on the commitment to faith accurately highlights the intensity of the religious experience, it is inevitably a two-edged sword.

That is first and most obviously because it encourages the assimilation of faith to mere opinion. That was certainly not the intention either of the Reformation or of the Counter-Reformation, which, on the contrary, demanded greater rigor and conviction from their adherents than ever before. However, as the crippling human toll of the wars of religion induced a horrified reaction against what was disparaged as religious 'enthusiasm', civil peace came to be viewed as requiring that religious claims be treated as matters over which reasonable people could disagree.

Particularly in the sixteenth century — when it was, as Herbert Butterfield put it, not an ideal to be pursued but simply the last resort "for those who often still hated one another but found it impossible to go on fighting any more" — toleration may have been little more than a begrudging acceptance of the other; but it nonetheless gave some legitimacy to the other's beliefs, and the greater the degree to which toleration became the norm, the greater the legitimacy it conferred.

The consequences were obvious to those who reflected on them. Kant had identified belief as the category of truth-claim that is "subjectively sufficient, but objectively insufficient," that is, which lacks objective validity and instead relies on judgement. Developing that insight, Hegel wrote that "The principle of the modern world at large is *freedom of subjectivity*," with "the right of the subject's particularity to find satisfaction" being "the pivotal and focal point in the difference between antiquity and the modern age." That "right of the subject" to "recognize nothing that I do not perceive as rational" allowed the unfolding of our highest moral selves. However, Hegel warned, it also meant that "the concepts of truth and the laws of ethics are reduced to mere opinions and subjective conditions," eroding — with what were certain to be fateful results — their authority.

Every bit as importantly, the stress on belief which emerged from the Reformation downgraded the other elements that form part of religion as a social phenomenon. Thus, reinvigorating an old distinction between the "things indifferent" (*adiaphora*) and the "fundamentals" (*fundamenta*) of religion, both Hobbes and Locke reduced religion's social practices — going from rituals to external signs and life practices — to external manifestations which could not be primary importance to the faithful. Rather, what mattered to the believer, they claimed, was what he believed, not how those beliefs were manifested in daily life.

It followed, said Hobbes, that it was fully within the sovereign's right to control the external signs employed in worship, including even the "motion of their tongues" by which men "show others the knowledge, opinions, conceptions, and passions which are within themselves." Locke was far more tolerant than Hobbes of religious diversity, arguing in his *Letter Concerning Toleration* of 1685 that "I cannot be saved by a religion I distrust, or by a worship I dislike;" but if he wanted to protect religion's external manifestations from the arbitrary powers of the civil magistrate it was not because he thought they were important but because he considered them as little more than trifles, especially compared to "that inner worship of the heart which God demands."

However, while viewing religion as mainly a credo came naturally to thinkers in the Christian (and especially Protestant) tradition, it did not sit at all naturally with other faiths. The Christian measures faith by the standard instrument of orthodoxy, the creed; Jews, however, measure their fidelity by a deeply considered and exhaustively articulated body of *halakot*, behavioral rules that are the touchstones not of an orthodoxy but of an orthopraxy. Indeed, despite the well-known attempt by Rabbi Moses ben Maimon (who is known in English as Maimonides and in Hebrew by the acronym Rambam) to summarise the heart of Judaism in his *Thirteen Principles*, there is a widely held view in Judaism that *emunah* (faith) requires not intellectual acquiescence to carefully defined statements of dogma but trust in God expressed in obedience to the Torah.

Judaism is, in other words, not a creed but a way of life; and in Rabbi Joseph B. Soloveitchik's words, even rites such as prayer "must always be related to a *prayerful life* which is consecrated to the realization of

45

the divine imperative, and as such [prayer] is not a separate entity, but the sublime prologue to Halakhic action."

Islam too is first and foremost an orthopraxy, whose demands are almost entirely defined in terms of what a Muslim is expected to do. Thus, of the Five Pillars of Islam, only one (there is no God but Allah, and Muhammad is his prophet) is a factual claim which could be regarded as a belief; the others are all imperatives about how to live one's life.

The Lockean definition of "true and saving *religio*" as "the inward persuasion of the mind" therefore impoverishes the social phenomenon — and it does so all the more by marginalizing its collective aspect. To say that is not to suggest that Locke ignored the collective nature of religion; on the contrary, an important element in the landmark clarity with which he distinguished the social from the political lay in defining churches as voluntary associations of individuals who adhere to a particular doctrine of salvation. He thereby placed them in a sphere of life that can be separated from other spheres, notably (and crucially) that of the public interest of the state, and so assimilated them to what Hegel would later call civil society.

But while both can be viewed as forming part of civil society, there is a difference between being a Jew and joining a golf club. As Roger Scruton put it, being a member of a religious faith is a matter of living in "a network of relations that are neither contractual nor negotiated." Rather, those relations are commitments that — to use Heidegger's metaphor — we are 'thrown into' when we come into the world, just as we are thrown into our family. And much like our family, the ties those relations define — even though they are neither chosen nor voluntary in a conventional sense — are intensely affective, foundational to the sense of personal identity, and shaped through ongoing participation in collective social practices.

They are also, importantly, inter-generational, with the faith community's temporal span stretching, in the case of the Abrahamic religions, from the covenantal origins into an unknowably distant future. As a result, to again quote Rabbi Soloveitchik, each member of the faith community stands "in an awesome awareness of responsibility to a great past which handed down the divine imperative to the present generation in trust and confidence, and to a mute future expecting this generation to discharge its covenantal duty conscientiously and honourably."

These are, in other words, communities of destiny, not of choice; they inherit social practices they are obligated both to respect and to themselves transmit.

In short, the concept of religion that emerged in the Reformation and its philosophical aftermath was reductive in three crucially important respects: it reduced faith to opinion; it reduced religious practice to worship; and it reduced the faith community to a voluntary association, bound together by shared beliefs rather than by a common destiny. This was to have far-reaching consequences as the concept of 'religious freedom' took shape.

The right to religious freedom

Whatever the issues it may later have posed, it is undeniable that narrowing religion from truth to opinion helped 'pacify' religion in the West, facilitating its movement from open strife to the relative tranquility of civil society and the private sphere. And it is equally undeniable that that shift facilitated first the growth of religious toleration and then the elevation of religious freedom into a 'right.'

Of course, those developments were part of a broader long-term process, whose components include the increasingly sharp institutional differentiation between the state, civil society and private life, the rise of nationalism and of nation-states, and the definition of new relations between the nation-state and its citizens. Importantly, the relations between individuals, and between individuals and the state, which had previously been specified in ascriptive terms — imputing rights and obligations on the basis of traits such as religion and inherited social standing — were gradually replaced by legal equality, in a move Henry Sumner Maine brilliantly synthesized as the passage from status to contract.

In turn, as equality before the law became the rule, and legal entitlements were formalized in written constitutions, all citizens —

regardless of their religion or social status — acquired 'fundamental rights' which the state could not override, although it could specify their precise content. Almost everywhere, religious freedom, variously defined, figured among those rights, with the Constitution of the new Commonwealth of Australia being no exception.

However, the gap between religion as it was imagined, and religion as the life-experience of the faithful, meant that this right was fraught with uncertainties. In effect, if religion is understood in the reductive sense described above, a right to religious freedom grants the religious virtually nothing they would not have as a result of the freedoms of conscience, expression and association, other perhaps than the recognition of a right to educate one's children in the tenets of one's faith. And viewing it as such — as properly entailing no more than the application to the religious of rights that are really no different in kind from those accorded (say) to pacifists or to promoters of vegetarianism — has been an important element in the secularist argument against a specific right to religious freedom, not least in Australia.

But if religion involves more than acceptance of a credo, and instead is an intensely-held commitment to a set of personal obligations, collective practices and social ties, then a right to religious freedom is rich in substantive implications, touching areas that go from the structuring and management of religious organisations through to issues such as the display of sacred symbols, religious dress, ritual slaughter and the ability to undertake mandated rites in schools and workplaces.

The tensions that creates were present from the start. As Teresa Bejan has brilliantly shown, when the invention and rapid diffusion of the printing press made it vastly easier to challenge the established order, the result was an outpouring of pamphlets, broadsheets and volumes in which the contending sects spawned by the Reformation attacked each other and the Catholic church as sinners, heretics and apostates.

Fearing that "contumelious words" and "persecution of the tongue" would fuel civil strife, ruler after ruler passed laws curbing freedom of expression, including the provisions against pamphleteering implemented in the German lands by the Peace of Augsburg (1555), the gag laws imposed in France in 1561, and England's prohibitions, enforced by the Star Chamber, on 'prophesying' (1576), conventicles (1593) and on any 'disputation regarding the Thirty-Nine Articles of the Church of England' (1621).

Even in the North American colonies, where a degree of toleration was the norm, similar restrictions were widespread, and were applied — at that times harshly — against groups, such as the Quakers, who, rather than being content with quiet worship, regarded assertive (and often aggressive) proselytism as a crucial religious duty. But the restrictions encountered a determined and effective opponent in John Williams, who ensured that the 1663 royal charter of the colony of Rhode Island and Providence Plantations, which he had founded, granted to all of colony's subjects the unprecedented right to the "free exercise and enjoyment of all their civil and religious rights" regardless of religious affiliation, in a colony with no established church at all. Piloting Rhode Island on what he called a "lively experiment" whose object was to show that "mere civility" — that is, civility without any added frills — provided a reliable basis for civil peace, Williams argued that accepting the cacophony, and occasional offensiveness, of discordant voices would not only avoid the violence required to silence them but would also allow the claims of true religion to be heard even by those, such as "a Jew, a Turk, a pagan, an Anti-Christian", who would otherwise have shunned the colony.

Williams' experiment was not without its challenges but his advocacy had widespread resonance. Even Locke, who had initially supported laws prohibiting dissident sects from proselytizing because their preachers so often used "reproachful, reviling, or abusive language against [other persons and beliefs], disturbing the peace, and engaging in quarrels and animosities," dramatically reversed course toward the end of his life. It was not just that those laws were so readily abused, making them "a matter of perpetual prosecution and animosity." It was also that they enforced hypocrisy, eroding the sincerity that must underpin the social bond.

For sure, a society in which people could speak freely would have plenty of bruised egos and heated tempers. But it was also the only one in which there could be genuine conviction. And the answer to the pains it caused lay not in repression but in teaching children that the "many inconveniences" they would inevitably encounter "require we should not be too sensible of every little hurt": "manly steadiness" was needed to sustain the "warfare of life" without jettisoning "Charity, Bounty and Liberality."

Ultimately, those views prevailed over the fear of civil strife, and formed an important part of the background to the sweeping guarantee of religion freedom embodied in the First Amendment to the Constitution of the United States. But as the jurisprudence associated with the First Amendment shows, the tensions between the narrow and the broader view of religion never entirely disappeared; now they have returned, and with a vengeance.

That largely reflects the wider forces that have reshaped social relations. The decline in religious observance, which accelerated throughout the advanced economies in the late 1960s and shows little sign of tapering off, was accompanied by a pervasive redefinition of personal identity, sexuality and gender relations in ways that are dramatically at odds with the teachings of the Abrahamic religions. At the same time, those new approaches have themselves been elevated into 'rights,' which include prohibitions on discrimination on the basis of sexuality and gender preferences. The result is a clash of rights, with many people of faith fearing that as the observant shrink into a minority, the right to religious freedom will fall victim to the tyranny of the majority. The fact that it is so difficult for those who do not live a life of faith to understand the intensity and significance of the religious experience for those who do only compounds those fears.

Greater foresight — and one might say, frankness — about the implications of thus extending non-discrimination rights to groups defined by sex and, especially, gender preference, could have made those consequences easier to manage. As a general matter, the new rights are ascriptive, in the sense of depending on a person's status, attaching, for example, to people who are transgender and giving them special protections. While such ascriptive rights are normally undesirable in a society based on equality before the law, there may be instances in which they are justifiable; nonetheless, careful thought about their nature and content is surely warranted *before* they are extended, rather than once they have been enshrined in law.

After all, every right imposes correlative obligations on third parties, i.e. on those who are required to observe it: to have a *right* to 'X' means nothing more nor less than to be entitled to claim that one has been *wronged* by those who withhold, deny or impede 'X.' It follows that if the new rights that were accorded, for example, on the basis of gender orientation, were to have any substance, they would allow claims to be made against those who fundamentally disagree with (say) 'gender fluidity,' do not believe they ought to be forced to legitimate it in matters such as the ethics that are taught to young people, and consider that giving in that respect would undermine their inner-most convictions about what is involved in living a life of integrity.

Since those consequences were predictable, a decision should have been made as to how they were to be handled; but instead of being tackled head-on, they were dealt with through exceptions and exclusions of uncertain scope and coverage, and in the case of same-sex marriage, largely ignored.

The problems that poses were acutely identified by Hannah Arendt when she warned, philosophically in *The Human Condition* (1958) and more polemically in her 'Notes on Little Rock' (1959), against confusing the *political*, which she defined as the area of human equality, with the *social*, which is the domain of life in which particularity has free play. "What equality is to the body politic — its innermost principle," she wrote, "discrimination is to society," where, "once we have entered it, we become subject to the old adage of 'like attracts like' which controls the whole realm of society in the innumerable variety of its groups and associations."

To use the coercive powers of the state to enforce non-discrimination in social interactions, she argued, cannot but threaten civil society, with the result that "very important possibilities of free association and group formation would disappear."

Moreover, the greater the extent to which rights were accorded on an ascriptive basis — empowering some groups over others — the worse the corrosion of civil society, and the undermining of civil peace, would be.

Nonetheless, as a practical matter, there is clearly no going back.

The question is therefore how the inevitable clashes between rights to religious freedom on the one hand, and the most contentious new rights on the other, should be addressed. Far from eliminating those clashes, a new statutory right to religious freedom — were one to be enacted in Australia — would only ensure they arose, making it even more important to have examined how they should be handled.

Managing the conflicts between rights

These are obviously difficult issues, and they are made no easier by the fact that 'rights' are generally regarded as much more than mere interests: they are, in Ronald Dworkin's terminology, individual "trumps that we can use against the state," and which as 'trumps' override all lesser claims. Moreover, nowadays 'rights' are widely viewed as inalienable, as compared to say Hobbes' belief that they are extinguished on the formation of political society or Locke's argument that they are transferred to the state when it is formed. Finally, the rights that embody fundamental freedoms are typically not seen as justified by the effect of their exercise in particular circumstances but as inherent in human dignity and in the nature of political society, so that they are — in the language of political philosophy — deontological rather than consequentialist.

Clashes between rights would therefore seem irresoluble, giving rise to what might properly be called tragic consequences — much as in the great tragedies of Aeschylus and Sophocles each ethical command struggles to avoid subordination to ethical commands that contradict it, with the outcomes inevitably involving the sacrifice of important values. But no matter how tragic the consequences may be, the fact remains that when rights clash the law must determine an outcome, and even accepting that outcome will never be fully satisfactory, the question is what should guide its selection.

At a general level, this question could be addressed in one of at least two ways. A first approach would rank rights lexically, allowing weightier or more important rights to 'trump' their less important counterparts. A second approach, that has been adopted by the international bodies such as the European Court of Human Rights (and seems to be endorsed by the recent *Religious Freedom Review*), considers each clash of rights through a balancing exercise that asks whether a restriction on a right is 'proportionate' to the harm which is to be averted and no more restrictive than necessary to actually avert that harm.

However, both these approaches are fraught with difficulties. Thus, even though the lexical approach seems attuned to the deontological character of rights, clarity is rarely provided as to how lexical orderings should be determined. Equally, the balancing approach is extremely open-ended, and has, in the European Court of Human Rights and elsewhere, led to decisions that are unpredictable, controversial and often inconsistent.

A way forward might seek to combine those approaches, using each one to temper the difficulties of the other.

It should, for example, be clear that the right of religious freedom has high priority relative to other claims.

After all, it is no accident that when John Rawls — whose work has had an enormous influence on liberal egalitarianism — sought to justify what he calls the "lexical priority of the basic liberties," he illustrated it by reference to the intolerable 'strains' which being forced to perform an action that promises eternal damnation in the afterlife would cause to the commitments to mutual accommodation that are crucial for civil peace.

And when the distinguished philosopher Charles Taylor, writing with Jocelyn Maclure, argued in favour of religious exemptions from many types of non-discrimination requirements, he and his co-author emphasized that matters of faith are not mere opinions: they are "moral beliefs which structure moral identity," that is "meaning-giving beliefs and commitments." Forcing a person to act contrary to those deep conscientious convictions constitutes a "moral harm" equivalent to the kind of "physical harm" that justifies citizens with disabilities being specially accommodated.

There is therefore a compelling case for stating, as the guiding principle of a statutory right of religious freedom, that in any consideration of possible restrictions on the exercise of that right, religious beliefs and collective practices which play a pivotal place in the life of faith communities must be given great weight, and only disturbed when doing so is indispensable to preventing a grievous and greater harm. There would, to that extent, be a strong presumption in favour of religious freedom, recognizing the damage that is caused when individuals are obliged, by the coercive powers of the state, to act against their life-defining commitments.

That would still leave room for that right to be qualified in particular instances. But it should be clear that in assessing those instances, the courts implementing that right would be required to conform to the guiding principle, even if they then rely on the tests of proportionality and minimum restrictiveness for its application. Moreover, in applying those tests, they should be required to ensure not only that the proposed restriction was proportionate and minimally restrictive, but also that the goal could not be achieved less harmfully by sacrificing other claims instead.

It is, for example, difficult to believe that the harm done to a gay couple when an individual baker, operating in competition with myriad others, refuses to supply them with a wedding cake is greater than the harm that baker would suffer in being conscripted to work against conscience.

And it is equally hard to believe that the harm done to the sensitivities of a few when a preacher, however floridly, condemns homosexuality as a mortal sin could possibly outweigh that done by stifling the free expression of sincere belief.

None of that would not appease the most ardent secularists, nor those who are as eager to suppress critics as they are aggressive in demanding toleration for themselves. The alternative, however, is to turn our back on liberties that have not only always been cherished as part of Australia's essential character but have also contributed to forging a society that, instead of pretending that social conflict can be avoided, has learnt to harness it as a creative force.

Conclusions

Ultimately, religious freedom is the freedom to live with integrity in the light of faith. Without that freedom, which was hard won, people of faith would not be accorded equal respect, instead having to subordinate their lives to the preferences and dictates of others. They would, in that sense, be dominated by others, rather than in fact being free. And unlike other citizens, they would be constantly confronted with a choice between disobeying the law and disobeying the demands of their legacy and the dictates of their conscience.

However, protecting religious freedom requires more than well-crafted rights of opinion, expression and association. Thus, for most faith communities, the dictates of faith are not solely creedal but encompass a whole way of life, whose demands form part of an inter-generational chain that extends both into the remote past and into the indefinable future. As a result, to assure religious freedom, there must be no less protection for collective practices than there is for individual belief, including the collective practices that cover matters such as religious symbolism, religious education, and religious burial.

Obviously, such rights are not absolute, and have never been held to be. But the role faith plays in determining one's sense of what is involved in living a life of integrity means they deserve the greatest respect, and should only be tampered with when the case for doing so is overwhelming. No doubt, the exercise of those rights will, at times, be offensive: but so too are the always robust and often rambunctious clashes that are the hallmark of Australian democracy. That is the price we pay for the liberties that make a free society. And with those freedoms giving us more than two centuries of peace and prosperity, it remains, as it has always been, a small price to pay.

Chapter 2

FROM LIBERAL TOLERANCE TO POSTMODERN (IN)TOLERANCE

Augusto Zimmermann

First Considerations: Locke and Religious tolerance

John Locke (1632-1704) is known as the 'Founder of Liberalism' due to his immense contributions to political philosophy. Those contributions provided a justification not only for the Glorious Revolution in England, but also to the United States' Declaration of Independence 100 years later. Above all, and for the purposes of this chapter, Locke was the leading philosopher of his time to deal with the problem of religious tolerance. Locke was a philosopher of the first order and an enormously influential political thinker and fierce advocate of inalienable rights of the individual. With the writings of Locke in mind, the early modern debate over religious tolerance began in the seventeenth century and it proceeds to this very day.

Locke was born in 1632 as the son of a Puritan family in the west of England. His father, who was a small landowner and supporter of Presbyterianism, fought on the side of Parliament during the English Civil War. Locke was raised according to the Christian faith and after attending the Westminster School in London, he went to Oxford in 1652 as a student at Christ Church College. Following his graduation with a M.A. degree, Locke became a fellow of Christ Church in 1658, a position he held until 1684 when he was expelled for political reasons.[1] Later in life, he would achieve an enduring reputation with his philosophical treatise, An *Essay Concerning*

Human Understanding (1689). In defence of the right of revolution and formation of classical liberalism, Locke also wrote *Two Treatises on Civil Government* (1689). As for his works on religious tolerance, these include primarily A *Letter Concerning Toleration* (1689), *Some Thoughts Concerning Education* (1693), and *The Reasonableness of Christianity* (1695).

During the late 1670s, Locke was associated with the Earl of Shaftesbury (Anthony Ashley-Cooper). Shaftesbury was a prominent politician during the reign of King Charles II. He eventually became the leader of an opposition movement. Such a movement was developed in Parliament as a result of growing fears that England was moving toward a form of Catholic absolutism akin to that of Louis XIV's France. Shaftesbury and his allies launched a campaign to exclude Charles II's Catholic brother and next heir, James, Duke of York, from the succession to the throne. When he eventually succeeded to the throne as James II, in 1685, and pursued the trend toward monarchical absolutism, it forced Shaftesbury to flee for political refuge to Amsterdam, where he died in 1683. Fearful for his safety, Locke also took refuge in Holland in the autumn of 1683, and returned to England only five years later, following the revolution against James II that replaced him with William and Mary as sovereigns.[2]

Locke's *A Letter Concerning Toleration* dates from his period of exile in the Netherlands. It was written during this exile, in 1683, and against the background of the *Edict of Nantes* (1598) and the Catholic reign of James II in Britain. There Locke censures religious persecution not only of Christians but also the persecution of pagans and idolaters, as well as the forcible conversion of Indians in America. Indeed, writes Perez Zagorin, "the incompatibility of religious intolerance with the spirit and teaching of Christ was one of his major themes."[3]

In this sense, Locke's defence of religious freedom (one which is certainly in line with the thought of the greatest thinkers in the classical liberal tradition) was not grounded on a doubt about 'truth' or a sympathy to the beliefs that he thought should be simply tolerated. Instead, Locke argued that the opinions he proposed to tolerate could be even completely "false and absurd," at least according to his opinion.[4] Although Locke was adamant that there is "only one way to heaven," and that humans should observe God's moral laws with the "utmost care, application and diligence in seeking out and performing them,"[5] still he believed that everyone is *individually* responsible for finding "the narrow way and the straight gate that leads to heaven."[6] Because he believed that "man cannot be forced to be saved,"[7] Locke then concluded that matters pertaining to religious truth should "be left to individual conscience and individual discernment."[8]

Locke applied: Religious tolerance in the American and Australian constitutions

Thomas G. West describes Locke as "a major theologian whose interpretation of Christianity was tremendously influential in Britain and America."[9] As noted by Alex Chafuen, "it is hard to read any work by Locke that does not bring up God or the Bible."[10] Indeed, as Locke stated in 1697: "The honour and veneration of the Creator, and the happiness of mankind. This is that noble study which is every man's duty, and every one that can be called a rational creature is capable of," stated Locke in 1697.[11] He also believed that freedom of speech and freedom of conscience are the very essence of the Christian defence of religious toleration. Such an understanding of religious tolerance is not grounded on any doubt about the 'truth' or sympathy to religious beliefs that Locke thought they should be tolerated. Instead, as mentioned above, Locke was adamant that most of the opinions he proposed to tolerate were, in fact, "false and absurd."[12]

The contemporary readers of Locke understood him as offering a consistent defence of religious tolerance that was fully compatible with orthodox Christian beliefs.[13] The Reverend Samuel Cooper, in preaching favourably about the American Revolution in 1779, remarked that the principles on which the American revolutionaries were acting were "to be found in the immortal writings of … Locke and other glorious defenders of the liberties of human nature."[14] It is undisputable that Locke's defence of religious tolerance ultimately inspired the drafters of the first amendment to the U.S. Constitution, which establishes the free exercise of religion and the principle of church-state separation.[15] In eighteenth century America, Locke was, after the Bible, "the principal authority relied on by the preachers to bolster up their political teachings."[16]

The American colonists aimed to enshrine Lockean principles of natural law and fundamental rights in their new system of government. The *American Declaration of Independence* of 1776 expresses a Lockean belief that "all Men are created equal, that they are endowed by their Creator with certain inalienable Rights," which perfectly reflects the belief in natural law and natural rights as described by Locke.[17] Accordingly, the Founders believed that it is the natural law enacted by God and discoverable by reason that the inalienability of fundamental rights is authoritatively prescribed — rights that are not conferred on people by government and so they cannot legitimately be denied by the political sovereign.[18] Ultimately, Locke's advocacy of religious tolerance inspired the drafters of the First Amendment to the U.S. Constitution to enact the establishment clause as well as the free exercise of religion.[19]

The Australian Founders considered very carefully the example of the U.S. Constitution when drafting section 116 of the Australian Constitution. During the constitutional conventions, it was noted that, in America, Christianity continued to be a major influence in the creation of federal law regardless of the First Amendment.[20] This was so regardless of the absence of explicit constitutional reference to the country as a Christian nation. Recognising, however, the potential for individual religious bodies to exploit the new federal system, section 116 of the Australian Constitution was designed to guard against a situation in which the members of one particular denomination might dominate the federal Parliament, thus enacting legislation which establishes their own body as the National Church, or introducing religious tests that favour admission of individuals from their own religious denomination to the federal tier of government.

This certainly does not amount to a rejection of religious sentiments. After all, there is an explicit reference to God in the Australian Constitution, one which actually received the strongest popular support of *any* part of the nation's foundational document. The insertion of an acknowledgment of God into the Preamble occurred in response to overwhelming public support coming from countless petitions as well as the colonial parliaments of Australia.[21] In their standard commentary on the Australian Constitution, John Quick (one of the drafters of the Constitution) and Robert Garran (who played a significant role in the Australian Federation movement) stated:

> This appeal to the Deity was inserted in the Constitution at the suggestion of most of the Colonial Legislative Chambers, and in response to numerous and largely signed petitions received from the people of every colony represented in the Federal Convention [...] In justification of the insertion of the words stress was laid on the great demonstration of public opinion in their favour, as expressed in the recommendations of the Legislative bodies and in the petitions presented.[22]

Also in their authoritative commentary, Quick and Garran explain that "[b]y the establishment of religion is meant the erection and recognition of a State Church, or the concession of special favours, titles, and advantages to one church which are denied to others. It is not intended to prohibit the Federal Government from recognizing religion or religious worship."[23] They further elaborated upon the implications of this section:

> The Christian religion is [...] recognised as a part of the common law. There is abundant authority for saying that Christianity is part and parcel of the law of the land [...] Consequently the fundamental principles of the Christian religion will continue to be respected, although not enforced by Federal legislation. For example, the Federal Parliament will have to provide for the administration of oaths in legal proceedings, and there is nothing to prevent it from enabling an oath to be taken, as at common law, on the sanctity of the Holy Gospel.[24]

Section 116 of the Australian Constitution precludes the federal parliament from making laws for establishing any religion. This is classically understood as the establishment clause in the Australian Constitution. And yet, it is profoundly erroneous, although increasingly popular, to assert that the establishment clause was aimed at enshrining a rigid secularism. Far from seeking to banish religion from government and society, the Founders intended a laissez-faire environment which ensured that no religious body would enjoy unfair advantage on account of federal endorsement. As noted by Stuart

Piggin, from the very beginning the Australian federation has rested on the principle of inter-dependence between church and state. These two institutions have co-operated considerably to build the nation, and the 'plural establishment' consisting of the public funding of Anglican, Catholic and Presbyterian churches established in the days of Governor Bourke was a visible sign of this.[25]

An accompanying benefit is that section 116 protects religious freedom from government encroachment. This is different from prohibiting the promotion of religious values. Indeed, such provision cannot be used to stop federal laws assisting the practice of religion, or to provide financial support to religious schools, hospitals, or charitable organisations. Its purpose is to limit the role of government and not to limit the role of the church or another religious grouping. In fact, section 116 does not even inhibit this government from identifying itself with the predominant religious impulses of the people, thus even authorizing religious practices where we could all agree on their desirability. According to Michael Hogan, who is Research Associate in Government and International Relations at Sydney University:

> Australia does not have a legally entrenched principle, or even a vague set of conventions, of the separation of church and state. From the appointment of Rev. Samuel Marsden as one of the first magistrates in colonial New South Wales, to the adoption of explicit policies of state aid for denominational schools during the 1960s, to the two examples mentioned above, Australia has had a very consistent tradition of cooperation between church and state.[26]

Liberal tolerance vs Postmodernist 'Tolerance': new tolerance in the absence of truth

In the *Oxford English Dictionary*, the verb 'to tolerate' means "to endure, sustain (pain or hardship)." One is tolerant if he or she, while perhaps holding strong convictions, insists that others must have the right to dissent and to argue their cases freely. This meaning of tolerance implies that objective truth exists and can be known, although the best way to ascertain this truth is via a spirit of mutual understanding and open-mindedness; for whilst truth may be discovered, the wisest and least malignant course of action is to adopt an attitude of 'benign tolerance' grounded in intellectual modesty which is capable of recognising our intellectual limitations.

Since our liberal tradition considers that truths can be known, freedom of speech can be accepted as an important mechanism through which falsehood can be eliminated. Regrettably, however, given the moral relativism of our time the old meaning of tolerance is rapidly becoming obsolete and replaced by another form of 'tolerance' which denies the attainment of truth. To be 'tolerant' no longer implies a desire for the attainment of the truth through trial and error. To the contrary, this 'new tolerance' operates under a postmodernist assumption that 'truth' is subjective since it implies that all beliefs possess an equal validity. According to D.A. Carson in *The Intolerance of Tolerance* (2012):

> Intolerance is no longer a refusal to allow contrary opinions to say their piece in public, but must be understood to be any questioning or contradicting the view that all opinions are equal in value, that all worldviews have equal worth, that all stances are equally valid. To question such postmodern axioms is by definition intolerant. For such questioning there is no tolerance whatsoever, for it is classed as intolerance and must therefore be condemned. It has become the supreme vice.[27]

Religious truths were for debating in the public square — robustly and without fear of offence. But these days the 'old tolerance' proclaimed objective standards of truth, the 'new tolerance' argues from a relativist perspective in which no values and beliefs must be challenged. We have moved away from the free expression of contrary opinions to the acceptance that all opinions are equality valid and acceptable, whatever such opinions might be. This obviously changes the meaning of tolerance in terms of religious freedom from an attitude of permitting the articulation of contrary beliefs to asserting that all religious beliefs are equally valid and acceptable. Thus any claim that there might be only one possible way and truth did becomes morally reprehensible.[28]

Because the 'new tolerance' proclaims that all values and beliefs are worthy of acceptance, desperate straits are no longer required from those who subjectively wish to claim the emotional status of being a victim of religious 'intolerance'. In such a context, all that might be required is 'the vaguest notion of emotional distaste at what another has said, done, proposed, or presented'.[29] When the meaning of tolerance can be distorted to such an extent, it practically signifies the impossibility of making reasonable judgement, and so the old link between tolerance and judgment has been lost due to the present cultural obsession with being non-judgemental.[30] As Frank Furedi points out, "when tolerance acquires the status of a default response connoting approval, people are protected from troubling themselves with the challenge of engaging with moral dilemmas."[31] Thus one might conclude that 'tolerance' has ceased to be a virtue so as to become "the superficial signifier of acceptance of affirmation of anyone and everyone."[32]

Postmodern 'Tolerance' and the Criminalisation of Truth-Telling

Although it is not easy to define postmodernism, one may loosely identify this as a label for a range of theoretical challenges to the objectivity of truth and knowledge. In Western societies, the idea of objective truth is traditionally linked to the relation between the real world and statements that correspond to the real world. Post-modernists, by contrast, deny that any objective truth can be achieved. For them, everything one knows is solely the subject of social context and cultural surroundings.

The sort of religious tolerance laws being enacted in our Western societies are directly inspired by the work of postmodern scholars. Whereas in the past our societies defined freedom in terms of freedom to seek for the truth, now "we put the emphasis upon creating a social, harmonious, and multicultural community."[33] A clear example of such a postmodern legislation is the notorious Victorian *Racial and Religious Tolerance Act*, which claims that in determining who might have committed 'religious vilification', "it is irrelevant whether or not the person who has made an assumption about the race or religious belief or activity of another person or class of persons, was incorrect at the time that the contravention is alleged to have taken place."[34]

In this sense, the motivation behind a person's statement is irrelevant for the purposes of the legislation.[35] In other words, one may be found guilty of vilification "by conduct which has the effect of inciting religious hatred even where the inciter had no intention to do so."[36] Such is the situation that unless this person falls within the exceptions of art, academic, religion, science, or public interest, such person is legally restricted in the manner whereby he or she can express an opinion on these important issues. This creates a distinction in which only the 'eloquent' forms of expression are allowed whilst the opinions of the average citizen are severely restricted.[37]

Why would the Victorian law state that the truth cannot be used as a defence against charges of religious vilification? After all, ascertainment of the truth has always amounted to an important element of defence in defamation cases, and so it should be. The answer seems to lie in the postmodern underpinning of religious vilification laws. Whereas the pursuit of the truth works as a primary element of defence in defamation cases, postmodern philosophy indicates that there is no objective truth and that 'truths' are socially constructed and invariably relative. However, if truth is relative to social context, then everything is always entirely relative and who are we to criticise different ideas? That being so, it is the criticism of any religion itself that deserves our moral condemnation, because the law in such a case operates under the philosophical premise that truth is always relative; and according to postmodern theorist Stanley Fish, there is 'no such thing as free speech' that should validate a person's strong criticism of religion.[38]

This explains why religious tolerance laws often sustain the premise that the truth of a statement cannot be relied on as a defence. Such law rests upon a postmodern premise that is sceptical of objective truth, which also means that such laws are not taking religion seriously. According to American law professor Carl Esbeck, "one who has never disagreed with others about religion is not ... commendably tolerant, but is treating religious difference as trivial, as if religious beliefs do not matter. That is just a soft form of religious bigotry."[39]

Our most influential postmodern thinkers have also been atheists, including Michel Foucault, Jean-François Lyotard, Pierre Macherey,

Gilles Deleuze, Jacques Lacan, and Jacques Derrida.[40] Macherey, for instance, was described as "a Marxist critic concerned with how texts act to reproduce the values of capitalism."[41] His philosophy rested on a 'loosely Marxist framework' that aspired to "bring Marx up to date."[42] Broadly speaking, he would agree with Friedrich Nietzsche's statement that "God" — which is to say, the supreme being of classical theism — "has become unbelievable, as have the autonomous self and the meaning of history."[43] Alister McGrath spoke of the intimate relationship between atheism and postmodern philosophy:

> Many Postmodern writers are, after all, atheist (at least in the sense of not actively believing in God). The very idea of deconstruction seems to suggest that the idea of God ought to be eliminated from Western culture as a power play on the part of churches and others with vested interests in its survival.[44]

Although Marxism can be described as a form of dialectical logic and postmodernism operates primarily as a reaction to all forms of dialectic, postmodernist philosophy actually emerged from the Marxist tradition of anti-Western philosophy. Karl Marx himself was a moral relativist. As evidence of this, he believed that human rights are neither inalienable or universal, but conditional and socially determined. The Marxist link is particularly evident with respect to all those French postmodernists who invariably emerged from the Marxist tradition. Macherey, for instance, was a Marxist critic "concerned with how texts act to reproduce the values of capitalism."[45] His theory rests almost exclusively on a "loosely Marxist framework" that aspired to "bring Marx up to date."[46]

Foucault provides another example of a postmodernist theorist who primarily addressed the relationship between power and knowledge from a Marxist perspective. He once was an active member of the Maoist *Gauche Proletarienne* as well as the French Communist Party, but left the latter when he discovered the traditional Marxist approach to homosexuality.[47] Despite this well-known aversion to a few aspects of Marxist theory, Foucault did not entirely abandon Marxist thought altogether. To the contrary, he remained under the profound influence of Marxist analyses of power relations and the role of economic inequality in determining social structures.[48] Mark

Lilla notes that Foucault felt a deep desire to develop something even "more radical" than orthodox Marxism. So he turned not only to Nietzsche and Heidegger, but also to avant-garde writers and Surrealists whose hostility to bourgeois life took a more aesthetic and psychological forms.[49] Inspired by these philosophical variants, Foucault argued that truth is not disinterested or neutral, but that truth is rather an instrument of power and, ultimately, an attempt to conceal biases under the mask of objectivity.[50]

In Foucault's view, "all knowledge rests upon injustice'"; and further, "there is no right, not even in the act of knowing, to truth or a foundation for truth; and the instinct for knowledge is *malicious* (something murderous, opposed to the happiness of mankind)."[51] Since he blamed Western Civilisation for colonialism and the oppression of other civilisations, he notoriously advocated for moral relativism on cultural grounds, thinking that Westerners were both the product and agent of a diabolical capitalist system which is inherently oppressive and exploitative. In a nutshell, Foucault embraced a critical view of Western Civilisation which condemned its citizens as irretrievably evil and corrupt, and, accordingly, a legitimate target of anti-Western terrorism.

This combination of Western self-hatred and cultural relativism resulted in Foucault's open support not only for Maoism in China but also for the Iranian Islamic Revolution, in 1978. As the Islamic protests against the Shah of Iran reached their zenith, Foucault visited Iran in order to lend unconditional support to the notorious theocratic leader of that Islamist revolution, Ayatollah Khomeini. After meeting with Khomeini in his capacity as a special correspondent for *Corriere della Sera* and *Le Nouvel Observateur*,[52] Foucault then produced numerous articles in favour of religious extremism. He interpreted the Iranian Islamic Revolution as a turning point in world history. According to him, such an oppressive Islamic revolution apparently signalled the end of Western hegemony that could "set the entire region afire" and forever change the "global strategic equilibrium." As Mervyn Bendle points out:

> Foucault's assessment became rapturous, describing the revolution as a mystical manifestation of 'an absolute collective

will' that has 'erupted into history', 'like God, like the soul'. He endorsed the Islamist claim that democratic political systems are inherently corrupt, and that Iranian theocracy, with all its brutality, expressed the 'collective will' of the Iranian people in a pure and uncorrupted fashion that Western democracy could never match. This is a view of democracy shared by many [postmodern] academics. Throughout his life Foucault was also fascinated with suicide and sadomasochistic sexuality. In Iran he was attracted to the ideal of revolutionary martyrdom and embraced its 'discourse of death'. He was mesmerised by the marching columns of black-clad men, rhythmically flagellating themselves in prolonged rituals of mass penitence, celebrating a 'political spirituality' that embraced death and would, he proclaimed with delight, overwhelm a decadent and materialist West.[53]

Foucault endorsed that Islamic Revolution because it was anti-modern, anti-liberal and, above all, anti-Western. He interpreted radical Islamism as a positive factor of upheaval at the heart of Western Civilisation. Because leftists such as him have a visceral hatred of Western democracy, they can sympathise with the radical Islamists as the enemy of their Christian mono-culture and as an anti-colonial and therefore 'progressive' force. Moreover, such leftists may attempt to establish a tactical alliance with the Islamists in order to further undermine Western democracy. They hope that Islam can become "the spearhead of a new insurrection in the name of the oppressed."[54] In the postmodern mind of the extreme Left, writes French philosopher Pascal Bruckner,

the hatred of the market is worth a few compromises regarding fundamental rights, and especially of the equality between men and women. The [Islamists], disguised as friends of tolerance, are dissimulating and using the Left to advance their interests under the mask of a progressive rhetoric ... Two currents of thought form temporary alliances against a common enemy: it is not hard to predict which one will crush the other once its objectives have been achieved. The Leftist intransigence that refuses any comprise with bourgeois society and cannot castigate too severely "little white men" actively collaborates with the most reactionary elements in the Muslim religion. But if the far Left courts this totalitarian theocracy so assiduously, it is perhaps less a matter of opportunism than of a real affinity. The far Left has never gotten over communism and once again demonstrates that its true passion is not freedom but slavery in the name of "justice".[55]

I am a legal academic who have personally witnessed the great fascination exercised by postmodern philosophy on many of my colleagues. This might explain why religious tolerance laws do not seem to take religious claims seriously.[56] According to postmodernist theory, what one takes as 'truth' is no more than a certain Christian, Jewish, Hindu, Muslim perspectives, for example. Such perspectives are 'correct' only in terms of corresponding to the socio-cultural context. And yet, they may sometimes be readily dismissed as naïve at the best and deceptive at the worst, in such cases as an attempt by any religious group to impose their own perspective on all the others groups.

Postmodernists often argue that religion is actually socially divisive. Allegedly, religious people believe in ideas of absolute truth that are intolerant of different opinions. This assumption was not shared by John Locke and other political philosophers in the classical liberal tradition. As previously demonstrated, one may display strong religious convictions and still remain entirely tolerant of the expression of 'erroneous' opinion. By contrast, the imposition by postmodernist legislation may engender quite serious limitations to the free expression of religious ideas on grounds of achieving religious 'tolerance.' Such is the case when 'un-enlightened' legislators embrace a postmodernist philosophy that denies objective truth and approaches any such matters according to the subjective lens of personal preferences.

Ironically, the postmodernist scepticism of truth claims allows religious tolerance laws to be more hijacked to a great degree by extremists who may claim that they — rather than their religious beliefs, per se — have been attacked. Indeed, some hard multiculturalists argue that a strong criticism of religious practices without regard for the traditional values of a particular group can be highly insensitive and even deserving a legal disapproval.[57] This allows religious organisations such as the Islamic Council of Victoria to remain committed to promoting practices that seriously affect the rights and freedoms of women, while using the language of multiculturalism to advance its illiberal argument. In a submission to the Commonwealth Parliament's Join Standing Committee on Migration, the Rev Peter Kurti reminds us that this Islamic council contended that in a 'tolerant and multicultural' society, "one should be able to observe religious Halal, wear the burqa, and build places of worship without hindrance."[58] Indeed, as Kurti points out,

> When a modern liberal culture is considered of equal value to a culture in which the freedom of women is so restricted, it diminishes the defining characteristic of that liberal culture as the defender of individual liberty. Clearly, the non-judgemental, tolerant freedom of expression defended by advocates [of hard multiculturalism] is, in fact, a circumscribed from of freedom.[59]

Kurti goes on to remind us how 'hard multiculturalists' resort to using anti-discrimination laws of Australia, "to secure precisely those kinds of 'cultural' rights" that undermine our liberal tradition of individual rights and freedoms. He correctly argues that the moral strength of a liberal democracy such as Australia, "which has the principle of individual freedom at its core, must not allow itself to be weakened by the cultural relativism and political correctness advanced by hard multiculturalists."[60] In a world where Islamic terrorism has become a major threat and where some radical Muslims express sympathy with the terrorists, the ability of our society to defend its interests is diminished by legislation which makes citizens particularly reluctant to make critical statements or give warnings about the adverse nature of religious beliefs, however well-based these warnings might be. This is the singular tragedy of a 'multicultural' society which allows legislation underpinned by postmodern philosophy to generate such a dramatic restriction of free speech and open deliberation on some of the most relevant issues of public morality.

If things weren't bad enough, some federal politicians are now effectively seeking to extend the reach of section 18C of the *Racial Discrimination Act* (Cth) to religious grounds. Under such a provision, it is unlawful for a person to do an act (other than in private) if the act "is reasonably likely, in all the circumstances, to offend, insult, humiliate or intimidate" a person where the act is done "because of the race, colour or national or ethnic origin of the other person or of some or all of the people in the group."[61] Chris Merritt, legal affairs editor of *The Australian* newspaper, reported that the Labor Party was considering a plan to extend the reach of litigation based on this provision to include people claiming they have been offended or insulted because of their religion.[62]

The proposal comes from the Egyptian-born Muslim MP, Dr Anne Aly, who seeks to expand the scope of anti-discrimination laws to religion, while simultaneously imposing significant restrictions on free speech. She contends that there was "scope to reassess" extending section 18C, saying the racism debate now "extends to religion".[63] Dr Aly also claims that extending 18C to cover religion is important because "we have definitely seen an increase in anti-Islamic rhetoric".[64] Effectively that would mean Australia has a federal blasphemy law because criticising Islamic beliefs in a way that offend Muslims could breach the law.[65] Not surprisingly, such a proposal has received the enthusiastic support from the Federation of Islamic Councils' president, Keysar Trad. "Of course we need religious protection. Section 18C should be strengthened and broadened … so that Australians can go about their legitimate daily business ... free from persecution on the basis of their religious affiliation," Mr Trad says.[66]

Fortunately, this appalling idea that the criticism of religion or religious beliefs should become unlawful in Australia has been rejected by the Ruddock Report, the Religious Freedom Review.[67] In fact, members of this expert panel appointed to examine whether Australian law adequately protects the human right to freedom of religion, recommended the *abolition* of the criminal offence of blasphemy, where needed, and the removal of some mentions of this offence from Commonwealth law.[68] These are sensible proposals because, as correctly noted by associate professor Neil Foster, "to enact laws making it a civil wrong to 'offend' on the basis of religion would unduly restrict legitimate debate about this important area, and run the risk that those who are frustrated because they cannot speak about their concerns, will in fact resort more easily to violence".[69] In the end, writes Foster, the best way of exposing the darkness of those who commit religiously-motivated harm against others, would seem to be to bring into play the strong light of full and frank dialogue, so that those views can be clearly challenged and exposed. Preserving free on these and other issues is virtually important.[70]

Final Considerations

Tolerance once meant the acceptance of contrary opinions that you may particularly dislike. That so being, the great Dutch jurist Hugo Grotius (1583-1645) advocated that religious tolerance should be based on the idea that there is no other way to defend the truth rather than by exposing truth itself to public scrutiny and critical assessment.[71] That nobody can be regarded as a free person unless he or she possesses the right to express their opinion constitutes the essence of a classical liberal defence of religious toleration. Religious tolerance as properly conceived leaves you free to believe and say it in public square, but also free to criticise and condemn as 'false and absurd' as per Locke. But given the moral relativism of our time, this traditional view of religious tolerance is gradually being discarded, and replaced as it is by a postmodernist approach which denies any possibility of truth. Such a contemporary approach declares the moral equivalence of all religious values and beliefs.

Western societies have therefore moved away from the free exercise of religious expression to the assumption that all religious beliefs are equally valid. Once our society slides from the classical liberal view of religious tolerance to a such a morally relativist postulation, tolerance ceases to signify the reasonable assumption that individuals have the right to express different opinions on such religious matters, and society starts to morph itself into a censor of opinions and statements that contradict the assumption that all religions are equally valid. To question such a relativistic assumption is therefore to commit a great 'sin' and to be guilty of the ultimate act of religious intolerance.

To conclude, the classical link between tolerance and judgment has been lost due to the refusal to pass valid judgment. A 'new tolerance' is therefore developed on the sole basis of celebration of religious diversity. This is done for diversity's sake and regardless of moral considerations. Such a premise reduces religious conviction to an entirely private matter as a result of legislation that embraces the postmodern fallacy that every religion must be tolerated simply because no religion can be entirely true. The legislators who have enacted such postmodernist law have accepted the postmodern denial of ultimate truth and have proceeded to perceive religious claim as no more than personal *preferences* that may even be ultimately illogical, absurd, and mendacious but which by itself does not allow for the rational manifestation of strong disagreement.

Chapter 3

A WATERSHED MOMENT: THE FRAGILE FUTURE OF RELIGIOUS FREEDOM

Julian Porteous

Change in the legal definition of marriage

The national debate on changing the legal definition of marriage was a watershed moment in Australian social history. The outcome was essentially determined by a non-binding, non-compulsory plebiscite that resulted in a large vote for 'yes' from those who voted — which was just shy of a majority of all eligible voters.[1] If the plebiscite had been conducted as a compulsory vote, my sense is that it would have been much closer. In any case, what this outcome shows is that Australian society has reached a tipping point.

Around half the population have rejected as normative the natural and biblical understanding of the nature of marriage; which has the complementarity of the sexes at its heart. This is not a sudden development. The importance of the complementarity of the sexes has been challenged vigorously since the sexual revolution of the 1960s. The 2017 plebiscite campaign and its success simply showed that the battle to defend this essential reality of human sexuality had been lost for some time. The actual 'yes' vote campaign for change did not really have to do much convincing — that work had already largely been done. It was simply a matter of reminding voters of how they already felt. The institutions of the society, including the churches and religious organisations, were largely ignored and considered irrelevant by the general public during this process.

This rejection of basic biological reality is unprecedented in human history and builds on a trend in western societies of de-linking the intrinsic relationship between marriage and the begetting of children. It touches on a foundational element upon which societies have been built. Throughout Judeo-Christian history it has been understood that human beings do best when raised by their biological parents in a relationship of lifelong committed sexual fidelity. This is why marriage was given special social and political recognition and protections. Marriage has been seen to be about procreation, about the nurturing and raising of children, about providing the next generation for society. Now, for the first time in the history of western civilisation, this understanding has been officially rejected and replaced with a new paradigm for human life and relationships based now principally on feelings.

The legal redefinition of marriage has been a significant turning point in Australian social history. The full negative implications of this decision will slowly manifest itself in the years ahead.

Christianity overridden

The vote and subsequent legislation rushed through parliament before Christmas 2017 has revealed another significant shift in Australian culture, which from the beginning understood itself as basically Christian. From the time of the first British settlements in the late eighteenth century, the Christian faith underpinned the spiritual and moral vision of the settlers. Being of British origins, the Anglican expression of Christianity provided the institutional religious base for the society. Indeed, being a convict settlement, the clergy were seen as essential to establishing and maintaining the proper religious and moral values for this new settlement. Convicts were compelled to attend Sunday services, as this was considered beneficial to their moral regeneration. Australian government was founded on principles of the Westminster system which upheld the ultimate authority of God over the exercise of political power. The rule of law was seen as necessary for social cohesion and the law was based on Christian principles, in particular the Ten Commandments.

The plebiscite vote of 2017 saw Australia turn its back on its Christian heritage. While opposition to the change in the legal definition of marriage was largely led by Christian voices, many who identified as Christians actually chose to vote for change. The leadership of the Christian churches were not able to convince their own members to hold to the traditional understanding of marriage. Many adherents of Christianity have moved away from traditional Christian teaching. Popular culture rather than the Church, now largely shapes how people think on important social issues.

What is certainly evident from the vote is that the Christian churches no longer enjoy the role of guiding the conscience of the nation. Again, this was not a recent phenomenon. For decades the standing and influence of the Christian churches in this country has been declining. The situation has been significantly exacerbated of late by the Royal Commission into Institutional Responses to Child Sex Abuse, with its damning findings of sexual abuse of children and of institutional cover-up and inaction in once trusted Australian institutions, especially the churches.[2] There is evidence of a significant loss of trust in church leadership as a result.[3]

Indeed, Christianity is fast becoming a minority religion in Australia; and its influence on the people and the culture will continue to be further marginalised in the coming years. The Christian teaching on many issues will be regarded by the Australian society as no longer relevant. Christians will quickly need to come to terms with a new reality as a minority.

Religious freedom

The plebiscite on the legal definition of marriage has exposed another issue of great concern: a growing intolerance towards those who hold the traditional understanding of marriage and human sexuality. Many who publicly expressed their opposition to changing the legal definition of marriage found themselves threatened or vilified. The debate was far from reasoned and respectful. Those who sought to defend the traditional understanding of marriage were subject to harassment. They were characterised as 'homophobes', 'bigots' and 'haters.' They were labelled and dismissed. This created a 'chilling effect' in that many of those who supported a traditional view of marriage found it was wiser to stay silent than to attract ridicule and derision. Venues for meetings of those supporting the retention of the traditional view of marriage were threatened. A number of meetings were forced to be cancelled. The practice of 'non-platforming' sought to silence those who wished to express their views in a reasoned and respectful manner.

The debate showed a nasty side of those who preached inclusion and diversity — except for those who disagreed with them. It revealed that there were individuals and organisations determined to shut down debate and simply impose their views on the society. The very notion of even having a debate on the question was referred to as 'hurtful' and 'offensive'. To allow the public expression of views that opposed the change in the legal definition was claimed to constitute an attack on those in same-sex relationships and their families.

Concerns about — among other things — the efforts of those from the 'yes' side of the campaign to prevent the expression of opposing views, gave rise to calls to protect freedom of speech and religious freedom. Up to this time, religious freedom was considered a given in Australian society. The debate revealed this was no longer the case.

Ruddock Report

Calls for protection of basic freedoms led to the decision of the Turnbull government to initiate a review of protections for freedom of religion in Australia. Phillip Ruddock was asked to head up an expert panel.

Their long-awaited report was finally released in December 2018. It was less than reassuring for those hoping freedom of speech and freedom of religion would be enshrined in some form of legislation. The report said: the Panel remained unconvinced there is urgent need to strengthen religious freedom laws; and it did not receive sufficient evidence that the existing framework was causing significant problems.

The Panel concluded there was no need for government to legislate to protect agencies run by churches providing services such as aged care, health and education from losing funding because of their religious beliefs.[4] It argued that if government tried to discriminate in this way on a practical level, it would struggle to find alternate service providers. However, the Panel was of the view that in geographic areas where there is only one government-funded service provider, the government should be able to insist that the agency disregard its religious charter and not discriminate to preserve its religious identity. This means a Christian organisation filling a need in a rural or a remote community where there is no other government funded service could be forced to go against its Christian beliefs with regard to employment of staff or the programs it delivers.

The Report also supported the Australian Law Reform Commission view that religious freedom protections should not extend to providers of goods and services for weddings.

In all, the Report was far from encouraging. There is little to be expected in terms of legislation to protect religious freedom in Australia. The panel said it did not support a Religious Freedom Act, and that the statutory protection of positive rights "necessitates a framework which provides equal treatment for a wide range of human rights."

We face a future, I believe, where religious freedom in practice will be curtailed and freedom of speech increasingly limited. There are already a number of examples from overseas where individuals have stated a traditional understanding of human sexuality and marriage and been threatened with prosecution.

Threats to Religious Freedom

When it comes to the question of the right to practice one's faith in public or in private, alone or in community with others, in worship or in the building and running of schools, hospitals and social services, Australian law does very little to positively protect religious freedom. Instead, it tends only to offer limited protection through particular exemptions to anti-discrimination law.

For example, Catholics can legally maintain a male-only priesthood because of a specific exemption in the federal *Sex Discrimination Act* and state anti-discrimination acts. We can insist that school principals of faith-based schools are themselves people of faith only because of a specific exemptions in law. In other words, it is always by exception rather than a legally protected human right.

This approach to protecting religious freedom through exemptions gives the impression that a person of faith is being given a legal way to discriminate against others. In other words, that they are really doing something wrong that the government is willing to tolerate. This is clearly far from satisfactory. In the public forum, it is difficult to argue for religious freedom as protected through exemptions because of the false impression of it being nothing more than legally sanctioned discrimination.

The public debate around the redefinition of marriage has indeed brought the issue of religious freedom into focus. Unfortunately, public discussion on this matter has often focussed on the issue of the baker baking a cake for a same-sex wedding, or the right of a photographer to decline to provide their services to a same-sex couple. While these are clearly important issues, there are many matters of deeper significance for our society.

One of these concerns the rights of religious schools to give preference in employment to those who share the particular religion. Currently a religious school has no absolute legal protection to insist that its teachers uphold the tenets of the faith upon which the school was founded. There are already moves afoot in the federal government to remove even the partial exemptions that currently exist.

Religious schools were established with the fundamental purpose of providing education within a particular faith or religious tradition. To seek to prevent them from upholding that tradition with respect to either employment practices, enrolments or curriculum, effectively renders the whole point for their existence null and void. There have been moves — for example by the Northern Territory government — to deny schools the right to preference Christian students for enrolment and instead enforce a first-come, first-served policy.[5]

On the matter of enrolment policies, pressure may be applied to religious all-girls or all-boys school to allow the enrolment of students who are seeking to change their gender. It is likely that religious schools will encounter challenges to their policies in relation to uniform, team sports, camping accommodation and toilet facilities based on a child's biological sex. We can expect transgender advocacy groups to demand that schools be required to fully support children who are seeking to change their gender identity, and be prepared to challenge faith schools that refuse to fall in line.

The right of religious schools to teach the tenets of the faith underpinning the school's identity has also come under threat. The Brindabella Christian College in Canberra received threats from the ACT Education Minister for expressing a Christian view on marriage.[6] In the United Kingdom, the government's integration expert, Dame Louise Casey, told a government inquiry it was "not okay" for Catholic schools to be against same-sex marriage, because she claimed it is not how children are brought up in the UK.[7]

I am very concerned that we will see a growing trend across the western world, where governments will prevent parents from removing their children from classes that present positions in conflict with their religious or moral beliefs. We have already witnessed the efforts to impose the promotion of homosexuality and gender transition under the guise of anti-bullying through the Safe Schools program in Australia. While the federal Liberal government withdrew its support for this program in June 2017, it and similar programs continue to be imposed by state governments.

In other countries like the UK, governments are trying to make it compulsory for all schools — including religious schools — to teach about LGBT issues. In 2017, the Vishnitz private Jewish school in the UK failed its third Ofsted inspection and was threatened with closure because, in addition to other issues raised, it refused to teach pupils about homosexuality issues.[8] More recently, the UK government published *The Independent Schools Standards: advice for independent schools*, which would more forcefully require religious schools to promote LGBT issues.[9] This set of standards is now being challenged by an Orthodox Jewish father, Straga Stern, who maintains that such standards violate his human rights under the *British Human Rights Act* and the *European Convention on Human Rights*.[10]

In recent years, we have also witnessed other western governments mandating that children receive indoctrination on LGBTI issues in state schools against the express authority of their parents. This happened in the case of Canadian parent Steve Tourloukis, who tried to remove his children from classes where such indoctrination was taking place and was prevented by the courts.[11]

Another significant threat to religious freedom that has arisen concerns the work of social welfare agencies run by religious communities. Historically, Christian churches have been at the forefront of the provision of social services; but in recent decades, the government has become very involved. Initially, the government itself sought to directly provide many social services, However, more recently it has chosen to outsource the provision of social services to various non-governmental agencies: Christian, not-for-profit, and now for-profit organisations.

There is also a possibility that faith-based agencies could be denied government contracts because of their commitment to particular religious beliefs. This is in evidence overseas. In Canada, Christian non-profit organisations have for years participated in the 'Canada Summer Jobs' program, (where the government provides a subsidy to not-for-profit organisations, the public sector, and private sector organisations with 50 or fewer employees) to create summer work experience for young people aged 15 to 30. In 2018, those employers who wanted to take part in the program had to attest or commit to support the position that: "Both the job and the organisation's core mandate respect individual human rights in Canada, including values underlying the Canadian Charter of Rights and Freedoms as well as other rights." The guide for applicants made it clear that this included "sexual and reproductive rights" and the "right to access safe and legal abortions."[12] This caused much controversy at the time and has been modified for the 2019 program, but still requires a commitment not to "undermine or restrict the exercise of rights legally protected in Canada."[13]

Catholic adoption and foster care agencies are already on notice that they cannot refuse to place children with same-sex couples. In the UK, Catholic Adoption agencies have had to close their doors.[14] The Family First organisation in New Zealand lost its charitable status after the Charities Board deemed, in their view, that the promotion of the traditional family was not for the public benefit.[15]

Faith-based charities could in the future be denied charitable or tax-deductibility status if they don't conform to mainstream beliefs about life, marriage, family, gender and sexuality. Other religious agencies which offer pre- and post-marriage courses and counselling may also come under threat if they do not accept same-sex couples. In Ireland a major Catholic marriage counselling service announced that it would counsel same-sex couples as well, because if it didn't, its government funding would be removed.[16] Christian agencies which promote chastity for those experiencing same-sex attraction could easily be targeted by activists. We have already witnessed efforts to ban so-called 'gay conversion therapy' by different governments throughout the world.

Exemptions to anti-discrimination laws apply to bodies established for religious purposes, but the case law is narrowing what that means. The Victorian Civil and Administrative Tribunal recently upheld a complaint against a company called Christian Youth Camps (CYC), established by the Christian Brethren for refusing a booking by Cowbaw Community Health for a suicide prevention workshop for same-sex attracted yout18h, because of this opposition to homosexuality. The Tribunal found that CYC had breached the Victorian Equal Opportunity Act by discriminating against the group on the basis of sexual orientation, for which there was no religious defence or protection. The Court of Appeal later upheld this ruling.[17] Christian conference and retreat centres could likewise find themselves subject to such a ruling if a similar case was brought against them.

Not only are Christian organisations now vulnerable to threats of being closed down, but there are a growing number of instances where individual Christians have found their jobs or businesses threatened.

During the marriage debate an 18 year old girl from Canberra lost her job for posting an "It's Okay To Say No" frame on her Facebook profile.[18] A Christian couple who had produced one of Australia's most successful wedding magazine, White, for a number of years was forced to close their business because of withdrawal of advertisers following a campaign by LGBT activists because of their decision not to feature same-sex marriages in their magazine.[19] A photographer in Western Australia was asked to do portraits of the children of a same-sex couple. He agreed to do the shoot, but mentioned to the couple that he believed in the traditional definition of marriage, in case they wanted to choose someone else. The couple lodged a complaint against the photographer in the WA Equal Opportunity Commission which has now been referred to the State Administrative Tribunal.[20]

Those in various professions find themselves threatened with loss of accreditation if they indicate that they have religious views on various matters. There is a silencing effect as doctors, psychologists, lawyers and others are aware that any public expression of their faith-based beliefs could threaten their livelihood. The body responsible for regulating all of Australia's health practitioners, including doctors and psychologists, The Australian Health Practitioner Regulation Authority, has put forward a new code of conduct which says that practitioners could be sanctioned, and even banned, if they express a public view on a matter that goes against the generally accepted view in the profession. This is troubling, given that the current position of the Australian Medical Association and the Australian Psychologists Association is supportive of same-sex marriage, so-called gender reassignment, and abortion.

Catholic university chaplaincies have experienced harassment and efforts at having them banned because of their stance on various moral issues especially their pro-life stance. In certain universities in the UK, faith-based student societies are not even permitted to hold stalls at the orientation days for new students, on the grounds that their presence may contribute to an unsafe environment.[21]

Finally there is the issue of the rights of parents to raise their children according to their beliefs. It is increasingly likely that the State could remove children from parents who fail to comply with education requirements that involve the teaching of homosexuality issues and gender fluidity.

The Future of Religious Freedom

So what does the future hold? In this section I would like to refer particularly to the situation of the Catholic Church.

While at the 2016 national census 52% of Australians still identified as professing a Christian faith, all the indicators suggest that Christianity will soon be a minority faith in this country. Although at 22.6% 'Catholic' was the largest actual religious category recorded, it was 'no religion' at 30.1% which came in first of all. This is a new reality for our society. One can expect that in the future the number of those professing no religion will continue to increase. It is also evident that many who would have considered themselves Christian in the past because of their family traditions now feel free to choose to not align themselves with any religious body. Among those who are still content to identify as Christian, many do not actually practice their faith. Only about 10-15% of Catholics in Australia currently attend Sunday Mass on a regular basis. Thus, many who claim to be Catholic, for instance, have only tenuous links with their church, and many lack a strong formation in the doctrines and moral teachings of their Church.

This will create a new paradigm for our nation. Various ideologies are now vying to be the dominant force directing and forming our culture. Secularist ideologies, particularly those inspired by the cultural left, are now quite vocal and aggressive in seeking to have their views imposed on society. They have essentially become the most dominant voice. They are promoted by the media in Australia and they have become effective in influencing all sectors of the society, from sporting codes, to the corporate and legal firms and government agencies. In recent years they have achieved great victories in influencing legislation.

In the current social and political climate the question of religious freedom has become even more pressing. There are now a variety of societal trends that point to a need to address the question of religious freedom. For example, there is political pressure on Australian governments to limit or remove the few religious freedom protections in anti-discrimination laws.[22] It will likely be the case as I experienced in Tasmania that activists will use anti-discrimination laws to punish or silence those with whom they disagree. There can be no doubt that there is a concerted effort on the part of activists to exclude a religious viewpoint altogether from public debate on the basis that such views are 'offensive'. However, it can be equally claimed that those advocating for various changes in society hold views that are just as 'offensive' to others.

Currently legislation in both Commonwealth and State jurisdictions which effects religious freedom is patchy and inadequate. There is a need for a much more extensive national and state review of legislation in the light of new issues impacting religious freedom. However, in the current climate such a review will probably not ensure protection for people who hold views inspired by their Christian faith.

Persecution of Christians

Christians across the world experience persecution in one form or another. In some countries the persecution is intense, in others it is subtler. The fact that Christians are suffering because of their faith should come as no surprise. Jesus Christ mentioned on several occasions that his disciples would be persecuted on his account. The history of Christianity is filled with stories of kings and rulers seeking to crush the Christian faith. Christian history is a history of martyrs for the faith. Often these martyrs were ordinary folk who just want to live quiet and unobtrusive lives. The Christian seeks to live within the laws of the society and be a contributing citizen, as long as these laws do not require acting against the teachings of one's faith. Increasingly, however, holding to Christian beliefs on certain moral issues is leading them into regular conflict with the civil authorities.

While we could say that the experience of persecution is the default position of the Christian, in a country like Australia we should expect that the Christian faith would be respected. The founding values of Australian society have their origins in Christianity and much that is good about our society has been derived from Christianity. The Christian understanding of the nature of human life, of human dignity, the centrality of marriage and family for the healthy nurturing of children, all have contributed immeasurably to the standards of life within our society.

It is also important that Christians are able to make their own special contribution to issues related to the way in which life is lived in our society. The Jesus Christ said that his kingdom is like leaven or yeast in bread. Christians can be an important leaven in society, enriching its quality by offering the vision of life inspired by the Christian faith.

Chapter 4

FREEDOM OF RELIGION AND EDUCATION

Paul Morrissey

Introduction

As Australia's polity moves to adopt a more progressive social order — liberal abortion laws, euthanasia, same sex marriage, transgender rights, etc. — freedom of religion is becoming a more contentious and urgent issue. This is especially true in education where a sizable number of Australian students are enrolled in religiously affiliated schools. These schools, in the vast majority of cases, are motivated by religious teachings that uphold a more traditional view of morality. In 2018, according to the Australian Bureau of Statistics, 3.9 million students were enrolled in 9,477 schools; 19.7% of these students were enrolled in Catholic schools and 14.6% in independent schools (approximately 90% of which are affiliated with a religion).

In the run-up to the 2019 federal election, religious freedom — especially as it impacts on religious schools — was very much a live issue. Christian Schools Australia demonstrated this concern by sending out flyers to parents of children at 329 schools outlining the parties' position on the issue. The flyer claimed: "This election will be the most critical for religious freedom in living memory." The Catholic bishops of New South Wales issued similar policy outlines of the different party positions. There was a fear among religious bodies that none of the major parties had clear policy direction on religious freedom. Both were keen to uphold in general the need to support religious freedom while at the same time ensure there was no discrimination.

There are two key aspects of the debate surrounding religious liberty and education. The first — and the one that has garnered the most attention — is to what extent a school can dictate its staffing and student body based on belief and lifestyle choices. This issue is addressed in the current exemptions to anti-discrimination legislation; exemptions that have come under fire since the release of the Ruddock report into religious freedom in 2018. In the wake of the same-sex marriage debate and subsequent legislation, the contentious example often given is where a teacher at a religious school promotes the good of same-sex marriage or enters a same-sex marriage him or herself.

The second key aspect, which is intimately connected to the first, is to what extent a religious school can teach its doctrines — including morality — when those teachings run counter to legislation. Again, this is especially pertinent in relation to same-sex marriage legislation as well as the more recent moves toward normalising transgender rights for young people of school age.

The current debate around freedom of religion is terribly frustrating. Religious institutions, especially Christian schools, have received a lot of heat for supposedly allowing discrimination, especially on the basis of sexuality and gender. This in turn has led many to suspect that arguments for religious liberty are just a thinly veiled cloak in which to cover over unjust discrimination. However, what is mostly avoided is any debate on the nature of freedom itself, and it is this that I would like to discuss first.

The Nature of Freedom

The lack of debate or theorising on the nature of freedom is as understandable as it is lamentable. Understandable in the sense that freedom is such a difficult concept to define and lamentable in the sense that the rather shallow understanding of freedom is what drives the debate on religious liberty. Theologian Servais Pinckaers nicely underscores the nebulous nature of freedom:

> Freedom is at the heart of our existence. It is at the core of our experience and is the source of our willing and acting. It is who we are at our most personal. It would seem that there is nothing about ourselves that we are more aware of. To hear us speak of freedom, to hear us incessantly defending it, it would seem to be quite familiar to all as a birth right and inalienable possession... Freedom is, therefore, what we know best, since it is at the heart of our most personal actions. At the same time, freedom is what we know least, for no idea can encompass it, no piling up of concepts reveal it adequately. The only possible definition, if there is one at all, would be to say that freedom always transcends the action it causes or the thought in which it is reflected.[1]

Education that is religiously motivated — and I speak here as someone from the Christian tradition — primarily understands freedom in a more classical sense, which sees freedom as having a two-fold meaning. The first is the most basic form of freedom: the freedom from restraint. This is the freedom *from* things that tie us down and restrict our ability to choose and act. This freedom is fundamental to what it means to be a human person as illustrated in the second account of creation in Genesis, where the Tree of the Knowledge of Good and Evil symbolises the gift of free will. Education, for example, is important because it frees us from ignorance. A job is important because it frees us from poverty. Laws are important because they free us from chaos.

The second type of freedom is far less discussed. This is freedom *for* what is good, noble, virtuous, and excellent. We are free 'from' restraint not so we can just do what we like but so as to be free 'for' what is good. This is a deeper, more real, and worthy freedom; but one that goes against our age — which exalts autonomy over the common good. "Don't tell me what to do!" is the teenage refrain that is the default position of just about everybody today. This is the freedom and individuality synonymous with the Enlightenment and such thinkers as Rousseau and Sartre, both of whom saw liberty as more constitutive of persons than human nature itself.[2]

This more contemporary view of liberty is built upon two anthropological assumptions: individualism and the voluntarist conception of choice; and human separation from and ultimate opposition to nature itself.[3] The divorce between humanity and nature begins with Francis Bacon and ends where we are today with efforts to go beyond our natural sex (transgender) and even our nature as humans (the futuristic trans humanist movement). A 'freedom' from our own nature is the natural endpoint for this vision of liberty. Unfortunately, seen through this reduced vision of liberty, religious teachings on morality are viewed as passé, 'restrictive' to human flourishing, and unwelcome in the public square. Religion naturally becomes, as it is today, essentially privatised.[4]

Liberty in its fullest sense is understood as something we learn through an education in virtue. Our birth right freedom, 'born free', is very limited and needs to grow and flourish through self-mastery, another word for virtue. If freedom simply means to do what you want then the prisoner is 'free'. However, common sense tells us freedom is only realised when it is constrained or ordered toward what is good and true. Real freedom, in the classical and Christian sense, is a freedom from our base selves and a freedom for an integrated human flourishing.

Democracy is reliant on a citizenry that extols both types of freedom. Alexis de Tocqueville, the great scholar of democracy, knew that a freedom from tyranny needed a virtuous citizenry lest it fall into a soft totalitarianism. Inherent in liberal democracy is the temptation to idolise the individual in the name of equality and eradicate universal notions of the good or the true. There is also the temptation to replace virtues with values, as Samuel Gregg outlined:

> The truth, however, is that democracies don't need "people with values." They require *virtuous* people: individuals and communities whose habits of the heart shape what Tocqueville called the "whole mental and intellectual state" of a people as they associate together, pursue their economic self-interest, make laws, and vote.[5]

How one understands liberty has consequences for how one understands education. A pioneer of modern education, Jean Jacques Rousseau was very concerned with freedom and individual authenticity and this was reflected in his philosophy of education, explored most thoroughly in his book, *Emile*. Rousseau held, contrary to the Judeo-Christian doctrine of original sin, that humans were born in a state of innocence and goodness. This natural goodness needed to be encouraged through an education that 'got out of the way' and allowed the child to be his or her authentic self. The child is not told what to think, etc., but the teacher's role is to create an environment whereby the student can arrive at knowledge on his or her own. The teacher is no longer a master passing on knowledge, skills, and wisdom, but rather education is about — in the contemporary jargon — student-focussed learning. His essential idea is that education should be carried out, so far as possible, in harmony with the development of the child's natural capacities by a process of apparently autonomous discovery.

In contrast, if one holds to a more classically liberal view, education is teleological, directed towards something greater than the individual. Liberty is taught through an education built upon universally held principles that accord with human nature. John Henry Newman understood this well, seeing a liberal education as an education directed towards a life of learning and freedom: With a liberal education:

> A student apprehends the great outlines of knowledge, the principles on which it rests, the scale of its parts, its lights and its shades, its great points and its little, as he otherwise cannot apprehend them. Hence it is that his education is called liberal. A habit of mind is formed which lasts through life, of which the attributes are freedom, equitableness, calmness, moderation, and wisdom, or what in a former discourse I have ventured to call a philosophical habit.[6]

Unfortunately, many today see education in utilitarian terms, which runs the risk of neglecting an education in true liberty. As Patrick Deneen laments: "To the extent that a fully realized liberalism undermines culture and cultivation into liberty as a form of self-governance, an education for a free people is displaced by an education that makes liberal individuals servants to the end of untutored appetite, restlessness, and technical mastery of the natural world. Liberal education is replaced with servile education."[7]

Educational institutions motivated and affiliated with religion, whether they are schools or universities have as part of their mission both a negative and positive understanding of freedom. They want to give their students a liberty from ignorance as well as the skills that will enable them to be free and flourishing persons, but they also propose a *telos* (goal) for this freedom that will require certain moral habits as well as religious doctrine. Their ultimate freedom is in God.

What has this to do with the discussion on religious freedom, especially the debate surrounding the freedom of religious institutions such as hospitals, schools, etc.? A society needs to allow as much basic freedom as possible: freedom of speech, freedom of association, and freedom of religion. These basic freedoms in turn allow for citizens within institutions to pursue a deeper more virtuous freedom. Now not everyone will agree with everything that these institutions propose as virtuous freedoms, but they are not compelled to join them or support them.

Thus a religious institution with a particular vision of the good should be given the freedom to operate without restraint. This is the first type of freedom; so as to allow the second type of freedom to be pursued by the members of that institution. A democratic state with many competing visions of the good is always in tension, but this tension is much better that a soft totalitarianism whereby only some visions are allowed.

Religious Liberty and Education – Contemporary Challenges

As already noted, religious based educational institutions educate a very significant number of students in Australia. They are motivated by the teachings of their faith. If the faith is compromised, that is, if they are not permitted to be who they are called to be, the very reason for the existence of these institutions disappear.

Although religious schools do seek a particular vision of the good, they do not see their mission in a sectarian or anti-world sense. They link their vision of the good to the common good of society and the nation. In other words, it would seem in the interest of the nation that these institutions are allowed to freely pursue their mission. Let us cite some examples. St Phillip's is an impressive network of schools in the Pentecostal Christian tradition that are flourishing in the Newcastle/Hunter Valley region of New South Wales. The first two mission statements of St Phillip's are that:

1. Every student develops a personal faith in Jesus Christ and is empowered to live with purpose, integrity and joy.

2. Every student achieves their God-given potential and is well equipped to make a significant contribution to society.[8]

Thus the administration and the teachers of these schools are religiously motivated, but also concerned with developing the skills and knowledge necessary to contribute to society.

To take another example, Sydney Catholic Schools oversees a vast number of schools that hold as central aspect of their mission the following: Catholic identity and recognising Jesus Christ as the centre of life, the passing on of beliefs and traditions of the Catholic Community, promoting schools of excellence in learning, and making a difference in the world by fostering the dignity and integrity of every person, and collaborating for the good of all.[9] To give an example from higher education, the institution which I lead, Campion College Australia, has as its central mission: "to provide a foundational education in the Liberal Arts that integrates the insights of faith and reason." This mission is elaborated on further stating that a Campion education:

> Entails systematic and integrated study across the humanities, stimulating genuine freedom of thought by opening the mind to truth. Religiously, it is recognisably Catholic in its affirmation of belief in the teaching authority of the Catholic Church. Students will receive a proper grounding in Catholic belief and thought, and be exposed to the richness of the Church's spiritual, moral, intellectual and cultural traditions. More broadly, its authority safeguards the search for truth by keeping in balance a range of intellectual freedoms.[10]

Each of these examples highlight the religious motivation of the institution's mission as well as the link this mission has to a broader good of society.

Within Catholic and Christian education in Australia, (and more broadly in schools of other faiths), there has always been support for the education and employment of those who are from outside the faith tradition. Those who elect to be part of the mission of the school are asked, quite reasonably, to support the mission and ethos of the School/College/University. The minimum of this requirement is generally accepted to be that students and staff not actively speak/act contrary to this mission. Without this requirement the educational institution is at risk of losing its *raison d'être*.

It is the very reasonable view of faith-based institutions that religious freedom as a basic human right should be positively protected in Australian law. One can understand, in our age, that in the popular mind there should be no right to discriminate against anyone. However, quite reasonably, many employers/groups are able to discriminate in employment (political parties, etc.). However, it would be far preferable for the religious freedom of institutions and individuals to be protected positively in law. It should be the right of religious institutions to freely act in accord with the teachings of their faith, which naturally impacts on anyone who will be in the employ or attend that institution, whether it is educational or otherwise.

In order that the vast number of religiously affiliated educational institutions can flourish, there must be a positive recognition of their freedom to operate, as they are constituted. Fundamental to this is their ability to recruit staff, especially teaching staff, who are supportive of the mission of the institution. In a Joint Statement from Australian Catholic Bishops Conference, Archbishop Mark Coleridge and Archbishop Anthony Fisher OP stated that, "Australians highly value the existing network of faith-based schools. It is not unreasonable for religious schools and the families who choose them to continue to expect that staff will support their school's mission."[11]

Archbishop Coleridge said staff in Catholic schools have a professional obligation to be supportive of the teachings of the Catholic Church, to act as role models to students and to do nothing publicly that would undermine the transmission of those teachings. The bishops go on to state that: "Those who seek employment or enrolment in a Catholic school will be asked if they understand and accept the values of that school. If employed or enrolled, they will be expected to uphold those values." Furthermore, "Catholic schools take seriously the duty that parents entrust to them in the handing on of the Catholic faith. It is therefore critical that Catholic schools are free to employ staff who are attuned to their mission in order to provide and promote the intellectual and spiritual formation of their students."

In other words, Catholic schools should be permitted to be Catholic. "We want to enjoy the rights that others — including political parties — have to employ people who support the organisation's values and beliefs."

Conclusion — The Freedom to Teach the Truth of the Faith

The right of religious educational institutes to hire is more complex than perhaps first thought; at least for some religious schools. In primary schools, with fewer class teachers, it would seem more important that a teacher support and uphold the religious tenants of the school. Secondary education can be more complex where there are many more subjects and subject specific teachers. At university level it gets even more complex. However, at the bare minimum one would expect staff to give support where necessary (in religious education for example) and at least not teach or promote anything contrary to the religion of the institution of their employ. There should be a basic commitment and respect of all at the school for its mission.

As Greg Craven has pointed out, a connected — but more difficult — question of religious liberty is raised when an existing staff member begins to promote something contrary to the school's religious teaching and mission. "Imagine," he writes, "two Catholic religious education teachers who discovered a same-sex attraction and married, publicly and proudly, and to the knowledge of the entire school and wider community."[12] Notwithstanding the potential difficulties a case such as this involves, the integrity of the school's mission would mandate that the continued employment of this couple be untenable. And as Craven correctly states, "this reality would need to be recognised under any legislation protecting religious freedom."

The infamous case of Archbishop Julian Porteous of Hobart has raised another central issue of religious liberty, namely the freedom of religious schools to propose and teach without fear the truths of their faith to their students. After simply distributing pamphlets outlining Catholic teaching on marriage to the schools of his diocese, Archbishop Porteous was told he had a case to answer before the Human Rights Commission on the grounds he was offending those who supported same-sex marriage. This question would seem even more pertinent now that same-sex marriage is legal. But surely where an educational institution cannot teach its doctrine about marriage then religious freedom does not exist. A guarantee in law on this question, one would think (and hope), is rather simple.

Chapter 5

PROTECTING RELIGIOUS FREEDOM IN AN AGE OF MILITANT SECULARISM

Patrick Parkinson

The legal weakness of 'freedom'

The freedoms that have long been enjoyed in western societies are cherished and often celebrated. They inspired the dedication that, in previous generations, has led countless young men to go to war — and to their deaths on the battlefield — to protect those freedoms their deaths on the battlefield. They have been the rallying cry for populist demagogues and political parties. They have been the shining light that has attracted millions to leave sites of oppression to try to migrate to countries where freedom is seen to exist.

It might then come as a surprise then, to assert that the protections for those freedoms in Australia are extraordinarily weak. We often speak of rights and freedoms as if they were of similar stature, similar efficacy; but a moment's thought should tell us otherwise. There is a vital difference between rights and freedoms. Rights can be protected in all sorts of ways. Fundamentally, they can be a shield or a sword. An example of a shield-right is the right against self-incrimination. A person cannot be compelled, under threat of punishment, to incriminate himself or herself.

Sword-rights are everywhere. They provide the basis for both entitlements and claims. An example of an entitlement-right is the right to receive welfare payments. In the modern welfare state, there is a right to support on the basis of various kinds of need, such as unemployment or disability. Other rights translate into the eligibility to make a complaint or to bring a legal action. The right, for example, not to be discriminated against, typically gives the aggrieved person a claim to a remedy against the person who is perceived to have engaged in discrimination. That remedy may involve a claim to damages.

Freedoms are, typically, neither swords nor shields, at least in countries without a constitutionally-entrenched Bill of Rights or a legally efficacious Human Rights Act. The United States provides an example of a constitutionally-entrenched Bill of Rights. It protects freedoms in important ways, not least by the First Amendment. Those constitutionally protected freedoms can act as a shield, allowing the courts to strike down laws that unduly interfere with those freedoms; they can also protect freedom in more nuanced ways, since judges will endeavour to interpret statutes and common law rights in ways that do not transgress constitutional boundaries, where it is possible to do so. Human Rights Acts can have similar effects, if they entitle people to appeal against interference with their rights to the domestic courts or to a transnational body such as the European Court of Human Rights.

However, the Australian versions of human rights Acts are not so efficacious. The ACT, Victoria and Queensland have human rights charters. They may well have significant impacts upon the way public servants view their duties and even on the crafting of legislation; but they do not confer legal rights or remedies. Courts can only give advice that legislation contravenes the Charter.[1] I might take some comfort from the judge's declaration that the law by which she needed to send me to prison for a statutorily fixed term was incompatible with the State's Human Rights Act; but that provides neither heat nor light to my prison cell.

In the absence of a constitutionally entrenched or statutorily conferred freedom, to claim I have a freedom to do something, provides no defence to a legal action except to the extent that I can assert successfully that there is no law against the impugned conduct. That is, to claim I have a freedom gives no entitlement, no power to lodge a complaint or bring a legal action. Indeed, it is almost a misnomer to talk of a 'legal freedom'. All that could be meant by this is that no law prevents me doing the thing I want to do, or saying the things I want to say, and no-one has a legal right to take action against me for those things that I do or say. Freedom, in other words, is the absence of restriction. A freedom which is more than this is actually a right, however it might be characterised. So, for example if I have the freedom to use a pathway to cross what would otherwise be private land, it is because I have a legal right of way over that land.

Freedoms may be little more than temporary vacuums that have not yet been filled by legal regulation or prohibition. They are like Crown Land, land which is open to all, but only because the government has not yet sold it into private ownership, leased it to a developer, or given exclusive grazing rights to a farmer. Freedoms last only as long as governments do not interfere with them, and they exist only to the extent that governments choose to leave that freedom in place.

In contrast, rights are — or can be — powerful. They compel the government to meet the entitlement; they confer claims or they act as a bulwark that defends liberty. Freedoms are pathetically weak in legal terms — in the absence of a constitutionally entrenched Bill of Rights, they are as powerful a defence as a wall of straw bales against a bulldozer.

Freedom and the values of the culture

It follows that the power of a traditional freedom rests only in a shared consensus about the importance of retaining it. It is therefore protected not by law, so much as by culture, by values and beliefs that are sufficiently entrenched within the society that legislatures refrain from interference. International human rights obligations, such as the commitments countries have made to the International Covenant on Civil and Political Rights, might also have a constraining influence. The difficulty is that rights may be in conflict with one another; and the application of those broad-based covenants to specific circumstances is open to contest. So international human rights are sometimes of more value as lampposts to lean upon in the cause of advocacy than lights to illuminate the pathway to a just resolution of a controversy.

For these reasons, freedoms are quite vulnerable to shifts in the culture — and not only shifts in the views of majorities. So much change in modern societies is actually driven by a relatively small proportion of the population who are politically 'woke', who join political parties or political lobbying organisations, become staffers to government ministers or have some level of editorial control in the media. They are in turn peculiarly responsive to the clamour of those few others who engage in campaigns and protests on their keyboards or phones, who establish organisations with a membership that may be smaller than their nuclear family yet purport to speak for thousands, and who write submissions to parliamentary committees.

Very small numbers thus have outsize influence in modern democratic societies. It should be recalled that Russia — a vast and culturally rich nation — fell to a few thousand Bolsheviks in 1917. It does not take all that many to storm the Winter Palace of a society, if they are mobilised by a cause, and support for the *ancien regime* has been seriously eroded.

The weakness of religious freedom in Australia

Freedom of religion is likely to be under threat, even in a society that has long respected it, if three conditions are satisfied. First, protection for it in law is weak. Second, belief in it as a cultural value has been eroded. Third, there are those with competing claims or ideologies who would wish to encroach on that freedom.

The weakness of legal protection

There can be little doubt that protection for religious freedom in Australian law is weak. The reality is that there is almost no protection for freedom of religion, conscience, speech and association anywhere in Australian law beyond exceptions and exemptions in anti-discrimination laws.

Yes, there is some protection in the Constitution (s.116) so far as the law of the Commonwealth is concerned. However, it is limited. As the Australian Law Reform Commission has explained, s.116 "restrains the legislative power of the Commonwealth to enact laws that would establish a religion or prohibit the free exercise of religion, but does not explicitly create a personal or individual right to religious freedom."[2] It does not prevent the states from restricting religious freedom.[3] Tasmania also has a constitutional provision that provides for the right of freedom of religion and belief,[4] but it is the only state to do so, and the Tasmanian Constitution is an ordinary Act of Parliament that can be amended by a simple majority.

By and large, freedoms are protected only to the extent that parliaments do not encroach upon those freedoms; but there is very little to stop parliaments doing so, and apart from s.116 of the Constitution, where it applies — domestic Australian law has no remedies for citizens if laws impact upon them in ways that violate international human rights standards.

The common law also provides no guarantee of religious freedom. At best, reliance might be placed upon the principle of legality as an interpretative principle where legislation is ambiguous.[5] Freedom of religion is not unique in the lack of protection that is provided in Australian law. The same is true for freedom of speech, freedom of association, freedom of assembly and freedom of conscience.

That said, there is a relatively broad scope for religious freedom in Australia. The Australian Law Reform Commission — reporting in 2016 on an inquiry into the protection of religious freedom in federal law— found that in practice there were few, if any, encroachments on religious freedom by federal laws at the time.[6] The Ruddock Review on religious freedom did not see the need for major changes to federal law.[7] Indeed, certain of its recommendations involved winding back exemptions for religious bodies within anti-discrimination statutes.

Nonetheless, there are more issues at state and territory level; arising from expansive anti-discrimination laws that make it unlawful to discriminate, for example, because of a person's lawful sexual conduct,[8] laws that violate the conscience of medical practitioners by requiring them to refer a patient to a medical practitioner who will perform an abortion,[9] and restrictions on the freedom to protest in the vicinity of abortion clinics.[10]

There are also provisions that make it unlawful to offend somebody.

Section 17 of the *Anti-Discrimination Act 1998 (Tas.)* is one example of a law with significant potential reach into freedom of speech, political opinion and religion. It has been weaponised to try to suppress certain points of view, on the basis only that the claimant has been offended — or believes that others would be offended — by some public comment.[11] The section makes it unlawful for a person to "engage in any conduct which offends, humiliates, intimidates, insults or ridicules another person" on the basis of various protected attributes, which include race, age, sexual orientation, lawful sexual activity, gender, gender-identity, intersex, marital status, relationship status, pregnancy, breastfeeding, parental status or family responsibilities. This is subject to the qualification that the conduct (which includes speech) must have occurred in circumstances in which a reasonable person, having regard to all the circumstances, would have anticipated that the other person would be offended, humiliated, intimidated, insulted or ridiculed.

This section was used to bring a complaint against Archbishop Porteous, the Catholic Archbishop of Hobart. He was summoned before a Tasmanian anti-discrimination body for distributing a booklet put out by the Australian Catholic Bishops Conference defending its traditional view of marriage. The Australian Catholic Bishops Conference was required to answer the complaint along with Archbishop Porteous. The basis was only that the complainant had been offended by a publication that was distributed nationwide, and which expressed a point of view on a matter of national public debate.

The complaint was eventually dropped; but what is remarkable and troubling about this case is not that the complaint was made, but that it was accepted by the relevant Commissioner, who saw it as a potentially valid complaint under the legislation. Other complaints have been brought against clergy under this section of the Act.[12] The defendant is typically put to a lot of effort and expense in responding to such complaints, even if they are eventually discontinued. This may have a chilling effect on freedom of speech. It should be entirely uncontroversial that Catholic bishops should be allowed to explain Catholic doctrine without fearing legal repercussions. These are foundational freedoms in any democratic society.

The erosion of cultural support

The weak legal protection for religious freedom — and indeed for freedoms generally — has not mattered in the slightest for as long as those freedoms have had strong cultural support. It is enough that legislatures would not wish to restrict or deny those freedoms. It is not necessary that they be restrained from doing so.

However, with the rapid secularisation of Australian society, illustrated by the strong vote in favour of same-sex marriage, religious freedom is culturally vulnerable — at least in certain respects. Illustrative of this is that in the wake of the Ruddock Report on religious freedom, a new organisation was founded with support from prominent human rights advocates, specifically to oppose whatever Ruddock might recommend by way of enhanced protection for religious freedom.[13]

Of course, the erosion of support for religious freedom should not be exaggerated. There is no threat to freedom of worship, for example. No-one much cares whether I go to church on Sundays, any more than they care if I spend Sunday morning playing video games.

However, there is no room for complacency. Freedom of worship was severely curtailed in the Soviet Union and most of Eastern Europe during the communist era in those countries. These were all nations where the Christian faith was deeply embedded in the history and culture of the society. A few thousand Bolsheviks ended that freedom in Russia. Countries such as Albania have experienced similar oppression at the hands of a relatively small number of people who seized power in the name of an atheistic ideology. Even freedom of worship can be lost if those in government, or those who seize government, have a reason to do so and an ideology that is hostile to faith.

I have the freedom to do what I want on Sunday mornings, and do not expect that to change, because my choice affects no-one else and therefore no-one has a reason to stir up a campaign to deprive me of that right. As Professor Stanley Fish once put it: "tolerance is exercised in an inverse proportion to there being anything at stake."[14]

However, increasingly, there is a mood of hostility towards people of faith to the extent that they express their beliefs in the public square. Former High Court judge Dyson Heydon recently observed that: "Among the elites is developing a hostility to religion which has not been seen in the West since the worst excesses of the French Revolution."[15]

This intolerance is expressed in terms of trying to drive people out of jobs or having them disqualified from professional occupations because of their beliefs about marriage or their opposition to some of the more extreme beliefs about 'gender fluidity'.[16] It was a hostility I experienced when it was announced that I would be taking up my current appointment as a Dean of a prestigious law school. The opposition was based on little more than a report I wrote on the wellbeing of children for the Australian Christian Lobby.[17] That report had nothing at all to say about homosexuality[18] — yet because the Australian Christian Lobby had been in the vanguard of the campaign against permitting same-sex marriage, there was seemingly 'guilt by association'. The suggestion was that anyone who did not support same-sex marriage was not fit to be a law school dean. The campaign involved attacks not only on me but on those who had been on the selection committee. Of course, like so many such media campaigns, the hysteria was whipped up by a mere handful (purporting to represent a much larger number) and quickly dissipated. However, this is far from the first time that I have come under attack in university life because of my public faith — and this is increasingly an issue for others I know.

Competing claims or ideologies

The erosion of support for religious freedom, and the associated freedoms of conscience, speech, and association, may not amount to serious threats to freedom as long as there are no competing claims or ideologies. However, religious freedom is now increasingly seen as being in conflict with other rights, notably 'equality' rights —in particular, freedom from discrimination. When anti-discrimination laws were first enacted to deal with issues of discrimination on the basis of race, gender, age and disability, there were few problems for people of faith. Indeed, religious leaders such as Dr Martin Luther King were in the forefront of campaigns for racial equality in the United States. Gender was an issue for certain religious organisations that have a theological commitment to male religious leadership. Sensibly, and in accordance with international human rights conventions, this problem was dealt with by providing an exemption for those faith communities that chose to rely on it.

As the scope of anti-discrimination laws expanded to prohibit discrimination on the basis of other protected attributes, so the need for such exemptions increased in order to make room, in religious organisations, for religious beliefs concerning sexual morality and the importance of (heterosexual) marriage as the basis for child-rearing.

In recent years, those exemptions have come under increasing attack. The Australian Law Reform Commission summarised a number of submissions to its inquiry into rights and freedoms as follows:[19]

> Other stakeholders opposed the exemptions for religious organisations entirely, or argue that they should be wound back — considering that the general application of anti-discrimination law is considered to be a justifiable interference with religious freedom.

Underlying this campaign against exemptions are two beliefs that are stated with a dogmatism as powerful and rigid as any belief system of religious groups. The first is a belief that all limitations on who is eligible to apply for particular jobs should be abolished or severely restricted in the name of one conceptualisation of 'equality', even if 99.9% of all the other jobs in the community are open to that person. This position involves taking a very restrictive approach to 'genuine occupational requirements' as a ground for exceptions to general anti-discrimination provisions.[20]

The second fundamentalist aspect of the campaign against exemptions arises from a belief that the only human rights that should be given any real significance are individual ones and not group rights. This can make advocates disregard competing claims that would justify a right of positive selection of staff in order to enhance the cohesion and identity of a religious or cultural organisation.[21] An example is seen in the response given to leaked recommendations of the Ruddock Committee on religious freedom. The Committee recommended that if religious schools wanted the freedom to discriminate on the basis of sexual orientation, gender identity or relationship status in their staffing policies, they should be permitted to do so, but only if the discrimination is founded on the precepts of the religion and the policy is made known publicly.

When the recommendations were leaked in October 2018,[22] a furore erupted over the perception that schools had a legal 'right to discriminate'. The Greens introduced a Bill into Parliament within days, seeking the removal of any discrimination in schools (whether in application to students or staff).[23] The apparent stance is that even if schools have a religious foundation, whether it be Christian, Jewish, Islamic or otherwise, it should not permit them to impose obligations or restrictions on the private lives of their teaching staff as a condition for employment.

When rights and freedoms conflict, the lack of parity between freedoms and rights has a practical effect. As the Joint Standing Committee on Foreign Affairs, Defence and Trade noted in its interim report on religious freedom, although "there is legislative protection for some ICCPR rights, notably the Article 26 right to non-discrimination, religious freedom has very little legislative protection and there is a risk of an imbalanced approach to resolving any conflict between the right to freedom of religion or belief and other rights."[24] That is, because there is no legal right to religious freedom, it is often seen to give way to a competing right.

Strengthening protections for religious freedom

The Australian Constitution is notoriously difficult to change, and hitherto, a referendum to incorporate certain rights, including freedom of religion, has failed quite decisively.[25] It is difficult therefore to see a constitutionally entrenched Bill of Rights as a way forward.

There are also enthusiasts for a Human Rights Act along the lines of the laws passed in the ACT or Victoria. Many lawyers see such a Charter as an indispensable feature of a modern democracy.

There are undoubtedly advantages of having such a Charter even if it is merely advisory, as in Victoria and the ACT, since sometimes rights need to be balanced with other rights — and compromises found. Having a Charter allows the courts to consider the different rights involved and to examine issues of proportionality.

However, Australia has only recently had this debate. A federal Labor government as recently as 2010 decided not to proceed with the implementation of the recommendations of the Brennan Committee[26] for such a federal Human Rights Act.[27] At that time, many churches expressed concerns about how a Charter of Rights, even of an advisory kind, transfers a lot of responsibility for balancing rights from parliaments to courts. That in turn may involve a much narrower consideration of the relevant issues than in a well-constructed democratic process. It also gives lawyers a disproportionate voice in determining public policy. There were other concerns as well.[28]

Since the Brennan Committee reported, the High Court has considered the constitutionality of a federal Charter of Rights in *Momcilovic v The Queen.*[29] While they are valid at state level, it appears from the judgments of French CJ, and Gummow, Hayne, Heydon and Bell JJ, that such a provision could not be introduced at the federal level, as it would represent a grant to the court of a non-judicial power contrary to Chapter III of the Constitution.[30] While these comments were not part of the reasons for decision in the case, they represent carefully considered thoughts nonetheless.

State charters of rights suffer from the deficiency not only that they are merely advisory, but also because judges are given quite a lot of discretion to hold that a right is not applicable. For example, s.7(2) of the Victorian *Charter of Rights and Responsibilities Act 2006* provides:

> "A human right may be subject under law only to such reasonable limits as can be demonstrably justified in a free and democratic society based on human dignity, equality and freedom, and taking into account all relevant factors including—
>
> (a) the nature of the right; and
>
> (b) the importance of the purpose of the limitation; and
>
> (c) the nature and extent of the limitation; and

(d) the relationship between the limitation and its purpose; and

(e) any less restrictive means reasonably available to achieve the purpose that the limitation seeks to achieve."

Religious freedom as a positive right

In the absence of a constitutionally protected right to religious freedom, the best way forward would be to move away from protecting religious freedom by means of exemptions in statutes, and to replace it with a positive right for religious organisations to recruit staff in consistence with their values. Religious organisations should also be permitted to require staff to adhere to a code of conduct that could include matters of private sexual conduct.

Another approach is to redefine what discrimination is. In a submission responding to a Discussion Paper about the consolidation of federal anti-discrimination laws in 2012, Professor Nicholas Aroney and I recommended that there be a new definition of discrimination that helps to define what discrimination is and is not.[31] It is based on the idea that differentiation of treatment does not necessarily mean discrimination. Paragraph 13 of the UN Human Rights Committee's General Comment 18 (Non-Discrimination) states that "not every differentiation of treatment will constitute discrimination, if the criteria for such differentiation are reasonable and objective and if the aim is to achieve a purpose which is legitimate under the Covenant."

That is, if different treatment is justified because of some other human right, it is not discrimination at all. Our new definition spells out when differentiation of treatment is legitimate and why it does not amount to discrimination.

Since then, their definition seems to have attracted a lot of support within churches and other faith organisations.[32] It was quoted in part by the Australian Law Reform Commission in its Freedoms Inquiry report (although the impression may have been given inadvertently that the Commission was quoting it in full).[33] The complete definition is as follows:

(1) Discrimination means any distinction, exclusion, preference, restriction or condition made or proposed to be made which has the purpose of disadvantaging a person with a protected attribute or which has, or is likely to have, the effect of disadvantaging a person with a protected attribute by comparison with a person who does not have the protected attribute, subject to the following subsections.

(2) A distinction, exclusion, preference, restriction or condition does not constitute discrimination if:

(a) it is reasonably capable of being considered appropriate and adapted to achieve a legitimate objective; or

(b) it is made because of the inherent requirements of the particular position concerned; or

(c) it is not unlawful under any anti-discrimination law of any state or territory in the place where it occurs; or

(d) it is a special measure that is reasonably intended to help achieve substantive equality between a person with a protected attribute and other persons.

(3) The protection, advancement or exercise of another human right protected by the International Covenant on Civil and Political Rights is a legitimate objective within the meaning of subsection (2)(a).

(4) Without limiting the generality of subsection (2), a distinction, exclusion, preference, restriction or condition should be considered appropriate and adapted to protect the right of freedom of religion if it is made by a religious body, or by an organisation that either provides, or controls or administers an entity that provides, educational, health, counselling, aged care or other such services, and either:

> (a) it is reasonably necessary in order to comply with religious doctrines, tenets, beliefs or teachings adhered to by the religious body or

organisation; or

(b) it is reasonably necessary to avoid injury to the religious sensitivities of adherents of that religion or creed; or

(c) in the case of decisions concerning employment, it is reasonable in order to maintain the religious character of the body or organisation, or to fulfil its religious purpose.

(5) Without limiting the generality of subsection (2), a distinction, exclusion, preference, restriction or condition should be considered appropriate and adapted to protect the right of ethnic minorities to enjoy their own culture, or to use their own language in community with the other members of their group, if it is made by an ethnic minority organisation or association intended to fulfil that purpose and has the effect of preferring a person who belongs to that ethnic minority over a person who does not belong to that ethnic minority.

The importance of this approach is that it provides a balancing of different human rights, including rights under Articles 18 and 27 of the International Covenant on Civil and Political Rights, within a comprehensive definition. The language used deliberately reflects that of the UN Human Rights Committee.

Conclusion

In its submission to the Ruddock Committee in 2018, the National Council of Churches said that it considered that "the human right to freedom of religion is in reasonable shape" in Australia.[34] That may be true, at least for most parts of the country. However, support for religious freedom is eroding, discrimination against people of faith is increasing, and freedom of religious organisations to organise themselves consistently with their beliefs and values is coming under challenge.

In these circumstances, the weak legal protection for freedom of religion and conscience is a problem. Living a religiously committed life is not just about freedom to worship. As South African Constitutional Court Justice Albie Sachs observed: "For many believers, their relationship with God or creation is central to all their activities. It concerns their capacity to relate in an intensely meaningful fashion to their sense of themselves, their community and their universe."[35]Religious freedom is under increasing threat from those who are not prepared to accept diversity of belief and opinion in a multicultural society and to 'live and let live'.

There is a line of continuity here with Lenin, Stalin and Mao. The history of the twentieth century demonstrates how fragile can be the freedoms and rights that western societies take for granted. It remains to be seen whether we will do better in the twenty-first century to protect religious freedom from the new Bolsheviks.

Chapter 6

MATCHING WORDS WITH ACTION: WHAT THE GOVERNMENT SHOULD DO TO STRENGTHEN RELIGIOUS FREEDOM

Lorraine Finlay

If we were to judge our parliamentary leaders on their words alone, there could be no doubting the central importance of religious freedom in Australia today. Prime Minister Scott Morrison has stated that "protecting freedom of belief is central to the liberty of each and every Australia."[1] The then Leader of the Opposition, Bill Shorten, described it as "central to our democracy and our society."[2] The Chair of the Joint Standing Committee on Foreign Affairs, Defence and Trade observed that whilst "Australia's record is not perfect ... most Australians have enjoyed, and continue to enjoy, a quality of life and a degree of freedom that is remarkable in a historical context. The right to freedom of religion, conscience or belief is one of the pillars of this liberty."[3]

There is, however, a considerable gulf between the words spoken by our political leaders and the actions taken (or not taken) by our parliament. This divergence is perhaps unsurprising, given how politicised the issue of religious freedom has become; particularly over the past two years during the course of the same-sex marriage debate. It also may not be an entirely bad thing, given that parliamentary inaction is surely preferable to deleterious action. On the other hand, as the Ruddock Review observed "religious freedom is precious and ... needs to be actively preserved."[4] For this to occur, our political leaders need to demonstrate that their belief in religious freedom is more than simply a convenient political platitude to be rolled out at a press conference.

The gulf between words and actions was never more evident than during the same-sex marriage plebiscite campaign and the subsequent passage of same-sex marriage laws in Australia. Concerns about way that same-sex marriage laws might impact on religious freedom were raised during the plebiscite campaign, with the then prime minister Malcolm Turnbull trying to assuage voter concerns by declaring that he believed in religious freedom "even more strongly" than same-sex marriage.[5] Despite this, amendments designed to provide greater protection to religious freedom were defeated during the subsequent parliamentary debate about the same-sex marriage laws and the question of protecting religious freedoms was instead left to be dealt with at a later date.

Before the same-sex marriage law formally came into effect, the federal government announced the establishment of an Expert Panel on Religious Freedom to "examine and report on whether Australian law (Commonwealth, State and Territory) adequately protects the human right to freedom of religion."[6] The Expert Panel received 15,620 submissions despite a relatively short public consultation period[7] — highlighting the public interest and concern with respect to the current state of religious freedom in Australia — and delivered its report to the Prime Minister on 18 May 2018. This report was not made public for almost seven months, with the report and the government's response both finally being released on 13 December 2018.

There were twenty separate recommendations made by the Expert Panel, with the government accepting (either directly or in principle) fifteen of these and indicating that further consideration would be given to the remaining five through a referral to the Australian Law Reform Commission. The government accepted "the central conclusion of the Religious Freedom Review, that there is an opportunity to further protect, and better promote and balance, the right to freedom of religion under Australian law and in the public sphere."[8]

So what should the Parliament do with respect to the question of religious freedom? This chapter will outline four important steps for parliament to consider, although it is important to note from the outset that none of these recommended steps actually involve the introduction of new laws. While in recent times some in Australia have measured the success of a Parliament by the volume of legislation is has passed,[9] good governance involves more than simply imposing new laws. If the next Parliament is serious about wanting to "better promote and balance" the right to freedom of religion then it should give serious consideration to resisting attempts to introduce a *Religious Discrimination Act*, revising existing anti-discrimination laws, recognising that there is no right not to be offended (and revising hate speech laws accordingly) and empowering civil society.

Of course, the complexity of this task is increased by the fact that Australia is a federation and many of our existing anti-discrimination and hate speech laws exist at the state level. This simply highlights the fact that religious freedom is not something that can be entirely protected by any one level of government or through any single law. While federal parliament clearly has an important role to play in safeguarding religious freedom, it is not a responsibility that lies exclusively with them.

Resisting attempts to introduce a Religious Discrimination Act

One of the recommendations made by the Expert Panel was that the parliament should legislate to make it unlawful to discriminate on the basis of a person's religious belief or activity, either through amendments to the *Racial Discrimination Act 1975* (Cth) or the introduction of a Religious Discrimination Act.[10] This recommendation was accepted by the government, who committed in their response to introducing a Religious Discrimination Bill into the parliament.[11] The Attorney-General described this as "the fifth and final pillar of an overarching architecture that prevents discrimination for Australians, directed to Australians, based on attributes which should never be the basis for discrimination."[12]

Given both the evidence that religious freedoms are increasingly vulnerable in Australia and the growth of anti-discrimination laws in Australia, it is easy to understand why the introduction of a Religious Discrimination Act might be seen as a desirable reform. However, it is a reform that carries a significant risk of unintended consequences and it is doubtful that it will actually end up significantly strengthening religious freedom in practice in the way that its proponents hope.[13]

The main outcome of any Religious Discrimination Act is to shift the responsibility for key decisions about the extent and limits of religious freedom from the parliament to the courts. Given that questions concerning religious freedom concern matters of deep personal conviction and conscience, and often involve divisive questions of social policy, community standards and personal morality, they are better suited to being decided by elected parliamentary representatives who are ultimately answerable to the people, rather than unelected judges who are not. This is particularly the case in Australia, where we have already seen the High Court apply a narrow and restrictive reading of the religious freedom provision that is already entrenched under s. 116 of the *Australian Constitution*.[14] There is no guarantee that any new religious freedom law in Australia would be approached differently by the judiciary and given a more expansive interpretation.

These same concerns apply to related recommendations that parliament should introduce a Religious Freedom Act. A Religious Freedom Act approaches the issue of protecting religious freedom from a more positive perspective than a Religious Discrimination Act — effectively creating a sword to pro-actively safeguard religious freedom as opposed to a shield to defend it against existing encroachments. While the specific details varied, the submissions to the Expert Panel that proposed a Religious Freedom Act generally suggested an Act that would formally implement the right to freedom of thought, conscience and religion that is outlined in Article 18 of the *International Covenant on Civil and Political Rights*.[15] The Expert Panel were not supportive of this proposal, finding that a standalone statutory enactment protecting freedom of religion "would be out of step with the treatment of other rights" and "would need to be carefully crafted having regard to the need to reconcile them with the full suite of other human rights."[16]

The problem of reconciling conflicting human rights is one of the key difficulties with the proposals for both a Religious Discrimination Act and a Religious Freedom Act. As discussed below, the question of how to deal with competing human rights is critical and a stand-alone Act aimed primarily at protecting one particular right or freedom would not only need to address this issue, but inevitably risks creating a problematic rights hierarchy by singling out that individual right or freedom for legal protection not offered to others.

Any Religious Freedom Act also raises the same concerns discussed above with regards to responsibility for key decisions about the extent and limits of religious freedom being shifted from the Parliament to the courts. Even though many of the groups who have proposed a Religious Freedom Act have sought to emphasise that this would not be "a mini-human rights Act nor a Charter of Rights by the back door"[17] the difference is essentially one of degree. While a Religious Freedom Act that could be amended or repealed by parliament means that the position of parliament is formally retained *vis-à-vis* the judiciary, experience shows us that, in practice, such an Act does still result in a significant movement of power away from the parliament. Yet, as discussed above, an unelected judiciary is not as well suited as an elected parliament to deciding issues that require conflicting human rights to be balanced, and divisive questions of social policy and personal morality to be decided.

In any event, examples from around the world clearly demonstrate that laws protecting religious freedom are not themselves enough to provide sufficient protection in practice. Of the ten countries designated in 2018 by the US Secretary of State as countries of particular concern "for having engaged in or tolerated particularly severe violations of religious freedom"[18] eight have some level of protection for religious freedom guaranteed in their national constitution.[19] If the leaders and people of a country don't value and respect religious freedom, then any legal guarantee will be worth little more than the paper it is written on. This is the "spirit of liberty" referred to by Judge Learned Hand when he famously said:[20]

> I often wonder whether we do no rest our hopes too much upon
> constitutions, upon laws, and upon courts. These are false hopes;

believe me, these are false hopes. Liberty lies in the hearts of men and women; when it dies there, no constitution, no law, no court can save it; no constitution, no law, no court can even do much to help it. While it lies there, it needs no constitution, no law, no court to save it.

Whenever there is a problem in Australia, the default position seems to be that the parliament should do something to fix it. Most often, this will involve a suggestion that some new law should be introduced. But a new law is not always the answer, and will not always be the best way to deal with an issue. Professor Carolyn Evans was absolutely correct when she observed that "sometimes the best protection that a government can give to religious freedom is to simply leave people free to make their own decisions about religious issues."[21] In my view, the introduction of a Religious Discrimination Act (or, for that matter, of a Religious Freedom Act) is not the best way to strengthen the protection of religious freedom in Australia.

Revising existing anti-discrimination laws

Rather than introducing a new law to protect religious freedom, a better approach would be revise existing laws that are restricting it. In fact, this is an important step even if a Religious Discrimination Act is introduced. Religious freedom does not exist in a vacuum, and it cannot realistically be considered in isolation from other rights and freedom. This is actually true for all human rights; as protecting the human rights of one individual almost inevitably involves restricting the choices and actions of another individual. The key challenge when it comes to strengthening the protection of religious freedom in Australia is how this one particular right is to be reconciled with other individual human rights; and how conflict between different rights is to be dealt with. This was recognised by the Joint Standing Committee on Foreign Affairs, Defence and Trade who recently found that "[a]n imbalance between competing rights and the lack of an appropriate way to resolve the ensuing conflicts is the greatest challenge to the right to freedom of religion."[22]

In terms of religious freedom, this conflict manifests itself particularly through the interaction with anti-discrimination laws. There are anti-discrimination laws at both the national and state levels in Australia, although the specific details of these laws vary in each jurisdiction. Anti-discrimination laws generally are designed to protect individuals with certain specific attributes against specified kinds of discrimination in prescribed areas of public life.[23] Existing anti-discrimination laws do provide some level of protection for religious freedom, although the Australian Human Rights Commission has noted that these protections "are inconsistent across jurisdictions and are quite narrow at the federal level."[24] Religious belief or activity is a protected attribute under the anti-discrimination laws of most States and Territories[25] and within most anti-discrimination laws there are a range of exemptions that apply, for example, to religious organisations and religious educational institutions in specific circumstances.

However, this current framework is problematic in terms of the rights hierarchy it establishes. For example, at the Commonwealth level, discrimination is prohibited only in relation to protected attributes such as age, disability, race and sex. These protected attributes are perceived to have a status superior to other attributes, such as religion, that are only protected through the provision of limited exemptions. As I noted with Joshua Forrester and Augusto Zimmermann in our joint submission to the Expert Panel:[26]

> Religious freedom is not sufficiently protected when it exists merely as a narrow exemption that is grudgingly accepted in anti-discrimination legislation. This implicitly undervalues the importance of religious freedom, with the consequence that it is consigned to a secondary role and is left vulnerable to removal at a later date.

One answer to this would be to establish religious freedom as a protected attribute through the introduction of a Religious Discrimination Act. However, in my view, the better approach is to revise existing anti-discrimination laws so that a better balance between conflicting rights is achieved, whilst also leaving untouched the greatest realm of freedom for each individual.

An additional problem is that anti-discrimination laws are not well suited to dealing with the nuanced interactions between conflicting human rights. They adopt a binary, all-or-nothing approach where the very purpose of the law is to decide which right is to be afforded priority over the other right. Instead of simply prioritizing one right at the expense of the other, the way in which conflicting rights could be accommodated should necessarily be more nuanced and will depend largely on the particular circumstances of the individual case example. The starting point should be that all human rights are important, and we should seek to give them all the widest scope of operation that is possible in each given case. This requires a degree of mutual respect and toleration to be demonstrated by all sides, something which has unfortunately been lacking in far too many recent examples where religious freedom has been in issue.

Of course, there will necessarily be times when conflicting rights cannot be reconciled, and it does become necessary for one to give way to another. In such circumstances, the relative weight to be given to each right is not absolute, but should be viewed along a spectrum depending on the individual circumstances. For example, where there is a conflict between freedom of religion and freedom of speech on the one hand and anti-discrimination laws on the other, the latter should be given priority if the relevant action involves any element of threats or violence. At the other end of the spectrum, if the relevant action is merely speech expressing an opinion that may offend the calculation is reversed and freedom of speech should take priority. As Jeremy Waldron has observed: "offensiveness by itself is not a good reason for legal regulation."[27]

A more fundamental problem when it comes to the growth of anti-discrimination laws in Australia is that they start from the premise that discrimination is a necessarily and unequivocally a bad thing, and that the absolute objective should be to eliminate discrimination as far as possible. A related concept embedded into anti-discrimination laws is that equality is an inherently desirable outcome to be promoted. For example, the *Equal Opportunity Act 1984* (WA) provides that its objects are "to eliminate, so far as is possible" discrimination and harassment on a range of grounds and "to promote recognition and acceptance within the community of the equality of persons" of protected attributes to others in the community.[28]

But discrimination and equality are not inherently positive or negative concepts in themselves. Instead, a great deal depends on the specific context and circumstances, and also on exactly what you mean when you adopt these terms. There are certainly many circumstances in which discrimination is morally repugnant and cannot be justified. Apartheid is one obvious example. But ultimately, discrimination itself is simply the making of a choice and can often be entirely justified. For example, electing to have surgery performed by a trained surgeon rather than a person with no medical training whatsoever is a form of discrimination that is entirely rational.

An important first step in revising existing anti-discrimination laws would be to reconsider the definition of discrimination. For example, Professor Patrick Parkinson and Professor Nicholas Aroney have recommended a new definition of discrimination based upon this idea that not every differentiation of treatment is discrimination in the wrongful sense. For example, under this new definition, different treatment would not constitute discrimination if (amongst other things) "it is reasonably capable of being considered appropriate and adapted to achieve a legitimate objective," with the "protection, advancement or exercise of another human right protected by the *International Covenant on Civil and Political Rights*" being specifically highlighted as a legitimate objective.[29] This would have the effect of recalibrating the existing relationship between conflicting human rights but, unlike existing exemptions in anti-discrimination laws, does so in a way that doesn't set up one right as being an inferior right that is granted only as a limited exception to the primary right.

The meaning and implications of a term like equality can also vary considerably depending on the circumstances. For example, equality of opportunity is not the same as equality of results, and they each carry with them vastly different implications. While demands for equality are very much a part of modern life, how can this be reconciled with the claims (confusingly, often made by the same groups) that diversity and difference should be recognised and celebrated? The entrenchment of anti-discrimination laws has occurred at the same time as the development of identity politics, and yet these two concepts are fundamentally irreconcilable when we are talking about human beings at the individual level.

Criticising the current anti-discrimination framework does not mean that you are opposed to its aims, or that you are in favour of all forms of discrimination. Simply recommending that laws should be reviewed to make sure that they are actually achieving their intended purpose and not over-reaching or resulting in unintended consequences should not be a controversial suggestion. In the case of anti-discrimination laws there are certainly important reasons for specific forms and instances of discrimination to be unlawful. But it is also important to ensure that we do not allow political symbolism to be prioritised over evidence-based analysis, and that we try to preserve as wide a scope as possible for individual choice and freedom. As Helen Andrews has observed:[30]

> Too often in their 50-year history, anti-discrimination laws have been expanded not for any logical reason, much less any evidence-based reason, but simply because a minority seemed to be 'next' or had 'come of age' as a pressure group. Too rarely have people stopped to ask whether anti-discrimination law is really the best means for accomplishing some new political goal, especially given that … anti-discrimination laws may not even be accomplishing the goals for which they were expressly designed anymore."

Revising current anti-discrimination laws is something that both national and state parliaments in Australia should do in order to strengthen the protection of religious freedom in Australia and, more broadly, to expand the realm of individual freedoms. Any such revision should consider, firstly, amending the definition of discrimination to make it clear that different treatment and wrongful discrimination are not necessarily the same thing. Secondly, the current growth trajectory of anti-discrimination laws should be reversed. Rather than continually expanding anti-discrimination laws to cover a greater number of protected attributes and to prohibit a wider range of conduct, these laws should be narrowly drafted so that they restrict as little as possible and leave individuals with the broadest possible realm of freedom.

Recognising there is no right not to be offended

The modern solution to fixing any perceived issue is usually to demand that the government does something, and that something is commonly a demand for a new law to be passed or an existing law to be strengthened. However, this focus actually disguises two important truths when it comes to the protection of human rights. Firstly, it is often the government that is responsible for infringing individual rights and whose power needs to be limited. Secondly, laws are just as likely (if not more likely) to restrict freedom as they are to protect it. The best way our political leaders can protect religious freedom is not by introducing new protective laws, but instead by refusing to introduce new restrictive laws and reducing the scope of existing restrictions. The widest realm of freedom will be achieved by having fewer restrictions imposed in the first place, rather than more allowances carved out in an attempt to address individual issues as they arise.

Viewed in this light, the terms of reference of the Expert Panel focused on only half of the equation. The Panel was asked to "examine and report on whether Australian law (Commonwealth, State and Territory) adequately protects the human right to freedom of religion."[31] An equally important question to ask is whether existing Australian laws undermine the human right to freedom of religion. To this end, existing laws that attempt to restrict 'offensive' speech potentially impose a significant burden on freedom of religion.

These laws are commonly referred to as 'hate speech' provisions, and yet this term masks the fact that the speech potentially captured extends beyond content that would be considered 'hateful' if that word was given its ordinary meaning. These provisions exist in various forms in all Australian jurisdictions. The most prominent example is s. 18C of the *Racial Discrimination Act 1975* (Cth). The most expansive is s. 17(1) of the *Anti-Discrimination Act 1998* (Tas), which provides that "[a] person must not engage in any conduct which offends, humiliates, intimidates, insults or ridicules another person on the basis of [a protected attribute] in circumstances in which a reasonable person, having regard to all the circumstances, would have anticipated that the other person would be offended, humiliated, intimidated, insulted or ridiculed." The protected attributes are outlined in s. 16 and encompass race, age, sexual orientation, lawful sexual activity, gender, gender-identity, intersex, marital status, relationship status, pregnancy, breastfeeding, parental status, family responsibility, disability, industrial activity, political belief or affiliation, political activity, religious belief or affiliation, religious activity, irrelevant criminal record, irrelevant medical record, or association with a person who has, or is believed to have, any of these attributes.

A high profile example of the way these laws can potentially restrict religious freedom came with the anti-discrimination complaint that was lodged against the Catholic Archbishop of Hobart, The Most Reverend Julian Porteous, in July 2015.[31] Transgender activist Marlene Delaney lodged a complaint under s. 17 claiming that a booklet distributed by the Church offended and humiliated same-sex attracted Australians. The booklet, *Don't Mess with Marriage*, was distributed at Catholic schools and churches. It outlined the traditional Catholic teachings about marriage, stating that marriage should be a "heterosexual union between a man and a woman" and outlining concerns about the effect of same-sex marriage on children.

The Tasmanian Anti-Discrimination Commissioner found there was a case to answer under Tasmanian anti-discrimination law, and accepted the complaint, with the parties then proceeding to a mandatory mediation process. Although the complaint was ultimately withdrawn in May 2016, this does not mean it disappeared without consequences. Archbishop Porteous was subjected to a formal complaints process for almost ten months, with all of the stress and pressure that must necessarily entail. There is also a broader chilling effect to consider, with the case raising the ongoing question of whether the Church — or any other individual or group — is at risk of future complaints being made to the Anti-Discrimination Commissioner in Tasmania if they publicly express views that support a traditional definition of marriage. The low threshold of "offends," "insults" or "ridicules" set under s. 17 must indicate that there is some level of continuing risk. In itself, this is enough to create a chilling effect on public debate and discussion, as highlighted by Angela Shanahan:[32]

> If people ... are forced to appear before an Anti-Discrimination Commission ... then this is a threat to one of Australia's greatest

freedoms, the right to free speech. This is a major disincentive to people making a contribution to debate across Australia. Anti-discrimination bodies should not be used as star chambers by those who simply don't like what someone else says

The characterisation of faith-based views as 'hate speech' is an emerging issue in Australia. During the same-sex marriage plebiscite a teenager was fired from her casual employment at a Canberra party entertainment company after adding a frame to her private Facebook profile picture that said "It's okay to vote no". In confirming that she had fired the teenager, the owner of the company posted on Facebook that:[33]

> Advertising your desire to vote no for SSM is, in my eyes, hate speech. Voting no is homophobic. Advertising your homophobia is hate speech. As a business owner I can't have somebody who publicly represents my business posting hate speech online.

This is an attitude also reflected by some high profile political leaders. The Australian Greens Senator Sarah Hanson-Young was quoted as saying: "The idea of marriage being only between a man and a women is not just outdated but extremely defamatory."[34] Recently, Queensland Deputy Premier Jackie Trad described Senator Amanda Stoker speaking at an anti-abortion rally in 2018 as having "taken to the streets to preach hate about women and their right to choose."[35] When the mere expression of traditional religious viewpoints runs a real risk of being characterised as hate speech, leading to possible legal complaints under existing anti-discrimination and hate speech laws in Australia, this represents a real challenge to religious freedom. As Professor Greg Craven recently observed: "A religion that cannot even speak its doctrines is merely a historical ritual, not a faith."[36]

While it is accepted that there is no absolute right to free speech, it is also important to acknowledge that there is no right not to be offended.[37] The question is where the line should be drawn to appropriately balance competing human rights. Current laws that prohibit speech on the basis that it may offend do not strike the right balance. Protecting free speech by revising existing hate speech laws and setting a higher harm threshold than 'offence' is essential to protect religious freedom in Australia.

Empowering Civil Society

The Expert Panel made a number of key recommendations that focused on data, dialogue and education. It noted that there is poor literacy concerning human rights and religion, with a "limited understanding in the general community about the human right to religious freedom, its application, and how it interacts with other human right."[38] To improve community understanding and engagement it was recommended that the federal government "should support the development of a religious engagement and public education program about human rights and religion in Australia" and should commission the collection and analysis of information concerning "the experience of freedom of religion in Australia at the community level," "the experience of freedom of religion impacting on other human rights," and "the extent to which religious diversity (as distinct from cultural diversity) is accepted and promoted in Australian society."[39] While the Expert Panel did not recommend the creation of a new Religious Freedom Commissioner position (although this has subsequently been proposed by the federal government), it did recommend that the Australian Human Rights Commission should take a leading role in the protection of religious freedom "including through enhancing engagement, understanding and dialogue."[40]

These are important recommendations. Religious freedom is best protected not through any single law, but through ensuring that the broader community understands why it is actually important and how it strengthens our nation. In particular, given the growing number of Australians who do not identify with a particular religious faith themselves, it is critical to explain that the protection of religious freedom is something that benefits everybody in our community — regardless of their individual religious views (or lack thereof). The challenge here is to understand that no single action will achieve this on its own. Instead, there needs to be a continuous commitment shown by not only our Parliament and political leaders, but also by civil society more broadly, to respect and preserve religious freedom.

There are numerous ways our political leaders can advance this aim. One obvious example was the first *Ministerial to Advance Religious Freedom* that was held in Washington D.C in July 2018, which brought U.S political leaders, international organisations, religious leaders, and civil society representatives together for a discussion about religious freedom and what can be done to better protect it. In Australia, a similar initiative could be seen in the national consultation on rights and responsibilities conducted by the Australian Human Rights Commissioner, which led to the establishment of a Religious Freedom Roundtable in 2015 "to provide a forum for constructive, respectful and trust-based dialogue about freedom of religion, conscience and belief."[41] These types of initiatives have an important role to play in strengthening religious freedom. Encouraging greater engagement, dialogue and education is essential to ensure that the value of religious freedom is more widely understood. It is also essential if we are to ensure that people understand that the responsibility for protecting religious freedom (and all other human rights for that matter) lies not just with the government, but more broadly with each and every one of us.

The controversy surrounding the "Keeping it Light" video in Australia shows, however, that encouraging dialogue and understanding is not always an easy task. This seven-minute video was produced by the Bible Society in March 2017 and initially linked with Coopers Brewery. It featured Andrew Hastie and Tim Wilson — two Liberal Party Members of Parliament with opposing views on same-sex marriage — discussing the issue of same-sex marriage with a moderator while drinking Coopers Premium Light Beers. Andrew Hastie observed that: "The whole point of this video was to demonstrate that two MPs can disagree on a very important issue and still be friends and still respect each other."[42] This message was evidently lost on some, with same-sex marriage supporters claiming it trivialised the issue, was homophobic and was evidence of Coopers Brewery pushing an anti-gay marriage agenda. There was an immediate backlash against the brewery, with a #BoycottCoopers push being launched on social media and a number of pubs indicating that they would no longer purchase any Coopers Brewery beer as a direct result of the video. A change.org petition calling for a boycott of Coopers Brewery gained 1,772 signatures in just over a day.[43] Coopers Brewery quickly issued a video apology distancing themselves from the video, emphasising their support for marriage equality and apologising for the offence that had been caused. As Tim Wilson observed, "I think it's a sign that there is a section of society that's very intolerant of a difference of

Forgotten Freedom No More

opinion on an issue like this today, and I think it speaks to the point of the video which is to have respectful disagreement."[44]

Religious freedom is not something that can ever be absolutely guaranteed through the law or by the government. Indeed, the ever-increasing reliance on government to solve these problems risks neglecting the vital role that civil society should play in this area. When we outsource responsibility for our freedoms to others, there is a real risk that those freedoms will be gradually eroded and diminished. As Helen Andrews has observed:[45]

> In a pluralistic society, different systems of values will inevitably come into conflict, but these conflicts do not have to be solved through litigation or legislation. Indeed, it is often better if they are not. One reason the culture wars are so bitter in Australia is that they revolve around government. When both sides know that the winner will be able to enforce their preferred outcome on the whole country via legislation, they approach the fight with winner-take-all ruthlessness and become reluctant to compromise or agree to disagree. A patchwork of organic solutions, worked out via civil society, does not incentivise radicalism in that way. It also yields more lasting and resilient solutions, since organic solutions are not coerced but freely chosen.

Conclusion

Australian political leaders have spoken frequently over the past few years about the importance of religious freedom, and have repeatedly promised to strengthen its protection. It is well past time for their words to be matched by actions. The parliament should take this opportunity, noting that strengthening religious freedom does not necessarily involve the introduction of new laws. Indeed, in my view, the parliament should resist attempts to introduce a Religious Discrimination Act, while also revising existing anti-discrimination laws, recognising that there is no right not to be offended and empowering civil society. But most importantly, we need to recognise that it is not parliament alone that bears responsibility for ensuring that religious freedom is protected. This is a responsibility that falls on each and every individual and, as noted by the Expert Panel, is a task that "requires constant vigilance."[46]

Chapter 7

A HUMEAN TAKE ON RELIGIOUS FREEDOM

James Allan

The editors have asked me to provide an atheist's take or perspective on the religious freedom debate in Australia. So first off let me be clear that I am indeed a non-believer in God. If labels and camps matter to you, then if anything I am a Humean when it comes to the question of the truth as to whether there exists a benevolent, theistic God. Along with the great eighteenth century Scottish philosopher David Hume, I think the answer to that query is "no."

Hume himself wrote one of the great books on this question; his post-humously published *Dialogues Concerning Natural Religion* (published in 1779, three years after his death). It is a magisterial piece of writing in the form of a three-person dialogue between what today might be classed as 1) the theist who relies in part on revelation ("Demea"); 2) the deist who argues, based on the evidence of design, for some sort of First Cause and Unmoved Mover type God ("Cleanthes"); and 3) the sceptic, who doubts human reason is up to the job of coming to any conclusions about a divine Being ("Philo"). When you take into account Hume's other writings on religion, it is clear Philo is very close to Hume's own views, though Hume himself was probably an outright atheist rather than an agnostic. Back then, it was still dangerous to take that position forthrightly; and indeed, even Hume's carefully crafted agnosticism — and no more than ironic jabs — at theism ensured that during his lifetime 'the great infidel' was precluded from holding any position at a Scottish university.

Remember, too, that Hume's demolition of the argument from design was written nearly a century before Darwin and hence before anyone could offer an evolutionary alternative for what looked like outcomes achieved by design. As I said, this book is magisterial. It is also subtle and sympathetic to the religious worldview in a way that, say, Richard Dawkins' writings on religion are not. It is all the more powerful for that too.

Hume is also justly famous for his writing on miracles (in his *An Enquiry Concerning Human Understanding* —a must-read). The gist of Hume's point there is that when some miracle has been claimed to have taken place (or any seemingly exceptionally unlikely event, so all of you alternative and complementary medicine adherents take note) one has to weigh up all of the empirical evidence on both sides — the case 'for' and the case 'against'. Since a miracle involves a supposed breach of the laws of nature (*ie.* of physics, chemistry, biology, etc), the evidence for it having happened will have to outweigh the likelihood that it did not happen because one was after all mistaken, or deluded, or that the people who vouchsafed it were in error or deliberately lying. And Hume then argues that the evidence that a miracle did take place — an n=1 event, if you like — is likely *always* to be outweighed by the evidence that it did not occur. Put differently, you are more likely to be wrong about what you feel sure you experienced or believe than that the laws of physics have been suspended this one time. In other words, you (and other miracle asserters) being wrong is more likely than is the possibility of the physical laws of the universe having been suspended.

Of course, if the number of people ultimately vouchsafing the miracle were higher than the number who provide evidence of the existence of this law of nature, or if the witness for the miracle were completely and 100 per cent reliable, then its claims could be supported as having happened. But Hume doubts the latter of those caveats could ever be met — not least because people tend to be too credulous, too gullible, too predisposed to want to believe it happened, sometimes too desperate, the list goes on... — while the former one just amounts to later-in-time or eventually realising that you had been wrong about what you thought the laws of nature actually are. An example of that might be how, after more than two centuries, the Newtonian view of physics gave way to a quantum view, due in part to new observations at the subatomic level. The laws of nature, in other words, were not what we had thought they were for some 225 plus years. A less grandiose example regards ulcers, which for quite a while the medical consensus believed to be caused by stress — wrongly we now know.

Hume was also well-known during his lifetime for being a very nice person to all and sundry. On his death Hume's good friend, Adam Smith, wrote that Hume approached "as nearly to the idea of a perfectly wise and virtuous man, as perhaps the nature of human frailty will permit."[1] About the sole person with whom Hume fell out was Jean Jacques Rousseau, and that was only after Hume had spent time and gold on rescuing the man from France and gaining him a pension, only to have the Frenchman turn nastily and publicly against the Scotsman. But of course Rousseau was anything but a nice person (I put the point as kindly as possible, you understand), a claim that can be made against a large number of other well-known philosophers — think Marx, think Schopenhauer, think Sartre, think Voltaire, the list goes on. Even Boswell, on seeing the atheist Hume on his deathbed and still content and unafraid, was impressed.

At this point, notice that non-believers in this Humean mould are merely making a truth-claim about the world; they say that in fact a benevolent, theistic God does not exist. However, they are not making any sort of claim about whether belief in God does, or does not, tend to promote good or bad consequences on average, over time. Far too many people elide those two questions. They assume that if you believe God does not exist then you must therefore also think that the belief in God by others (or more generally by most of society) tends to have an overall negative effect. But of course these are separate questions. The former does not entail the latter.

Moreover, there are solid grounds for having more than a few doubts about the latter assertion. Sure, some pretty horrific things have been done in the name of religion, including religious wars, forced conversions, sectarianism, an Inquisition or two, and the like. But on the other hand, some pretty wonderful things have emanated from the religious worldview. Slavery in the modern world was first stamped out because of non-conformists in England, and then the Royal Navy enforced a ban on slave-trading across the open seas because it was pushed to do so by the same sort of religiously inspired people. For certain, this was not done because of atheists like me.

Likewise the comparative charitable impulse, which seems not to produce too many atheist Mother Theresas dedicating their lives to helping those in the slums of Calcutta, to say nothing of those who are prepared to give 10 per cent of their incomes to those less well off. And there is the wonderful music, art and literature. Nor can one plausibly argue that the modern world's embrace of the notion of human rights (for good or for ill) has historical roots in anything other than Christianity, with its treatment of each individual as one of God's children and hence as deserving of respect and of a hefty degree of autonomy.

Here's another factor that gets little attention. In the absence of a Christian (or other mainstream religious) worldview, how many people are likely to be content or able to function at all with what looks to be a corollary of atheism, namely a fairly bleak picture of a meaningless world where a human "is of no greater importance to the universe than that of an oyster" (to quote Mr Hume again)? Your Bertrand Russells and your David Humes, yes. But one suspects the vast preponderance of people who forswear the religious mindset with one hand will, with the other, have a deep need to welcome it back into their lives in some different guise. They might substitute worship of the planet, of Gaia, and instil that with some deeper significance — though truth be told, why some tiny dot of a planet in an obscure, far-flung galaxy in an ever-expanding universe should warrant that sort of souped-up, steroid-enhanced level of concern (absent a benevolent, theistic God) is not wholly clear.

As a subset of that they might re-direct the religious impulse towards, say, lowering carbon dioxide emissions, again with a near religious impulse. Or they might infuse vegetarianism with this redirected spiritual vigour. The possibilities are many. And more than one commentator has suggested that most (perhaps almost all) non-believers will not actually jettison Christianity or Judaism or Islam for some bleak Bertrand Russell-like atheism, but rather for some version or other of these modern day types of Paganism. It won't exactly be a return to the Roman Republic before Christ; but there will be parallels — possibly including the tendency to live in the here and now, gratifying what you can as soon as you can. And if there be any truth in that, then the cost-benefit analysis of whether a widespread belief in a benevolent, theistic God be an overall plus or minus must include the consequences of that sort of redirected Paganistic zeal as well.

As I said, then, there are solid grounds for having more than a few doubts about a society's loss of belief in the existence of God being something that generates overall net good consequences. This seems to be even more the case if one believes that not all competing mainstream religions are created equal. Societies that lose faith in one may find another takes its place (given the above mooted widespread human need to find meaning imposed by or into the universe). And that other might look to non-believers to be a good deal less benign on all sorts of fronts.

At any rate that is a quick sketch of my non-belief and the type of issues that sort of worldview can, and does, throw up. Let me turn now to the question of how such a perspective (or at least how my non-believing perspective) views the issue of religious freedom in Australia.

A non-believer's perspective on the issue of religious freedom in Australia

Start with a liberal (at least liberal in the progressive, US-sense) conceit: the Rawlsian notion that religion is best kept confined to the personal realm so that a sort of public neutrality can be maintained in the political realm.[2] The idea here is more or less along the lines that the state should not reward or penalise any particular conception of the good life; instead it should provide a neutral framework of sorts under which any person can pursue his or her own conception of the good life. Rawls gets to this by reinvigorating the old social contract worldview (which, as it happens, Hume had powerfully critiqued two centuries ago, not least because "it wasn't worth the paper it wasn't written on") and imagining what someone would pick from behind a veil of ignorance.[3]

From there, goes the claim, no one would know even their own conceptions of the good as it were. But of course Rawls and others of like mind stack the deck. Their 'public reason' and allowed public sphere for debate patently favour those who, for instance, hold personal freedom to be the highest ideal and (to be unkind) would, *mirabile dictu*, fit in at any present day Harvard University faculty philosophy seminar.[4] The supposed neutrality aimed at allowing us all to get along in fact works to rule out certain first principles or core worldviews.[5] It stacks the deck, as I said, in favour of those who think personal autonomy is the greatest moral good. As a consequence, it excludes from the public square much of the core positions held by (amongst others) traditional religious believers — say, views that might include an opposition to abortion or to giving the state's stamp of approval to same sex marriage.[6]

But I have never understood why that Rawlsian or US-style liberalism claim to being neutral is remotely plausible. For many people the most important values and motivating principles in their lives, with all sorts of downstream practical implications, flow from a deeply held belief in a benevolent, theistic God. And why should their views be simply ruled out of order because of their source? Good luck trying to answer that one with a straight face. And yet much of the progressivist's opposition to input into public debate from those with religious worldviews flows from precisely that sort of stacking of the deck. Or so it seems to me. Such stacking is self-serving tosh, though not the least effective rhetorical and polemical tool in the armoury of those who see themselves at the vanguard of promoting 'needed' changing social mores.

By contrast, I am a democrat.[7] Count each of us as equal and let the numbers count, say I; allowing people to come to the vote however it is that they happen to have been shaped by genes or social inculcation or religiously-inspired (or not) thinking. That, I think, is a much more neutral starting point, at least procedurally and in fact, than one that implicitly feeds into an imaginary construct all sorts of presuppositions that the author him or herself happens to share. Of course that sort of 'democracy is the least bad option' starting point means that sometimes — perhaps often — one's fellow citizens will vote for parties I don't much like.[8] Alas, that is the cost of democracy. If you don't like it spend a few Saturdays working for a political party that looks more aligned to your own worldview — don't delusionally pretend the public realm can legitimately be restricted by what flows from starting premises that you just happen to share, and that you no doubt believe are neutrality and reason incarnate.

Be that as it may, we democrats are unfortunately on the retreat across much of the developed democratic world and factors such as the above progressivist conceit have moved the issue of religious freedom to near the top of the "how do we deal with this?" table. So let me now run through what I think about those policy-making issues here in Australia.

Policy for religious freedom in Australia

First off, I am adamantly opposed to any sort of Bill of Rights-type 'freedom of religion' provision, however it might be disguised.[9] This, in my view, is a horrible mistake and one no centre-right or Bill of Rights-opposing government should ever make. It can only plausibly be justified on the premise the unelected top judges would clearly and consistently favour religious freedom concerns over, say, equality type concerns. And that is palpably false as the empirical track record of top courts around the Anglosphere makes clear (where both entrenched, constitutionalised and enacted, statutory bills of rights do exist).

As a class (I speak in general terms you understand) the lawyerly caste from which the top judges will be chosen will overwhelmingly side with equality concerns over freedom of religion concerns; some might go so far as to say that the archetypical modern Australian judge has the political opinions of the Italian left circa 1910. Hence any sort of constitutional or statutory grant of 'freedom of religion', however drafted and however brought into being, is undesirable. It will do nothing when push comes to shove.

That is a prediction upon which I am happy to take bets. So any government seriously concerned about religious freedom in Australia, and wanting to do something to protect it, is grasping at an illusion —

at fool's gold — if it travels down this road of opting for some sort of freedom of religion type legislative provision.

At least as bad in my view, any such move would also increase the pressure for the grant of a bundle of other rights; in other words, it would re-open the whole stalled Bill of Rights debate in Australia and make life noticeably easier for proponents of such an instrument. I have written at tedious length as to why I am against such instruments and will not repeat myself here. Suffice it to say this. A Liberal Party that has been consistently and strongly opposed to a Bill of Rights will find such a position much harder to maintain if it — when it thinks (wrongly in my view, but that does not affect the principle here) that some partial Bill of Rights-like micro provision will further its preferred goals and possibly get it out of a self-imposed political jam — hops onto the 'give this to the unelected judges to deal with' high speed train. In the larger scheme of things, a worse 'own goal' is hard to imagine.

What will do something to help, or so think I, are the following two broad courses of action. I give them in order of importance.

Firstly, rather than adding any new statutory provisions, a few extremely illiberal classes of provisions need to be repealed. Three immediately spring to mind, namely: the 'no offence' provisions in Tasmania (the ones in which Archbishop Porteous was enmeshed);[10] the various anti-discrimination laws which effectively prohibit religious schools and welfare agencies from discriminating on the basis of religion (because the exemptions that used to exist have been narrowed and are these days narrowly interpreted by the courts);[11] and Australia's national hate speech laws, s.18C.[12] (It would take a bad situation and make it worse, much worse, were religion added as a s.18C grounds, as requested by the Grand Mufti).[13]

Removal of those three classes of existing statutory provisions would go some considerable distance towards emasculating any disabilities suffered by those with religious worldviews. Take away their attendant administrative penalties (which have real bite and in various ways apply to those whose world views are based on deeply held Christian or other denominational beliefs) and there would be plenty of scope to speak out against, say, same sex marriage or to comment on transgender issues. Or on nearly anything else for that matter. Most of the problem disappears with the disappearance of these type of provisions.

I would have thought that was pretty clear. Alas, one suspects the percentage of the federal Liberal Party's party room prepared to fight for such a repeal of 18C is unlikely to reach even a third. And I may be something of a Pollyanna in putting the percentage as high as that! Meanwhile at the state level, the same would be true of Liberal party rooms as regards winding back anti-discrimination laws and 'no offence' provisions. The irony is that many state laws[14] give political parties the right to discriminate on the basis of politics while not (or not to the same extent, as interpreted by today's judges) giving religious organisations a corresponding right to discriminate on the basis of religion — leave aside the question of whether viewing all of this through the prism of 'discrimination' is even a good idea. (Hint: No, it's not).

The second, longer term course of action I think needs pursuing is for those concerned about religious freedom to take the appointment of top judges a lot more seriously. The Liberal Party in this country, over the past two decades at least, has made appointments to the High Court ranging from ordinary at one end to awful (meaning noticeably worse than Labor would do) at the other. The last two really good High Court of Australia (HCA) picks by a Coalition government were the choices of Ian Callinan and Dyson Heydon.

I have written about this whole judicial appointments problem at length as well, and so won't repeat myself here either. Just realise that whatever happens in the immediate future, over time the top judges in this country are likely to have a not insignificant role to play on the religious freedom front. It is bad enough that the last few Coalition governments haven't been bothered to pick a single HCA judge with tolerable federalist credentials, or not a one sceptical of the HCA's judicial activism on the implied freedom front, it also has not picked anyone of late likely to go to the wall to support religious freedom against the progressivist equality crusade (if I can be forgiven for using that term). On any scorecard of how the recent federal Coalition governments have done on this judicial appointments front, I doubt that anything higher than a D+ could be defended — with all the massive grade inflation in today's Australian universities, make that a C-.

Those, then, in broad terms are the two classes of actions I would recommend — and that I think any Coalition government should do — to help ensure there is plenty of scope for those of a religious bent to act and speak as their consciences dictate, freely and without legal constraint. Having said that, this particular non-believer does not for an instant believe that the elected politicians currently making up today's federal (or state) Liberal and National parties would have anywhere near enough joint party room support to do either of them when they are next back in power. Indeed, it would come close to qualifying as a miracle if they did.

Chapter 8

ON RELIGIOUS FREEDOM AND ITS CULTURAL DESPISERS: AN ANGLICAN PERSPECTIVE

Michael F. Bird

We are worshippers of one God, of whose existence and character nature teaches all men; at whose lightning and thunder you tremble, whose benefits minister to your happiness. You think that others, too, are gods, whom we know to be devils. However, it is a fundamental human right, a privilege of nature, that every man should worship according to his own convictions: one man's religion neither harms nor helps another man. It is assuredly no part of religion to compel religion — to which free-will and not force should lead us — the sacrificial victims even being required of a willing mind. You will render no real service to your gods by compelling us to sacrifice. For they can have no desire of offerings from the unwilling, unless they are animated by a spirit of contention, which is a thing altogether undivine.

- Tertullian (155-240) writing an open letter to Scapula, Roman Proconsul of Africa who had begun persecuting the Christians, in 212 AD

Religious Freedom: The State of the Problem

According to the Magna Carta (1215), *Anglicana ecclesia libera*, "the English Church shall be free." A wonderful aspiration, but one that falls foul of the fact that, historically speaking, the English Church has not always been free from foreign intervention, royal interference, and political manipulation. Even worse, the Church of England and its colonial off-shoots have not always treated other Christian denominations and other world religions with liberty and charity. If we burned our own bishops like Nicholas Ridley and Thomas Cranmer, you could only imagine what fate befell those poor souls judged to be apostate or unbelieving. It was only with the establishment of religious rights for non-conformists in 1689, and then later with the advances of individual liberties, that the English legislated religious toleration and religious freedom for itself and its colonies. Even in Australia, which was established as a nation without a state-sponsored church and with an ostensibly secular government, the Church of England always received preferential treatment at the hands of the political class up and until the 1970s.

Thankfully, over the past 200 years, the Church of England and its Anglican expressions around the world have progressively championed religious liberties for other Christian groups, as well as for other world religions — and to those of no religion at all. It is refreshing these days to see senior Anglican and Catholic archbishops joining together to call for an end to religious persecution and to promote religious freedom.[1] Indeed, whereas Henry VIII was given the title 'Defender of the Faith' by Pope Leo X in 1521 for his anti-Lutheran tractate, it would be fair to say that today's English royals and Anglican bishops would be happy to embrace the title 'Defender of Faiths'.[2]

Religious freedom is a burning issue and it is out of the Anglican tradition that I wish to voice my own concerns about the paramount importance of religious freedom in Australia for a fair, just, prosperous, and flourishing society. As the Second Vatican Council's *Dignitatis Humanae* stated in 1965:

> The human person has a right to religious freedom. This freedom
> means that all men are to be immune from coercion on the part

of individuals or of social groups and of any human power, in such wise that no one is to be forced to act in a manner contrary to his own beliefs, whether privately or publicly, whether alone or in association with others, within due limits.

I would also affirm the words of Jan Figel, the European Union's first Special Envoy for religious freedom, that "Religious freedom is litmus test of overall freedom in society and overall universal human rights so it is important to pay due attention."[3] Or as Rex Ahdar and Ian Leigh claim, religious liberty is the "ultimate freedom," a cornerstone of modern political rights.[4] And yet, if religious freedom is an intrinsic good and necessary for pluralistic and participationist democracy, why does religious freedom feel so under threat? Why do people say things like 'religious liberty' is merely a code word for "discrimination, intolerance, racism, sexism, homophobia, Islamophobia, [and] Christian supremacy."[5] Why is there remarkable resistance to bolstering Australia's religious freedom protections among the media, the chattering class of elites, on social media, and even among some of our politicians?

When it comes to the Australian context, the reasons for the hostility towards religion and religious freedom are I think complex and revolve around several things: (1) The rise of the 'nones', i.e., a significant percentage of the Australian demographic have no religious affiliation, means that many people are religiously illiterate, they do not grasp the intricacies and nuances of secularism, and they have little contact with people of faith; (2) In popular imagination, religion mostly conjures up notions of Islamic terrorism and Catholic church clerical sex-abuse scandals, which is not conducive to a fair hearing; and (3) There is an on-going cultural war that pits religious liberty against LGBTI rights. The result of all this is that in Australia there is "a thin veneer of resentment toward Christianity on top of a sea of apathy!"[6] In such a context, where religion is matter of apathy and antipathy, it is hard to persuade segments of the public that religious freedom needs legislative attention precisely in the public interest.

I argue that there are valid reasons for strengthening Australia's religious freedom protections. The protections laid out in s116 of the Australian Constitution comprises a Westminster appropriation of the

US Constitution's non-establishment of religion by government clause and the free exercise of religion clause. However, s116 is inadequate for several reasons:

Firstly, the provisions pertain only to federal law and not to state law. In fact, there has been two referenda to extend the protections to state laws but they were both defeated in 1944 and 1988 respectively; In legal cases s116 has been interpreted very narrowly by federal courts which entails a narrow exercise of religious freedom. Secondly, the only other protections for religious freedom are a pastiche of state-level legal exemptions to anti-discrimination legislation which are themselves problematic because: (a) they vary markedly between the states; (b) they define religious freedom by what is exemptive to a legal norm rather than as an intrinsic good in its own right; and (c) they are very unpopular as they give license to religious bodies to discriminate against persons on the basis of religion, marital status, and sexual orientation; A Pew-Templeton research report in 2016 noted that Australia had low levels of government restrictions on religion, however, the same report gave Australia a high rating on its social hostility index, measuring acts of religious hostility involving individuals, groups, or organisations. While government generally does not itself pose an immediate threat to religious freedom, there are factors and actors in the wider social fabric that are overtly hostile to religion and religious people;[7] and Instances of Islamophobia, anti-Semitism, and attacks against Christians – including verbal attacks, vilification, vandalism, discrimination, and assault – means that religious persons need protection from both rival religious groups and from anti-religious antagonists.

The fact of the matter is that our current federal laws are not fit to deal with the complexities of faith and freedom in twenty-first century multicultural Australia — a land of all faiths and none, where sectarian tensions and anti-religious fanaticism, as well as government interference in religious bodies, are a real threat to our relative peaceful co-existence with one another.

The Ruddock Religious Freedom Review of 2018 was meant to deal with some of these legal lacunae, but its recommendations fell short of advocating a wide-ranging and effective mechanism for safeguarding religious freedom.[8] Perhaps, in the aftermath of the 2019 federal election, where religious freedom, and even the existence of hell was a live political issue, we will see a concerted and comprehensive proposal to ensure religious freedom in Australia. This could conceivably happen in two stages. In the short term, legislation to dismantle some anti-discrimination exemptions so that religious entities cannot discriminate against LGBTI children, yet combined with legislation to reinforce the rights of religious entities to maintain their ethos and to discriminate in their hiring practices. Then n the medium term, legislation to ensure freedom from discrimination based on religion and to enshrine liberty to practice religion privately and in community.

That is an optimistic reading of the situation, one that might even eventuate. While this might represent the best-case scenario, I believe that we must prepare for the worst-case scenario, where a minimalistic approach to religious freedom is exercised and where potential for government encroachment on religious liberties continue. It must be borne in mind that the greatest threat to religious freedom and to the secularism which undergirds it is not the conflict with LGBTI rights — that itself is a skirmish in a larger socio-political conflict — the larger threat is far more menacing. If a threat is defined between the poles of capability and intent, then, the single greatest threat to religious freedom in Australia is *civic totalism*.

Civic Totalism: The Real Threat to Religious Freedom

There was an age, not so long ago — let's call it the 1990s — when champions of liberal democracy believed in protecting religious freedom because such freedoms were good for religion and good for a pluralistic democracy. Religion was 'good' because, as everyone knew, liberal democracy was rooted in a Christian framework and Christianity provided the moral capital that modern liberalism routinely spent in its quest for social betterment. In other words, liberalism knew and respected the moral order which preceded it, even if space was created for those who were not religious adherents or not the normal sort of adherents. However, classic liberalism has been eclipsed by a mode of progressive politics that takes a more sceptical or even adversarial position on religion. We might say that there has emerged a pharaoh who knew neither John Locke nor Thomas Jefferson.

In the latest permutation of political progressivism, gone is the fear of government overreaching its authority, gone is the fear of state encroaching upon religious space, and instead we encounter political agents who advocate an expansive and activist government to implement its policies, if necessary, over and against religious convictions. This amounts to a progressive vision of the state and its apparatuses as able to impose its will and values upon private associations and even into religious communities. Among the progressive intelligentsia, the state is no longer conceived as a set of political arrangements with derivative freedoms guaranteeing that persons of different perspectives can live in relative harmony with one another. Instead, the state is now prophet, priest, and king and seeks to regulate as much of civil society as it is able to dictate.[9]

While progressive leaders are far from monolithic — compare Terri Butler with Elizabeth Warren! — generally speaking, they see in traditional Christianity a moral framework that must be resisted because it represents to them the cathedral of the western evils of capitalism, patriarchy, and white supremacy. Indeed, traditional Christianity, including its institutions, cultural influence, and moral vision, is *the* number one enemy progressives believe they are struggling against. Progressives know that Christianity's enduring legacy in western culture can only be defeated by realigning institutions towards a sanitised and secularised morality, by redefining the parameters of religious freedom, by a coercive catharsis of religion itself, and by deconstructing the permanent structures of human existence like family and marriage. Such a social transformation requires far-reaching control over civil society in order to be effective. Thus, the progressive social vision amounts to what Stephen Macedo calls *civic totalism* where the plenipotentiary state is invested with all power and seeks to regulate as much of public and private life as possible.[10]

Civic totalism has antecedents in various philosophical, social, and political theories where individual rights are subordinate to the objectives of the state to promulgate a certain social vision that aggressively supplants any competing visions such as those found in religion.[11] The person who is probably the primary forerunner to modern versions of civic totalism is John Dewey.[12]

Dewey was a philosopher and educational theorist who believed the state should sanction a scientifically informed public morality that made comprehensive claims to truth. Such a morality would be comprehensive in the sense of including the public and private domain, be rooted in the state education system, required the subordination of the church to the state, and would effectively dissolve traditional religions in order to enable religious energies to be transferred to the advancement of progressive state culture. In the end, Dewey's political project envisaged a society unified around what Macedo labels "a progressive democratic religion."[13]

Key to civic totalism is the view that public institutions are supreme, and civil society is reduced to a plethora of pliable people to be artfully managed — and for whom liberties are granted, modified, and revoked as the state so decides the expediencies necessary to advance its progressive agendas. As a result, the distinctions between the public and private increasingly shrink, independent institutions become increasing susceptible to government coercion, and the gap between church and state narrows. For political progressives this is not only reasonable but even necessary because the very survival of the state depends on a convergence of private and public values which requires government to be empowered with the "ability to turn people's deepest convictions — including their religious beliefs — in directions that are congruent with the ways of a liberal republic."[14]

Thus, varieties of political progressivism have a quasi-religious view of the state as the deliverer from a forthcoming eco-economic-equality Armageddon, i.e., the state must be deity, priest, and cathedral in order to save people from imminent disaster. According to this civic totalist vision, religion is regarded as dangerous since religion ascribes notions of ultimacy to something other than the state and the state's eschatological vision for manufacturing utopia. Religion creates a competing social vision and an alternative morality, which divides the loyalty of citizens away from the state's salvific designs, rendering certain forms of religion as hostile to the state's mission. In civil totalism, religious persons who are not suitably progressive, who do not align themselves with the state's progressive vision, and who do not embed themselves within the state's progressive apparatuses, become, in either soft or hard forms, enemies of the state.

The claim I am making might seem alarmist, hyperbolic, and an exercise in catastrophising. However, I offer several philosophical and legal examples to demonstrate my concerns are genuine.

Firstly, the German philosopher and social theorist Jürgen Habermas provides a very accurate summary of civil totalism vis-à-vis religion when he suggested that the "consciousness of the faithful" must be "modernised" and forced to acquiesce and accept "the individualistic and egalitarian nature of the laws of the secular community."[15] Habermas offers a brutally transparent expression of civic totalism.

Secondly, the idea of forcibly changing religious bodies to correspond with progressive ideology is not a mere hypothesis, it is already on the table. According to Carolyn Evans and Beth Gaze, "There is an increasingly powerful movement to subject religions to the full scope of discrimination laws, with some scholars now suggesting that even core religious practices (such as the ordination of clergy) can be regulated in the name of equality."[16] It was precisely this sort of thinking that led Hillary Clinton to say, in the context of a speech about women's access to reproductive services, that "laws have to be backed up with resources and political will; and deep-seated cultural codes, religious beliefs and structural biases have to be changed."[17] Civic totalism is not a thought bubble... for many, it is already party policy.

Thirdly, clear examples of civil totalism as it pertains to religion are already apparent in Australia. To begin with, in 2015, the Catholic Archbishop of Hobart, Julian Porteous, released a booklet entitled *Don't Mess with Marriage* explaining the Catholic Church's position on same-sex marriage.[18] It was a pastoral and nuanced description of Catholic teaching on marriage that was disseminated to parents with children at Catholic schools. However, a local LGBTI activist took issue with the booklet and made a complaint to Tasmania's Human Rights commissioner on the grounds that the booklet was insulting and offensive to LGBTI people. In a shocking move, the commissioner agreed that the bishop had a case to answer. Now consider this, we had a Catholic bishop about to be hauled before legal proceedings because he did with (apparently) malice and heinousness of forethought conspire to teach Catholic beliefs about marriage to Catholics and even had malevolence to defend what was at the time the current marriage law of Australia. The complaint was dropped, not on account of any reconciliation, but due to political expediency on the part of the complainant. Yet we still do not know if, in the state of Tasmania, teaching Catholic beliefs about marriage to Catholics is a crime.

To give another example, the Queensland Anti-Discrimination Tribunal determined in 2008 that the St Vincent de Paul Society of Queensland had discriminated against a non-Catholic who was elected president of a local conference of the society, when the person was required to convert to Catholicism or to lose their position. The society argued that it was a religious body and therefore exempted from the relevant anti-discrimination laws. It was further claim by the society that being a Catholic was a genuine operational requirement of the position as president of a conference of the society. The tribunal, however, rejected both of the society's arguments. The tribunal judged that the society was not a religious body and that while there was a religious dimension to the position, being Catholic was not a necessary operational requirement of the position. It is pertinent to observe that a state body had determined that a Catholic charity was not a religious entity and prohibited an overtly Catholic organization from insisting that its senior officers be Catholic.[19] A decision that is palpably and positively Erastian!

In sum, civic totalism advocates the subordinations individual freedoms, especially religious freedom, to the state and mandates social conformity to state-sponsored political principles by all tiers of society. In the end, civic totalism seeks the near-unrivalled supremacy of the state to govern public and private spheres, to indoctrinate its views without question, and to even change people's religion.

Religious Freedom as a Civic Necessity

Despite common misconception, Australia is not a secular country. To the contrary, Australia is in fact a pluralistic country with a secular government and with a decidedly Christian social and religious heritage. Added to that, Australia is a multicultural success story. It is a *pot-pourri* of Indigenous, post-colonial, and ethnic groups that live together in relative harmony; even if there remain unresolved issues related to Indigenous recognition and occasional sectarian tensions imported from overseas.

What must be acknowledged is that a multicultural nation is inevitably a multi-faith nation and the continuing success of Australian multiculturalism is dependent upon ensuring the capacity of people of all faiths and none to live out their beliefs in private and in community with others in relative freedom. If multiculturalism means anything it means the right to be different without fear of reprisal from mobs, media, or state management. To this end, secularism, when properly understood, is imperative in multiculturalism, since secularism ensures that religion is free from government interference and government is likewise free from religious domination. Although there are different species of secularism — contrast France and Turkey![20] — benevolent secularism seeks to preserve rather than inhibit religious liberty. In which case, the temptation of the progressive political bloc to embrace a form of civic totalism, characterized by the subjugation of religion to ends determined by the progressive state, represents the greatest threat to religious freedom and multiculturalism in Australia and it must be resisted and refuted at every juncture.

Government has the job of ensuring basic human rights for its citizens, including religious freedom, and establishing mechanisms for a fair and equitable resolution when competing freedoms come into conflict with one another. Ultimately, government would be well served to see in the words of US President George Washington, when writing to the Hebrew congregation in New England, a template for their own approach to religious liberty for religious minorities:

> All possess alike liberty of conscience and immunities of citizenship It is now no more that toleration is spoken of, as if it was by the indulgence of one class of people, that another enjoyed the exercise of their inherent natural rights. For happily the Government of the United States, which gives to bigotry no sanction, to persecution no assistance requires only that they who live under its protection should demean themselves as good citizens, in giving it on all occasions their effectual support. It would be inconsistent with the frankness of my character not to avow that I am pleased with your favourable opinion of my Administration, and fervent wishes for my felicity. May the Children of the Stock of Abraham, who dwell in this land, continue to merit and enjoy the good will of the other Inhabitants; while everyone shall sit in safety under his own vine and fig tree, and there shall be none to make him afraid. May the father of all mercies scatter light and not darkness in our paths, and make us all in our several vocations useful here, and in his own due time and way everlastingly happy.[21]

To put that in an Australian idiom, government should ensure that everyone can sit on their own veranda, with a sacred text and cold beverage at hand, among friends and family in the shade, confident that nobody will ever make them afraid. Hopefully with appropriate legislation, Australia can establish and preserve religious freedom, so that, to rehash the Magna Carta, *Et omnis populus erit religione liber*, "The religion of all people shall be free."

CHAPTER 9

RELIGIOUS FREEDOM IN AUSTRALIA TODAY: A JEWISH PERCEPTION

Benjamin J. Elton

Introduction

Jews have been part of Australian society since the very beginning of European settlement. Although the exact number is difficult to determine, there were certainly Jews on the First Fleet. Those first Jewish transportees — along with other convicts and free settlers who followed them — began to organise themselves as Jews in the early nineteenth century, with a Jewish burial in 1817 and Jewish collective worship in the 1820s. I have the honour to serve as the Rabbi of the congregation which is the linear descendant of those first prayer meetings, which evolved into synagogues and eventually The Great Synagogue.

I am a representative of the Orthodox branch of the Jewish community. There are other denominations within the Progressive spectrum, and of course secular or cultural Jews. these different groups disagree about the nature of revelation and the binding nature of Jewish Law. Although some of the issues I will raise will have a greater impact on the Orthodox, almost all Jews would support their rights and freedoms of their co-religionists, even if they are not scrupulously observant in every regard.

The question of religious freedom has always been an important one for Jews in modern Australia. We have always been a religiously distinct minority, governed first by a nation with an established church, and then in a colony, state and Commonwealth with an almost entirely Christian population and where the churches were powerful. Many Jews came to Australia from countries where their religious liberty had been severely restricted — and their lives had been endangered. They arrived looking for peace and freedom and were anxious that these positive features of Australian life be maintained, a concern which was shared by the rest of the Jewish community. Religious freedom is therefore an ongoing area of interest for Jews in Australia, even if it is not a cause for immediate alarm.

Any discussion of the Jewish view of anything has to go back to the sources of Judaism, the Bible, Talmud and Rabbinic Codes, and to the history of the Jewish People. I will turn first to that context before examining religious freedom and its impact on the Jewish community in contemporary Australia.

The Bible and Rabbinic Literature

The society envisioned by the Hebrew Bible always had a place for the 'stranger'. The Israelites who settled in their tribes in the Land of Israel expected to find themselves living alongside people from other nations. While the Israelites were not permitted to tolerate idolatry within the Land of Israel, other monotheists were to be allowed to live there in peace. The Bible recognises their existence and grants them rights and benefits. When the Israelites were told to observe the Sabbath, the Book of Exodus records that the non-Israelite too shall be allowed to rest. When the system of tithes for the poor and weak was established, non-Israelites were also given material support through a tithe. Furthermore, the non-Israelite was included in the national legal system, and was to be treated with especial care because of their vulnerable status. Deuteronomy (27:19) warns, "cursed be he that perverts the judgment of the stranger, fatherless, and widow."

At the same time, it was understood that these strangers could not be included in the full religious life of the community; they were not to be circumcised, to eat of the Pascal Lamb on Passover or dwell in booths on the Festival of Tabernacles. Their religious distinction was respected, but their civil inclusion was also honoured. This was possible because Jews do not believe that adopting Judaism is necessary for all peoples. In the Jewish view, it is possible to be a good, even a saintly person, without being Jewish. As long as a person leads a righteous and holy life, they can be close to God and receive immortality. One classical Rabbi taught "I call heaven and earth to witness, that whether one be Gentile or Jew, man or woman, slave or handmaid, the Holy Spirit will rest upon them according to their deeds" (*Tanna devei Eliyahu* 9). The Jewish position was therefore always inherently tolerant of other faiths, allowing them their freedom — and simply wished for the same in return.

This tradition of created a shared civil space continued after the fall of Jerusalem and the end of Jewish independence. When the Israelites were exiled from their Land, the Prophet Jeremiah (29:5-7) advised them on how to live in their host nations. His prescription has been the basis for the Jewish Diaspora experience ever since: "Build houses and live in them; plant gardens and eat what they produce...seek the welfare of the city where I have sent you into exile, and pray to the Lord on its behalf, for in its welfare you will find your welfare."

While never advocating religious assimilation, Jeremiah counselled secular integration. This prophetic call became reflected in established Jewish law. The Talmudic ruling (in *Nedarim* 28a and elsewhere) that *dina demalchuta dina*, the law of the land is the law, became the basis for Jewish financial dealings with wider society. Our greatest jurist, Maimonides (1138-1204), ruled (*Hilkhot Gezelah veAvedah* [laws of theft and lost objects] chapter 5) that once a government is accepted by the people, once there is an acknowledged authority then its laws and decisions become binding on everyone, Jew and non-Jew alike.

Jewish History

This long tradition has provided Jews with the intellectual tools to manage the question of religious diversity and the religious freedom problems it throws up. That ability has also been developed by the often tragic course of Jewish history. Although the vision of Jeremiah, the Talmud and Maimonides was that of lending spiritual and material support to the societies where Jews found themselves living, it was also usually the happy arrangement desired by the rulers of those societies. In Muslim lands in the medieval period, Jews were given the status of *dhimmi*, second class citizens. They enjoyed certain legal protections, including freedom of religion, although not all the benefits that came to Muslims, and they had to pay an additional tax. Of course, on some occasions, conditions became much worse, and forced conversions to Islam were imposed. This is what caused Maimonides to flee from Spain to the Middle East in the second half of the twelfth century. In the same period in Christian Europe, conditions were usually worse, with severe restrictions on trades, freedom of worship, place of settlement and mode dress, the imposition of rapacious taxes and regular massacres and expulsions.

In the modern period, full emancipation came only in the late nineteenth century. In the United Kingdom, the first Jewish Member of Parliament was only able to take his seat in the House of Commons in 1858; before that the price of admission to Parliament was conversion to Christianity. The situation on the European continent was even slower to change. The German-Jewish poet Heinrich Heine (1797-1856) converted to Christianity on the basis that it was the 'entry ticket to European culture'. Jewish emancipation was only completed in Germany in 1871, and in France the Dreyfus Affair (1894-1906) showed the great limitations of tolerance for Jews, who could not rely on impartial justice. Perhaps paradoxically, this was at the same time that Jewish communities across Europe were building imposing and ornate synagogues, demonstrating their self-confidence and comfort in wider society. Almost all of these synagogues were destroyed by the Nazis, as part of the greatest repudiation of Jewish religious freedom, the Holocaust.

Jewish internal life also had to change with the advent of both emancipation, which gave Jews civil rights, and the Enlightenment, which opened up their minds. In several European states, Jews were not integrated, but were instead granted internal self-government — at least in civil matters — and expected to deliver up a tax (and often additional fines) through whatever internal mechanism they felt appropriate. This was a denial of religious freedom because it created a choice between Jewish affiliation and access to the same rights as every other citizen. When that was overturned (and it lasted until 1863 in Altona, then a Danish possession) Jews had to work out how to live as full and equal members of society, no longer under the jurisdiction of their fellow Jews — and Jewish hierarchies had to work out how to operate without coercive power over members of their community. Whereas previously excommunication was a real threat, because it meant exclusion from the only community open to Jews, after emancipation it became a much less worrying prospect. When Baruch Spinoza was excommunicated by the Amsterdam Jewish community in 1656 for heresy, he carried on much as before. He continued as a private scholar living in tolerant Holland, and did not feel the need or inclination to convert to Christianity. In other words, the attempt to curtain his religious freedom failed. In London in 1842, a group of Jews inclined to Reform were also condemned and driven out by the Rabbis of the traditional community. They built their new synagogue anyway, appointed a Minister and attracted a congregation. In liberal England there was nothing that could stop them. Over a century and a half later, that synagogue is still functioning. More significantly, that was the last occasion that an excommunication was issued in London, because it had been shown to be futile — and frankly embarrassing in front of general British society, from whom the Jewish community was seeking full liberty and inclusion; if Jews could not tolerate each other, why should the Christian state be asked to do so?

The root of these developments was only partly emancipation itself. The deeper cause was Enlightenment, the rationalist movement that swept Europe in the eighteenth century. Whereas before Jews had been confined in an intellectual ghetto as well as a physical one, those walls now collapsed. As Jews ceased to be fluent solely in Jewish languages, they were able to read the latest ideas and have their existing notions challenged and undermined. This was the greatest aspect of religious freedom; the ability to think as never before. The nature of God, the authorship of the Bible, the authority of Jewish Law, all of these essential elements of traditional Jewish life and thought were now on the table, and could never be taken off again.

Some Jewish groups responded by seeking to self-impose restrictions, hence the antagonism to secular education, modern languages and even contemporary dress. Yet, people could, and people did, choose to leave such communities. This was often at great personal cost, but they could make that decision if they wished. Solomon Maimon was a Talmudic prodigy born in mid-eighteenth century Lithuania. He gained access to German scientific and philosophical books, made his way to Germany and became a Kantian philosopher. He did not adopt Christianity but was also entirely separated from the Jewish community. He made a new life as an intellectual of no particular religious affiliation. That possibility was a direct creation of the Enlightenment.

In this new reality, insightful rabbinical leaders altered their postures towards their own communities. The generation of Rabbis that led the newly emancipated and enlightened Jewish communities of the late nineteenth century understood that in a world of freedom, faith, even the outward observance of faith, could not be forced. As a great twentieth century American Rabbi, Joseph Soloveitchik, often observed, "religious coercion is an oxymoron," because true religion comes from within, from the heart. Or, as the Chief Rabbi of the British Empire from 1913-1946, Dr Joseph Herman Hertz expressed it the only means of enforcing his will was "moral influence" which could be either accepted or rejected; what was clear, was that the age of forced religiosity was over.

Religious Communities in Modernity

The position in Western liberal democracies today, including in Australia, stands on these two developments of the eighteenth and nineteenth centuries: Jewish religious freedom vis-à-vis the non-Jewish community and the State, and vis-à-vis the Jewish community itself. Both have to be guaranteed by the State. If a person, of whatever faith, wishes to leave a particular religious community, it is the responsibility of the State, as the protector of the rights and liberties of its citizens, to allow them to do so. Similarly, if a Jew wants to ignore the religious leaders or institutions of their own community, they should not be subjected to undue pressure to conform. There are means other than physical force or financial penalty that can coerce an individual, including shunning and shaming. Those sorts of activities should be guarded against.

Religious freedom also has to be safeguarded in the way that religious communities interact. For example, if Christians wish to go knocking door to door to evangelise, even in Jewish areas, provided they do not infringe any more than, say, a political campaigner might, that liberty should be defended — even if it is tiresome or offensive to the householder. Religious freedom should include the right to proselytise, but not the 'right' not to be challenged, argued with or offended. That is not to say we should tolerate gratuitous insults, intimidation or violence, but within the boundaries of civil, robust interaction, the freedom to encourage others to join a religion is one that ought to be upheld.

Major Aspects of Jewish Religious Freedom

Communal and Personal Security

Freedom within and between communities are of concern, but the major challenges facing Jews and other wishing to exercise religious freedom lie elsewhere. The first and most important is the freedom to lives openly and safely as Jews and to practice Judaism, so that, as Jeremiah expressed it (30:10), "Jacob will again have peace and security, and no one will make him afraid." There is a much greater problem in some countries outside Australia, but it is still significant here. There are regular incidents of anti-Semitic graffiti, individuals who act suspiciously and are identified as threats by the police, and opportunistic incidents. There are some cases of vilification on religious grounds and incitement to violence. The Jewish community has invested in the Communal Security Group, which works closely with the police, to guard Jewish buildings using trained volunteers. There are other security measures including CCTV, bollards, alarms, armed commercial guards and controlled entry and exit systems which have been installed to protect members of the community.

There are still two senses in which this does not fully address the issue of religious freedom. First, all of these security measures cost money. The state and federal governments help with some of these costs, but the Jewish community still spends a large amount of money each year on its own security. That money could be used for religious, education or cultural initiatives, or to help financially struggling members of the community. The security threat has necessitated the diversion of limited communal resources; simply in order to stay safe, the community is unable to do everything it would like to do in other fields — , and that is a diminution of its religious freedom.

The second aspect concerns the impact of these security measures. When a Jew who wishes to attend a synagogue service is stopped at the door, questioned, has their bag searched, perhaps is turned away because the person speaking to them is not convinced of their bona fides — or is put off from attending a service because of the process needed to gain entry — that is a restriction on religious freedom. The fact that synagogues cannot simply have an open door, the way many churches do, and the barriers they have to put in front of those who simply want to pray, means that religious freedom for Jews has been curtailed. While there is currently no alternative, we still should not lose sight of that fact. What can the State do about these aspects of religious freedom? The Jewish community would not expect total financial support, but as citizens at risk as they go about their lawful business, they should be considered for generous funding, and the technologies used should be as effective but unobtrusive as possible, to reduce the friction experienced by people who merely want to pray as Jews.

Scheduling and Exceptions

A second stream of religious freedom concerns how Jews go about in wider society. For the most part, living a full Jewish life is totally compatible with aspects of Australian citizenship, at least in theory. It is not illegal for a man to wear a Jewish head covering (*kippah*), but in some areas he might be subject to abuse or attack if he did so. Jews often fulfil the obligation to place a mezuzah, a small scroll containing Biblical verses on the doorposts of their homes; if they do so, the mezuzah should not be stolen or vandalised.

Observant Jews will want to leave school or work early on a Friday evening during the winter months so that they can be home in time for the onset of the Sabbath. In schools and universities where sport is largely played on a Saturday, observant Jewish students are excluded from that activity, with all its health and social benefits. Observant students will also want to be absent for the festive days of the year, which often fall during the working week. In some cases they will miss lectures and even examinations. It is an important aspect of religious freedom that arrangements can be made so that they will still be able to pass all their requirements and take a degree, and that they will not be pressured to work at times which go against their religious beliefs, and that they are not discriminated against in the recruitment process because of the flexibility they will need for religious reasons. We should not adopt here in Australia the French approach of *laïcité*, which is not just a state of neutrality regarding different religions, but actually drives religion from the public sphere. That is not the Anglophone tradition, is a threat to religious freedom and ought to be resisted.

One aspect of Australian civic life which does impinge on Jews' freedom of religion is the timing of elections. Since election day is always a Saturday, on those times of the year when the Sabbath ends after 6 pm, observant Jews cannot vote on the same day as everyone else, because they cannot make a mark on a ballot paper. Of course, they can vote earlier, but that is not entirely satisfactory either, because anything that takes place in the final days of a campaign will be too late to affect a Jewish citizen's vote, and they will have taken their decision with less information than the rest of the voting population. That is a direct consequence of Jewish observance, and is surely regrettable.

Jewish Schools

An alternative to Jewish students working round school timetables that are not devised with Jews in mind, is to attend a Jewish school. The ability to run faith schools is an important religious freedom. All schools, whether overtly religious or secular should comply with the same standards of education. The situation is more complicated in matters of admission and employment. A Jewish school will only want to admit Jewish students, in order to ensure the Jewish ethos of the school, including its student body. That discriminates against non-Jews who wish to attend, but is important in an attempt to create a Jewish school. Similarly, a Jewish school will wish to appoint teachers who uphold its values. For non-Jewish teachers this is a less significant issue, but Jewish teachers will be expected to be role models, and conform to the requirements of the religion at least in public. In these instances, the religious freedom to run and attend a faith school also impacts on the freedom of others. An enhancement of the religious freedom afforded by faith schools would be to follow the British model, and allow them to be included in the state system, so that the secular education is paid for as in every other public school, and parents only have to pay for religious education. That would make a Jewish school education much more widely available.

Jewish Practices

As a religion of complex and numerous laws, Judaism has some practices that differ from societal norms, but which are essential to the maintenance of Jewish life. Life cycle events are one example. On the eighth day after his birth, a Jewish boy is circumcised by another Jewish male. This is a surgical procedure on a very young child, and would normally be restricted to a hospital or similar environment. It is not medically necessary, but except in rare cases there are no negative effects, and there may even be benefits. Most significantly, circumcision is an absolute religious necessity for Jews, is almost universally practiced and is defended forcefully by Jewish communities everywhere. There are campaigns in Australia and elsewhere to ban circumcision, and non-religious cosmetic circumcision is already illegal. Were it to be banned, that would constitute a major blow against the religious freedom of Jews, to such an extent that it might persuade Jews to leave a particular country.

The food eaten by observant Jews must comply with kashrut, the laws of kosher consumption. A particularly exacting element of these laws concerns kosher slaughter, which must be conducted by a highly skilled and trained specialist. A ban on kosher slaughter, which has already been implemented in New Zealand and some other countries, either deprives Jews living in that country of the ability to eat kosher meat, or makes them dependent on imports which raises the price. In either case, Jews are disadvantaged when compared to non-Jews. There is an argument that if the animals are suffering as a result of the kosher slaughter technique, then that should take precedence over access to kosher meat. There are several points to be made in response to that. First, there are leading experts who affirm the humaneness of kosher slaughter. Secondly, there are ways to mitigate possible suffering without impairing the kosher status of the slaughtered animal: for example stunning immediately before slaughter, and this is the practice in Australia. Thirdly, many of the most egregious aspects of animal cruelty have no connection whatever with kosher slaughter, and therefore a focus particularly on that one small aspect of the animal industry is misplaced. Finally, all slaughter involves taking the life of an animal, and some distress to the animal in the process. For as long as any slaughter is permitted, and allowing that we should make every effort to reduce animal suffering, we should not pretend that any method of slaughter is ideal as far as the animal is concerned. Projecting concerns disproportionately onto kosher slaughter is inappropriate.

Marriages and Weddings

When a person comes to marry, Australian Jews are in a fortunate position that a wedding performed according to Jewish rites also effectuates a civil marriage. Jews therefore do not have to undertake two marriages, one civil and another religious, which at least makes the wedding process more convenient. Since the 2018 change in the law, there is now another aspect of religious freedom connected to weddings. Orthodox Rabbis will not be able to marry two people of the same gender in a religious ceremony, because Jewish law does not recognise same sex marriage. At the moment, a Rabbi cannot be compelled to marry two people whose marriage is forbidden in religious law, for example a Jew and a non-Jew or a Cohen (member of the priestly tribe) and a divorcee. If this approach was maintained for same-sex couples (and there is every indication that it is being maintained) then Orthodox Rabbis should have nothing to worry about. This is not the same issue at all as providing services for people celebrating weddings. I am not convinced by any means that religious freedom means the ability to refuse to serve a paying customer — for example by providing a cake, even one with a particular inscription — as long as it is celebrating a legal activity.

Burials

At the end of life, Jews are buried a quickly as possible, and with as little invasion as possible. Post mortems are therefore avoided as much as possible, because they both delay burial and interfere with the body. Cremation is forbidden according to Orthodox practice. If post mortems became even more obligatory or invasive than at present, or if burials were no longer allowed because of a shortage of cemetery space, then Jewish religious freedoms would be imperilled. There does not seem to be any indication that would take place, although a Coroner in London was recently behaving in a way that did restrict this aspect of religious freedom for Jews and complaints were made.[1] Therefore, even if the law remains as it is, problems can still be caused by individual decisions.

Concluding thoughts

Jews have been a religious majority in their own state (and those living in the State of Israel are once more), but for most of Jewish history we have been a minority religion. That has made the Jewish community particularly thoughtful in matters of religious freedom. Jews carry an understanding of its necessity, tempered by a realisation of its proper limits. Religious freedom cannot mean unreasonably limiting the rights of others, and determining what is reasonable takes careful thought. Jews have had to negotiate their way through pre-modernity, modernity, and perhaps now, post-modernity. In each era, the aim has been to be able to live as Jews, make a positive contribution to wider society and create an atmosphere of both religious freedom and social responsibility.

Chapter 10

MUSLIM PERSPECTIVES ON RELIGIOUS FREEDOM

Tanveer Ahmned

Islam and Freedom

Muslims in Australia comprise a relatively small — but scrutinised (in light of the terrorism age we live in) — section of the community. Their migration has been apparent since early settlement, starting from the Afghan camel traders to the wave of post-civil war Lebanese migration to, more recently, a greater proportion from Asia.

Religious freedom in the Islamic community is of considerable significance. Much like the wider Western world, there has been great debate about the place of Islam in Australia. This has led to controversies around the building of mosques, appropriate limits on free speech and the wearing of the hijab.

I grew up being taught that freedom was a dirty word. It was the undergirdle of Western decadence; the force that ripped families apart, destroyed long-held cultural traditions and laid waste to sexual morality.

Islam's moral axis was one of honour of shame; not of redemption and sin, as existed within Christianity. At its heart, this implied a strong collective culture where the needs of the group held sway over the individual. Unlike Christianity's emphasis on sin and the parallel, internal experience of guilt, the primary emotion that encouraged

167

appropriate social regulation in Islam was that of shame.

The religion grew within the clan-based culture of the Arabian desert, where anything that weakened tribal cohesion spelt death. Even today, we see that spectre in the upholding of tribal codes through despicable practices such as honour killings. In combination with the intense policing of behaviour that Islam potentially imposes upon its followers, freedom is not a word that comes to mind in discussing its virtues.

Yet the intermingling of Western style freedoms and a new generation of Muslims growing up in the West lies at the heart of the expression of Islamic extremism. What is sometimes known as identity Islam is about the assertion of a public, political self — a practice fundamentally derived from Western notions of the individual.

In a speech delivered to the world's Muslims from Cairo in 2009, then United States President Barack Obama spoke of religious freedom as an universal principle rooted in human dignity. "Freedom in America is indivisible from the freedom to practise one's religion."[1] Obama praised Muslims for what he described in the main as tolerance, but also chided those communities where the dominant group of Muslims were intolerant of other minorities or sects. This latter criticism is held much more forcefully among Islam's strongest critics, who see violent extremism rooted in the founding texts of the religion. When combined with the belief that the Koran is the unfiltered word of God transmitted via the Prophet Muhammad, tolerance and a distinct opposition to what might be considered freedom appears to be the norm within Islam.

The topic of religious freedom in Islam should be seen amidst the background of individual Muslims, as well as Muslim countries, responding to the West and its freedoms in a variety of ways. The subject should also be seen within the pattern of the declining place of traditional religion within Western societies, and the increasing hostility to religion by the secular, progressive left.

I want to first review the scriptural basis for religious freedom, its practical application throughout the Islamic world and then consider the implications for Muslims living in Australia.

Scripture

When we consider the scriptural basis for religious freedom, there are contradictory elements in the Koran that open up battles in interpretation.

Australian academic Abdullah Saeed is a prominent advocate of the possibility of religious freedom within Islam. Saeed argues in his book *Religious Freedom and Apostasy in Islam* (Routledge 2004) that the bulk of the Koran and the Hadith — which is a recollection of the Prophet Muhammad's sayings and actions — support the idea of religious freedom.

He quotes lines such as "there shall be no coercion in the matters of faith." Saeed believes the bedrock of the Koran supports an idea enshrined in the Abrahamic religions of humans having the dignity and intellect to make free choices. By this reckoning, Islam has scriptural grounding that belief is a free choice involving the individual and God.

However this does not sit so well when Mohammed himself is quoted making statements such as "Whoever changes his religion, kill him."[2]

Saeed and Islamic theologians argue that even the Prophet himself could not impose or force people to convert to Islam; citing a Koranic text: "Your task is only to exhort, you cannot compel them to believe." There is also evidence that the Prophet's successors embraced this view. In a recorded example, a Christian woman came to visit a caliph Umar to refuse his invitation to convert to Islam. The Caliph became anxious that his request may be seen as a directive: "O my Lord," he said, expressing his remorse, "I have not intended to compel her, as I know that there must be no compulsion in religion ... [R]ighteousness has been explained and distinguished from misguidance."

The Koran emphasises the Prophet's job as teaching people about God, rather than forcing conversion. "The Apostle is not bound to do more than clearly deliver the message [entrusted to him]" (24:54). Similarly, it urges readers to "pay heed, then, unto God and pay heed unto the Apostle; and if you turn away, [know that] Our Apostle's only duty is a clear delivery of this message" (64:12).

The Koran also offers considerable freedom to non-Muslims under

Islamic rule; particularly Jews and Christians who are referred to as "people of the Book." There is a clear delineation made between non-Muslims hostile to the Muslim community, and those who were willing to live peacefully. Even where there is a command to bring hostile forces under the rule of the Muslim state, Koranic verses encourage a recognition of state authority but not an enforced change of religious belief.

In drawing upon these characteristics, Saeed argues that the concept of religious liberty is enshrined within the primary sources of Islamic thought. But centuries of debate among Islamic legal scholars defining the meaning of Muslims and community — along with parallel debates about free will and predestination — produced multiple schools of thought that led to greater limits on religious freedom. The progressive thinkers on the issue lost. Saeed hopes they are making a comeback, although critics can point to the fact that the vast majority of reformist thinkers live outside the Islamic world.

There are also critics of the idea of religious freedom within Islam, arguing that it is a Western concept. Chief among them is the Arab-American academic Talal Asad, who believes the concept overlaps closely with secularisation. He outlines his ideas forcefully in the book *Formations of the Secular: Christianity, Islam and Modernity* (Stanford University Press 2003).

Asad argues the concept of religious freedom has a strong Western bias and threatens to sideline religion as an entirely private, inner matter. This understanding of religion is borne of the Enlightenment view that genuine faith cannot be coerced by the state. Asad argues that religious freedom debates have the potential to enforce the West's view of religion upon those who conceptualise it differently, and not as the Protestant, secular march through global institutions. As a result, the idea of religion is no longer viewed as embodied community through rituals and practices but is characterised instead by an individual's belief and sincerity of faith.

While recognising this criticism, for the purposes of this essay I have applied the definition of religious freedom as it might apply locally and argue that — much like Obama in Cairo — religious freedom be seen as a universal principle.

Muslim Nations

Given there is a basis for religious freedom within the sacred texts of Islam, it is reasonable to consider whether there are countries with Muslim majorities that are religiously free.

At the administrative level, religious freedom is best considered by thinking about the varieties of government that Islamic countries have decided to adopt. They range from those that might be considered religiously free, those where religious rights are stifled within a secular nationalist framework and those where religious expression is actively limited or coerced in an Islamic legal structure.

When considering whether a country is religiously free, characteristics include whether there is any state interference with religious practices, whether public preaching is allowed and whether conversion away from Islam is permitted. Consideration must also extend to whether religious broadcasting is controlled by authorities, whether foreign missionaries are allowed, what laws surround the wearing of religious symbols, bans on any religious groups, and whether certain religious groups need to be officially registered.

There are 47 Muslim majority countries. Some key surveys or quantitative indexes that have been used to measure religious freedom include the Pew Government Restrictions Index (GRI) and the Social Hostilities Index (SHI), which measure conflict amongst different religions or sects.

By such measures, three quarters of the Islamic world fall into the category of moderate or high restrictions on religious freedom.

The religiously free ones are most likely to be in one particular region, that of West Africa. There — in countries such as Senegal or Sierra Leone — Muslims live side by side with Christians, sects like Sufism are common, and traditional animistic practices are often practised in parallel with Christianity or Islam. People are free to seek religious education or refuse it. The laws are largely secular. Some Islamist uprisings have occurred but have been resisted by authorities. The trends are not related to Muslim proportion, as the countries vary considerably. Overall, there is a stronger inter-religious harmony. While it cannot be proven, several academics argue that the history of colonialism in the region is important to why the countries have a greater deal of religious freedom. From the outset, France also had more experience and possibly greater respect for Islam, according to Princeton academic Daniel Phillpott in his book *Religious Freedom in Islam: The Fate of a Universal Human Right in the Muslim World Today* (2019). Historian Lamin Sanneh writes in *Beyond Jihad: The Pacifist Tradition in West African Islam* (2016) that the Islam in West Africa is of a more spiritual quality; partially diluted by indigenous animistic practices.

The most common model suppressing religious freedom is the secular repressive model. Most Islamic countries in the Middle East have taken on the negative secularism inspired by the French model of religious freedom.

The standard bearer of such a model is Turkey, which after the death of the Ottoman Empire after World War I, aggressively attempted to sideline religion from the public square. In 1924, the Caliphate was abolished and the Diyanet or the Directorate of Religious Affairs established. In 1928, references to Islam were removed from the Constitution and the word secular was inserted in 1937. Symbolically, the top hat replaced the Fez and there were attempts to curtail the freedom of the Sunni majority and other sects of Islam.

Pew ranked Turkey the 14th worst in the world in terms of religious freedom in 2009. It is likely things have since declined further, given President Tayyip Erdogan's rule. He has led an economic boom and pried away a degree of secularisation. Erdogan has cracked down on popular protests, curtailed judicial independence, and restricted the press and social media. He has also made religious education compulsory and lifted rules limiting headscarves.

Other practitioners of the secular, repressive model have been authoritarian rulers such as Saddam Hussein in Iraq, General Nasser in Egypt or the Assads in Syria. The wider population is usually more religious and brute force in combination with repressive government have been required to subdue the masses. The governments in such models closely monitor the governance of mosques, universities, and expression of religion in the public square. The courts are governed by secular laws.

The idea of secular repressive patterns is also linked to the pan-Arabism that inspired the Middle East half a century ago. The inspiration was to unite the Arab world as a bulwark to Western power and imperialism. Now there is a resurgence of Islamic parties promising to restore Islamic faith and law. A wider trend across the Arab world is the decline in Jewish populations.

While the Arab uprisings were in part a challenge to such repressive regimes, religious freedom has since worsened across the Arab world. For example, the current Egyptian leader Abdel Fattah el-Sisi — who has strongly suppressed religious opposition — has recently had his term as president extended to 2030 by a constitutional change. .

The other key model for Islamic countries is when the country classifies itself as an Islamic state. Pakistan was the first such country, while Iran and Saudi Arabia are also classic examples.

In these situations there is usually something in the Constitution declaring Islam as the official religion and that other laws should not contradict Islamic law. This results in the direct denial of religious freedom. Terms like apostasy or blasphemy are often loose; leading to exploitation. In countries like Pakistan, entire sects — such as the Ahmaddiyah — are pronounced as blasphemous. There may be laws forbidding conversion from Islam and there is usually a government body overseeing mosques, the public expression of Islam, and religious education. The courts are conducted, at least in part, through Islamic law.

Saudi Arabia is the classic model of an Islamic state. In addition to the above characteristics, there is also a religious police enforcing norms — and little room for the practice of other religions, including within its army of foreign workers. The only public practice of religion allowed is if it conforms to the official interpretation of Islam. Under this regime, the Shias suffer great discrimination. Mosque preachers openly speak of killing non-Muslims and such ideas are incorporated into school textbooks.

The Asia Bibi example illustrates the potential exploitation of laws in Islamic states. Pakistan was the first country to declare itself an Islamic state. Bibi was a Catholic woman in rural Pakistan. She professed her beliefs in Christianity after being challenged; and asked what Mohammed ever did to save mankind like Jesus. She was reported for blasphemy; a crime in Pakistan. The governor of Punjab, Salman Taseer, defended her and was promptly killed by his bodyguard in the process. Large crowds demanded her death. The Supreme Court suspended her sentence but she remains in prison.

My home country of Bangladesh is a nation that began as a secular democracy but has moved towards Islamisation in parallel with a slide towards authoritarianism. The Supreme Court has guarded secularism and — unlike Pakistan — the country has never passed laws against apostasy or blasphemy. Fatwas were banned in 2001. The most zealous Islamists exist outside government and attempt to impose vigilante justice — a problem across the Islamic world. The murder of atheist bloggers in recent years is a clear example.

Among our neighbours, Malaysia and Indonesia are important examples worthy of examination.

Malaysia guarantees religious freedom but codifies Islam as the state religion. Article 11 in the Constitution allows government to "control and restrict the propagation of any religious doctrine or belief among persons professing the religion of Islam." Non-Muslims are allowed to practice their faith as long they don't interfere or say anything against Islam. Pew judged Malaysia the sixth-worst for religious freedom in 2015. There is a dual court system, with Muslims going through traditional Islamic-style family courts, and there are laws against apostasy.

Indonesia has a healthy tradition of pluralism grounded in its Constitution, which guarantees religious freedom. However, the country has become more unfree over time. In 2016, there were protests across the country against Jakarta's first Chinese Christian governor, Basuki Purnama, citing anti-blasphemy laws. Religious freedom has suffered since the fall of Suharto. In 2014, Pew ranked Indonesia as the fifth-highest violator of religious freedom. The government imposes heavy restrictions on other sects, such as Ahmaddiyas, regarding building houses of worship. There has also been the steady rise of Islamist parties such as PKS (Prosperous Justice Party).

Muslims in the West

In summary, the concept of religious freedom does exist scripturally within Islam and occurs in practice in only limited corners of the Islamic world. The two key models otherwise tend to be secular repressive ones and those with some version of an Islamic government. The overall trend within the Islamic world is for less religious freedom — not more — inviting a degree of pessimism regarding the future.

As a result, most Muslims come to Australia with little experience of freedom in a Western sense, especially around speech or robust political contest. They are grateful for the chance to practise their faith, but in the age of terror, there are controversies around the wearing of religious symbols or building houses of worship. There is evidence that those women wearing veils and niqabs are more likely to be targets of racial abuse.

While there has been little appetite to ban religious symbols in the Australian public sphere — as has happened in countries like France or Switzerland — there have been controversies around some Muslims refusing to remove the niqab in court hearings. When Victorian Judge Christopher barred a woman from giving evidence while wearing a niqab in 2018, he was criticised by the Islamic Council of Victoria. Such cases have been relatively rare, but are equivocal and determined by individual magistrates. At the heart of the issue is the significance of the human face in human interaction, and especially in appropriate court process.

Houses of worship are also a potential source of tension. There have been several cases in the past decade where mosques have been approved by relevant local authorities, but protests have arisen from unhappy local residents. A case in point was in Bendigo in 2015 as well another 2018 row in outer Melbourne in the municipality of Melton.

Locally, Muslims have come to be seen as a marginalised group in the face of discrimination; so much so, that there are calls to include them as racial group under the Racial Discrimination Act.[3] An important work by American author Asma Uddin, *When Islam Is Not a Religion: Inside America's Fight for Religious Freedom* (Pegasus

175

Books 2019) paints the dilemma for Muslims, who are viewed with suspicion by many conservatives but engaged by the Left primarily as a marginalised group. Uddin argues that, for her, Islam is not defined by the expression of a public identity but in terms of theology and religious practice. This is an important concept; and justification for rejection of inclusion of Muslims as a category within the Racial Discrimination Act. As Uddin writes: "As the Left embraces Muslims "as a group notable primarily for its marginalization," Islam in America may in time become secularized."

Uddin's fundamental point is that progressives have the potential to increasingly construct Islam as a left-wing political stance. This is especially underlined when middle class feminists wear the hijab as some kind of solidarity stance, or homosexuals march about issues like Palestine in an unholy alliance with Muslims.

The debates around free speech often involved Muslims, who were constructed as the most vulnerable community by opponents of any loosening of the Racial Discrimination Act. However, examination of the Islamic world illustrates that most Muslims come from countries where there are strict limits on speech, including a large percentage of countries which have blasphemy laws. This makes Muslims not the best allies when debating the benefits and necessity of free speech.

Recent tragedies like the Christchurch bombings also raise fears among Muslims about their ability to freely practise their religion without inviting suspicion, interference or worse. Much like other faith systems, the tension between discrimination and the freedom to teach value systems will remain an issue within Islamic schools; the fastest rising segment of the religious education sector. What to do with gay students or teachers is especially sensitive among Muslims, who retain the most traditional views regarding homosexuality — as evidenced by the large No vote for gay marriage in Muslim majority areas, especially in western Sydney.

Religious freedom for Muslim minorities living in the West is an ongoing source of tension. While some areas of concern overlap with other religious groups, especially Jews and conservative Christians, the unique conflicts that arise amidst the sensitivities of better managing cohesion and the threat of terrorism show no sign of abating.

Chapter 11

TAKING THE RIGHT WAY BACK: THE TRUTH IN AN ERA OF CHALLENGES TO FREEDOM OF RELIGION IN AUSTRALIA

Michael Quinlan

It was a great joy to me when some brothers came and told of your faithfulness to the truth, and of your life in the truth. It is always my greatest joy to hear that my children are living according to the truth.[1]

The question of why religious freedom in Australia is important and still an issue has been addressed elsewhere in this book. The challenges to freedom of religion in Australia can be overwhelming and cannot be ignored.[2] Rather than dwelling on those challenges, this chapter looks at what can — and should — be done to address them.

As Christianity remains the largest faith tradition in Australia, the chapter concentrates on that faith.[3] This chapter argues that while the law can, and does, present impediments to religious believers' ability to live their lives in accordance with their faith, there are limits to the extent to which the law can solve all of the challenges faced by religious believers today. There are also limits to the extent to which religious believers should seek to rely on the law to do so.

Having first looked at the limits of the law, the chapter looks to the early Christians for inspiration and makes some suggestions for actions that individual believers, their families and the Christian religious traditions might take in Australia. The chapter concludes by arguing that to change the mood of Australian society, and in doing so to change the political climate — and if it remains necessary, the law — Christians in greater numbers must first live more fully as Christians.

The limits of the law

Christianity's influence on Australian law is undeniable.[4] It can be seen in the requirements in criminal law to prove intention (*mens rea*), in the rule of law and the idea of equality before the law, in human rights law, in contract law and the sanctity of promises,[5] in negligence law,[6] in the principles of equity[7] and in many other aspects of the law. While the influence is there, the law has never been, and never could, be an enforcer of the full manifestation of a lived Christian life. As Deagon has pointed out, while the Court references the parable of the Good Samaritan[8] in the seminal negligence case of *Donoghue v Stevenson,* it set limits on the obligations owed at law by one citizen to another in a manner that is absent from the love of neighbour shown by the Samaritan:

> Christ's commandment to love your neighbour as yourself extends to showing mercy to people in peril not caused by you (such as the example given in the parable, which we are called to imitate), but this is not the case in the legal adaption of the theological principle.

> So the law of love in the revelation of Christian theology was appropriated by Lord Atkin [in *Donoghue v Stevenson*] as the foundation for a duty of care in modern negligence. However, despite its promise, it is a mere trace, a distorted, pagan version of the 'law of love.' Atkin's appropriation of the theological principle to love one's neighbour applied to the legal principle that one should not injure one's neighbour implies a far more restricted sense of conduct than Christ advocates in the parable...'[9]

Deagon here demonstrates that references to Christian scriptures and the influence of Christianity on the law has not resulted in a set of laws that seek to ensure by force of law the love of both enemy and neighbour demonstrated by Christ. There are limits to what the law can achieve. and to what it should seek to achieve:

> The laws of a state can never provide the transformative love that Christians find in Jesus Christ. The law cannot require and it cannot inspire people to be kind to one another, to treat each other as they would wish to be treated, to visit the sick or the imprisoned or to feed the hungry. Religions, not laws, inspire religious groups to provide education, welfare, medical, nursing and hospice care, aged care and works of everyday charity.[10]

While the law should not, and cannot, compel such acts, it should at a minimum not unnecessarily act to prevent Christians from living their lives in accordance with the dictates of their faith.[11] This is increasingly not the case in Australia today; and our legislative representatives' immediate reactions in late 2018 to leaks from the Ruddock Report inquiring into religious freedom provide little basis for an expectation that laws to protect — rather than further restrict — religious freedom are imminent.[12] If Kristina Keneally is correct in her view that Australian politicians are significantly more involved in religion than the average person, these adverse legal developments are occurring at a time when religious believers may have more friends inside parliaments than outside.[13] This chapter argues Christians should look at themselves and their own communities to find the root causes of the current legislative malaise. It suggests it has much to do with the failure of contemporary Christians — including some in positions of authority within their churches as exposed in the hearings and the findings of the Royal Commission into Institutional Child Sexual Assault (the Commission) — to live their faith. This has turned the Christian faith — which, when lived well, is very attractive — into something seen by many in our society as unattractive.[14] Christ was scathing of the Pharisees for their hypocrisy.[15] Christians are just as capable of hypocrisy and as capable of drifting away from the message of love central to the Gospels. As Francis Collins has observed:

> Frequent examples of gross hypocrisy among religious leaders, made ever more visible by the power of the media, cause many sceptics to conclude that there is no objective truth or good-

ness to be found in religion. Perhaps even more insidious and widespread is the emergence in many churches of a spiritually dead, secular faith, which strips out all of the numinous aspects of traditional belief, presenting a version of spiritual life that is all about social events and/or tradition, and nothing about the search for God.[16]

How can Christians behave so badly?

As to how this kind of behaviour can occur, Collins provides this explanation, which — although correct — may not be altogether satisfying to contemporary critics of Christianity:

> The church is made up of fallen people. The pure, clean water of spiritual truth is placed in rusty containers, and the subsequent failings of the church down through the centuries should not be projected onto the faith itself, as if the water itself had been the problem.[17]

What can Christians do?

It is always tempting to endeavour to blame others for such things as the downward trend in religious identification — particularly Christian religious identification — in each national census, in what appears to be an increasing animus towards faith and the lack of adequate national protections for religious freedom in Australia. There is no doubt that the serious and sustained failures of Church leaders and of the institutions of the Church to protect young people from the scourge of child sexual assault has damaged the credibility and the place of the institutional Church and of Christianity as a whole in our society. These failures must be addressed openly, honestly and comprehensively. The failures of many Christian religious institutions and agencies from many religious traditions were exposed by the Commission. These manifest failures of prominent Christians and of Christian institutions are very visible and symptomatic evidence of the broader failure of Christians to live their faith; which is the subject of this chapter. The causes of the decline in religious affiliation, in animus towards religious belief — particularly Christian religious belief — and the lack of adequate legislative protections for religious freedom in Australia, cannot all be sourced to failures by Church institutions and Church leadership. Blaming others has the distinct benefit of not necessitating any change in ourselves. However, the reality is that all these problems ultimately stem from the individual decisions and behaviours of individual religious believers. There are specific appropriate responses to be taken by the institutions and agencies examined by the Commission, which will vary and are beyond the scope of this chapter. This chapter looks not at institutional responses, but at the decisions and behaviours of individual believers. It argues that it is the actions of individual Christians in all their roles in society that can really staunch and reverse the downward trend in religious affiliation, and the animus towards Christianity; and revitalise the place of religious freedom in Australia. To make good this point, it is worth considering the experience of Christians in the early Church.

Can we learn anything from the early Church?

Sometimes we erroneously consider the world that Christ lived in and the world of the early Christians was a place in which the Christian message resonated because of its synergies and reinforcements of then contemporary views. The reality is that the Christian message was at least as challenging, counter-cultural and surprising — shocking, even — in the Greco-Roman world in which Christ and the early Christians lived as it is now. As Williams has observed, "[t]he Greco-Roman establishment was not attracted but repulsed [by the behaviour of Christians]."[18] At the time of Christ, men preferred the single life to the commitment of marriage and divorce was common.[19] Several Roman emperors sought to address the low marriage rate by decrees requiring men to marry.[20] Male and female prostitution, promiscuity, adultery, homosexuality, abortion and contraception were common.[21] The birth rate was significantly below the generational replacement level despite governmental steps taken to punish childless men and to reward those with three or more children.[22] As Percy has observed:

The world at the time of Christ, and at the time of the early

Church, was not unlike ours. Yet Christ did not hesitate to speak the truth.[23]

While Percy is right to identify the similarities, there were also differences. These might have made the Christian message even less amenable to adherents of the then prevailing moral zeitgeist. Owning slaves was an accepted part of Roman life. Cruelty and violence were celebrated as part of male Roman culture and Roman wives were confined within their homes.[24] Infanticide (particularly of baby girls) was common in Rome and when marriages did occur they often involved very young girls.[25] The methods used and dangers posed to pregnant woman undergoing an abortion and the methods of contraception then employed were different to those employed today. Abortion was more likely to cause death or sterilisation than today and contraceptive methods were less reliable.[26] In short the prevailing moral worldview at the time of Christ shared some striking similarities with today but was even more antithetical to the Christian moral worldview than today.

Indermaur has observed that:

> Most people, it seems, want to have an opinion that is in keeping with the majority, particularly in relation to subjects where there is a risk of social isolation from proclaiming an unfashionable or unpalatable view.[27]

Given the hostile world in which early Christians found themselves, it might have been expected that a small new religious group with less than 50,000 adherents by 120 AD would conform to the prevailing cultural norms. Instead, these Christians adopted radically different lifestyles to the communities around them. In doing so they exhibited the criteria required for a religion to be recognised as such for legal purposes in Australia today. These are twofold:

First, belief in a supernatural Being, Thing or Principle; and second, the acceptance of canons of conduct in order to give effect to that belief, though canons of conduct that offend against the ordinary laws are outside the area of any immunity, privilege or right conferred on the grounds of religion.[28]

This test is not intended to identify the prospects of the faith having any particular longevity or sustainability. The religious behaviours of early Christians went beyond that definition to clearly exhibit the complex cognitive, affective, behavioural and developmental aspects of religious systems which have been identified by sociological and anthropological literature across cultures:[29]

> These are: Belief in supernatural agents and counterintuitive concepts; Communal participation in costly ritual; Separation of the sacred and the profane; and importance of adolescence as the life history phase most appropriate for the transmission of religious beliefs and values.[30]

Alcorta and Sosis describe these traits as "basic elements of religion."[31] They find that while these traits are expressed differently across cultures, all religions share them.[32] These act to maximise the retention and transmission of the faith, and affective engagement with it.[33] Despite the risk and reality of imprisonment, execution and the confiscation of their property during many periods of persecution,[34] the early Christians continued to escape from the profane world to the sacred and gathered every Sunday to do so. They did so not to engage in orgies or bacchanalia but to pray, to read the scriptures, to raise funds for the poor, widows and orphans, to sing hymns, and to break bread in memorial of their founder, Jesus Christ, who they claimed had been crucified, died, buried and resurrected.[35] The counterintuitive belief in a crucified and then resurrected Christ was a serious obstacle to those from the Jewish tradition — and stupidity to the Greeks and Romans.[36] However, it was a clear and honest signal of commitment by a Christian to the Christian community, which shared in that belief.[37] Participation in rituals like the Sunday worship of the early Christians empowered them.[38] Ritual gives religious beliefs motivational force and emotional salience.[39] As Alcorta and Sosis observe:

> Ritual not only promotes more efficient and effective group functioning for politically and socially sanctioned endeavours, it simultaneously creates motivationally coordinated coalitions that can surmount existing in-group/out-group boundaries and provide a mechanism for social and political change.[40]

Key to the success of the early Christian church was its fidelity to the teachings of Christ. These early Christians rejected infanticide, promiscuity, adultery (by men or women), prostitution, contraception and abortion.[41] Valuing all people — men, woman and children, rich, poor, free and enslaved — equally they cared for the poor and the sick (even placing themselves at personal risk of contracting diseases such as smallpox in so doing).[42] As Williams has observed:

> It is an historical fact that, like Jesus Himself, the early Christians extended kindness to the lowest members of society, even those outside their immediate circle. Widows, prostitutes, tax collectors, slaves, beggars, orphans, cripples — all were welcome. So were unwanted babies. The early Christians spoke up strongly against the widespread Greco-Roman practice of infanticide.[43]

The life experience of many early Christians especially during the periods of persecution would no doubt have confirmed to them the accuracy of those Christian scriptures which warn that Christianity will be a faith which can be an ordeal and present significant challenges.[44] They would also have been aware that lived Christianity involves making choices; and that Christianity is not an inoculation against danger or hardship — given that bad things do not only happen to bad people.[45] They would also have been aware of the teachings of the early Church against abortion[46] and of the many scriptural passages that consider children to be a blessing.[47] In Edward Gibbon's view, Rome just could not compete against the "pure and austere morals" of these early Christians.[48] Their commitment to their faith was there for the surrounding community to see, and ultimately to admire. Seeing the family as central to their lives, they married; and rejecting divorce, abortion. contraception and infanticide, they had children and reared them in stable families.[49] Carlson has observed that one consequence of this way of life was population growth:

> Where the Roman pagans faced a great shortage of fertile females—due to infanticide and botched abortions—the Christian movement had an abundance of young, fertile women: an estimated sixty percent of early believers were female. Even after accounting for early practitioners of celibacy, this was a community open to the propagation, protection, and rearing of children. This openness to new human life had consequences. While

hard numbers on differential fertility do not exist, circumstantial evidence affirms that a novel Christian family and sexual ethic, tied to the abundance of young women, produced a significantly higher number of births and the survival of more offspring to adulthood. Along with conversions (particularly among pagan men married to Christian women), this accounts for the growth in Christian numbers from a negligible figure in 100 A.D. to 32 million by 350 A.D., representing half of the Empire's population. As Rodney Stark concludes, "superior fertility contributed to the rise of Christianity."[50]

The benefits of the approach of the early Christians to their faith

A multiplicity of empirical studies demonstrate something the early Christians could not have known other than intuitively or by reliance on the Scriptures: their way of life has many benefits. This reality seems little known by contemporary Christians and less known by the general community. Most Christians living in the Western world today tend to live lives that are more or less indistinguishable from the lives of their fellow citizens. Focusing on material wealth and prosperity, and on providing for vocational education and economically for their children, many Christians fail to learn their faith and so do not practice or pass on the Christian tradition. A 2007 study of Catholics who had ceased attending mass regularly found that:

> Many participants displayed a poor knowledge of certain Catholic teachings. When asked whether they agreed with the Catholic position on a particular issue, some said that they did not know what the Catholic position was. Others expressed disagreement with specific Church teachings despite having only a hazy idea of what those teachings entailed. Nuances in Catholic thought — for example the distinction between condemnations of homosexual acts and compassion for the homosexual person — were often completely missed.[51]

Given the significance of a religious upbringing to the likelihood of later religious participation, not knowing the reasons for their faith's teachings or practising their faith, many modern Christians downplay, ignore and effectively deprive their children of the legacy and statistically significant life benefits of the faith and of living a traditional Christian lifestyle.[52] This is not to suggest that contemporary Christian parents should adopt Pascal's wager as their guide to raising their children; but to recognise there are rational and empirical grounds for believing that passing on traditional Christian beliefs will, on a statistical basis at least, be likely to be beneficial not harmful to their children in this world and of course if the faith itself is true of potentially infinite value in the next. For example, there is ample evidence that stable marriages between a man and a woman are good for their mental and physical health and wellbeing.[53] Statistically, children reared by their biological father and mother in a stable marriage also do better than their peers — educationally, in emotional health, familial and sexual development, and in their behaviour both as children and as adults.[54] There is also much statistical evidence that regular church goers are happier,[55] enjoy greater health and well-being[56] and have lower blood pressure than the general community.[57] Chan and VanderWeele found that:

> Compared with never attendance, at last weekly service attendance was subsequently associated with greater life satisfaction and positive affect, greater volunteering, greater sense of mission, more forgiveness, and lower probabilities of drug use and early sexual initiation.[58]

Those who regularly participate in religious services have reduced mortality risks[59] and some studies show that even irregular participants live longer and are healthier.[60] Research also shows that university students who engage in religious activities enjoy better social integration and emotional well-being.[61] Studies have shown that depression and anxiety decrease as religious convictions increase.[62] Chan and VanderWeele also found that prayer was beneficial:

> Compared with never praying or meditating, at least daily practice was associated with greater positive affect, emotional processing, and emotional expression; greater volunteering, greater sense of mission and more forgiveness; lower likelihoods of drug use, early sexual initiation, STIs and abnormal Pap smear results, and fewer lifetime sexual partners.[63]

In short, according to the empirical evidence, religious belief and practice is good for us.

How do Christians today compare with the early church?

For reasons discussed earlier, this chapter is here not concerned with the institutions of the Church but with the behaviour of modern Australian Christians as a whole. The comparison to the early Church is sobering and helps to explain the animosity that many in the surrounding society feel towards Christians — and why the Christian faith is in numerical decline. The thesis advanced here is that Christians are no longer a distinctive and readily identifiable force for good in society, displaying a coherency of approach and living the 'pure and austere morals' of the early Christians — and that this, in and of itself, is a source of numerical decline. When Christians do not live their lives in an identifiably different and attractive manner to the rest of the population, their calls for religious freedom to enable them to hire others who share or live their beliefs, or their seeking to use their religious beliefs as a political weapon and campaign for laws to reflect their view of morality, can appear to be toxic, bigoted and "on the wrong side of history."[64]

Unlike the position in the early Church, it does not appear that the population of Australian Christians is growing disproportionately to the rest of the population. While some official Church doctrines in major Christian traditions such as Catholicism continue to proscribe abortion[65] and contraception, the practice of many who self-identify as Christian from such traditions is not consistent with those teachings.[66] Looking at the Catholic population, for example, and taking into account the official teachings of that Church, if all Catholics were following official Church teachings they might be expected to have a significantly higher birth-rate to the general population — but this seems not to be so. According to United States statistics, there has been a widespread rejection of many of the official teachings of the Church among Catholics who attend the Novus Ordo Mass (NOM).[67] This is the most common form of the mass and is celebrated in the common language of the congregation.[68] Surveys of such Catholics in the United States have shown that — contrary to the official teachings of that Church — 89% approve of contraception and 51% approve of abortion.[69] Similarly, 67% of these American Catholics approve of same sex marriage70 in contrast to the official teachings of the Catholic Church.[71] While the official teachings of the Catholic Church mandate attendance at mass every Sunday and on holy days of obligation[72] and at least annual confession,[73] 78% of these American Catholics do not attend mass weekly and 75% do not make an annual confession and attend weekly mass.[74]

American Catholic women in this group had a fertility rate of 2.3% and overall Catholics worshipping in this rite donated 1.2% of their income.[75] The Catholic population across Oceania[76] grew at the same rate as the total population in the period from 1980 to 2012.[77] Like their American Catholic NOM counterparts, unlike the early Christians, most Australian Christians no longer regularly communally participate in rituals — even rituals such as setting aside time each week for public worship. As a consequence, they fail to regularly separate the sacred and profane; to use Alcorta and Sosis' indicia of religion. As Lewis and Able observe "Australia is reputed to have one of the lowest rates of church attendance (or the equivalent) in the Western world."[78] The rates have been falling in Australia for decades.[79] Around 24% reported monthly attendance of a religious service in 1990, but this had fallen to 17% by late 2016.[80] In the same period, self-reported weekly church attendance fell from 10% in 1991 to 6% in 2011.[81] In the Catholic Church, weekly mass attendance in Australia and New Zealand fell from 28 % in the 1990s, to 25% in the 2000s to 21% from 2010 to 2012.[82] Australian figures indicate that while over 35% of people 70 or older attended mass weekly at the turn of this century, only 6–7% of Catholics in their twenties did so.[83] Between 1980 and 2012, there was a slight increase of 4% in baptisms in the Catholic Church in Oceania. This sacrament is usually celebrated at infancy in that Church.[84] The numbers of Catholics receiving the other sacraments in Oceania has been falling significantly, with first communions falling from 96,147 in 2000 to 84,594 in 2012, confirmations falling between 89,893 in 2000 to 84,270 in 2012 and the number of marriages celebrated sacramentally in a Catholic Church falling from 39,224 in 1990 to 21,399 in 2012.[85] The decline in confirmation rates is most significant, as for centuries in the Catholic Church, confirmation has been celebrated at "the age of discretion."[86] A decline in this sacrament reflects a decline in the recognition of the "importance of adolescence as the life history phase most appropriate for the transmission of religious beliefs and values" to return to Alcorta and Sosis' "basic elements of religion."[87] No doubt the loss of significant religious events in adolescence has been one factor contributing to the reality that young Australians are the most likely to report having no religion — with 39% doing so in the last census.88 The substantial decline in sacramental marriages suggests a hollowing-out of the significance that Catholic Christians place on this sacrament.

Whilst Kristina Keneally may well be right in suggesting Australian politicians are more religious than the general community, there are prominent examples of politicians who are public about their faith and equally public about their support for moral positions antithetical to the official teachings of their tradition.[89] There are also prominent Australian clergy who have done the same.[90] In an Australian context there are also prominent politicians who have failed to live up to the way of life they espouse in well publicised respects.[91] Within the leadership and institutions of the Church, the Commission found copious evidence of egregious behaviours by clergy and others, who professed to be Christians but manifestly acted in ways completely at odds with the teachings of their faith[92] All these behaviours contribute to Australians associating Christianity with negative characteristics such as hypocrisy (17%).[93] Well-publicised hypocritical behaviour by prominent Christians[94] makes Christianity unattractive; and where there is not a clearly identifiable body of believers living consistently with their traditions, these aberrations are the 'Christians' known by the general community. In turn, this contributes to a distorted picture of Christianity. This leads to 4-5% of Australians disclosing negative attitudes towards Christians in interviews and 12% disclosing such attitudes in self-administered surveys that may be more reliable indicators of their true feelings.[95] While there are certainly Christians who do lead authentically Christian lives in the manner of the early Christian outlined above, the Christian community as a whole in Australia does not demonstrate the characteristics of the early Church. The family no longer occupies the central position it held in early Christianity where Christians had models in their own life experience of family life and of love. Eberstadt opines that this is central to understanding the Holy Family, the Trinity and many other Christian concepts and moral principles; and that is it critical to the passing on of the faith to the Christian community.[96] She observes that the life experience of many today makes traditional Christian teaching appear not only judgmental but positively offensive — and that is not a promising soil in which to plant and grow the Christian faith:

> [I]f your parents are divorced, you might find positively offensive Jesus Christ's injunctions against divorce...If you spend your alternate-custody weekends happily with your father and his new wife you may find intolerable the traditional Christian idea that so long as you mother is alive, your father is committing adultery and risking hell. Similarly, the very idea of being punished in eternity for formication may strike you as bizarre under any circumstances — especially if you've been sexually active and on the Pill since you were fifteen years old.[97]

Stability and growth of strict churches

Those churches that are the strictest and demand the most from adherents — and in so doing continue to exhibit the basic elements of religion identified by Alcorta and Sosis — appear to be the religious success stories of the United States.98 In Australia, if stricter churches are not growing, unlike their less strict cousins, they are at least not declining as a percentage of the population. They must therefore also be considered success stories. In the period from 2011 to 2016, there was a decline in the proportion of Australians identifying as Catholic (25.3% to 22.6%), Anglican (17.1% to 13.3%) and as Uniting Church (5.0% to 3.7%). In the same period, the numbers of Latter-day Saints (0.3%), Seventh-day Adventists (0.3%), Jehovah's Witnesses (0.4%) and Pentecostals (1.1%) remained stable. Members of such churches live differently and are less likely to drink, engage in pre-marital sex or experiment with 'new age' or alternative religions — and they attend church services more frequently, donate more, have firmer religious beliefs, join more church groups and are more likely to identify as being strong members of their faith.[99] Such strict churches, much like the early Christian Church, require the sacrificing of pleasures, the forgoing of opportunities and the risk of social stigma more than their more liberal cousins.[100] Iannacone argues that:

> [S]trict demands "strengthen" a church in three ways: They raise overall levels of commitment, they increase average rates of participation, and they enhance the net benefits of membership.[101]

Another example of the phenomenon discussed by Iannacone can be seen within the Catholic Church. Since 1984, it has been clear that the Traditional Latin Mass (TLM) was authorised as a means of worship within the Catholic tradition; albeit with the approval of the local bishop.[102] Since July 2007, TLM has been an authorised means of worship for any priest within the Catholic tradition without the need for additional approval.[103] A survey of parishes in the United States celebrating the TLM in 2018 revealed substantial conformity with the official teachings of that Church, and stark differences in their behaviours and attitudes to those of Catholics worshipping with the NOM liturgy discussed in 3.3 above.[104] Only 2% of TLM worshippers approved of contraception, 1% of abortion, 2% of same sex marriage, 99% attended mass weekly and 98% attended confession yearly as required by the Church.[105] In contrast with other Catholics, worshippers attending TLM parishes had a fertility rate of 3.6% and donated 6% of their income.[106] Here, worshippers within the same church who have elected to worship in a manner using a traditional language of worship, no longer commonly spoken as their liturgical language, adopt a greater separation of the sacred and the profane and almost uniformly participate communally in a weekly ritual, believe, and behave differently to those worshipping in their usually-spoken language. This form of worship has experienced substantial growth in Italy and the United States.[107] There are good reasons to believe that there is stability and growth within the Australian Catholic Church among those Catholics attending the TLM compared to those who attend the more common NOM.

Taking the right way back

The numbers of Australians who identify as Christians is on the decline. At the same time, many Christians no longer accept the official teachings of their Church or live in a manner that is obviously different to the prevailing culture. Religions that no longer exhibit the 'basic elements of religion' and that make no significant demands on believers, are not likely to survive, to be attractive to potential followers or to the general population. Hypocrisy and behaviours inconsistent with Christian ethics by those claiming to be Christian are perhaps inevitable — given that — as Collins has observed: "[t]e church is made up of fallen people"[108] — but those behaviours should readily be identified as aberrations from the Christian calling. The challenge for those Christians calling for religious freedom and tolerance in Australian society today is the need to demonstrate by lived example the value and benefit of the Christian life not only to those who follow it but also to the broader community.

The process of achieving genuine religious freedom — if necessary by way of legislative reform — starts not with politicians or laws, but with everyday Christians. If the benefits of Christianity were at least demonstrably visible through the lived examples of those who profess the faith, there would be far greater prospects of our society recognising that protecting religious freedom is reasonable, if not laudable. Christians living honestly and truthfully as Christians transformed the Roman Empire; and so can Christianity — if lived with vitality and commitment — transform contemporary society. The transformation of the Roman Empire did not happen immediately and this chapter does not suggest that its advocated response by Christians is likely to result in any immediate or short-term transformation of society and any immediate blooming of recognition of the value of religious freedom. However, to use Gibbons' phrase, this chapter argues that the "pure and austere morals"[109] of Christianity — if really lived —would prove equally as irresistible to contemporary society as they did to the Romans.

CODA:
RELIGIOUS FREEDOM - A CONTEST BETWEEN BELIEFS AND ORTHODOXIES

Peter Kurti

When first writing about religious freedom in the course of my work at the Centre for Independent Studies, I was frequently asked why I thought this was even an issue worth investigating in contemporary Australia. Although I was concerned that the increasingly aggressive implementation of anti-discrimination laws was beginning to have an adverse impact on religious liberty, few seemed to share my concerns. That was in 2011.[1] Eight years later, religious freedom is regularly front-page news in Australia's daily newspapers and it featured prominently in the 2019 federal election campaign. What can explain how such change has come about so quickly?

One factor — as recounted in the essays in this book — is that anti-discrimination laws have, indeed, been applied in ways that restrict religious liberty. Provisions intended to protect people from discrimination on the basis of race, gender, and sexual orientation when applying for jobs, housing, or education have increasingly been applied far beyond the scope intended by legislatures.

Today, it is faith-based institutions — especially Christian ones — that bear the brunt of this sharpened application; because some religious traditions maintain conservative positions on matters relating to gender and sexual orientation. These doctrinal views can come into conflict with the law when faith-based organizations seek to order their affairs in accordance with their religious doctrines and beliefs —

for example, by hiring staff sympathetic to a particular faith tradition. This exercise of the fundamental human right to religious freedom is dismissed by opponents as nothing more than a supposed freedom to exclude and vilify. As a result, a decline in bad discrimination — based on race and gender — has been accompanied by a decline in the capacity to exercise fundamental freedoms such as that of religion, speech, and association.

The advancing reach of identity politics is another factor that helps explain the emergence of religious freedom as a pressing issue. Whereas the initial intention of legislators was to ensure anti-discrimination legislation minimised differences based on race, gender or sexual orientation, identity politics only accentuates those differences by insisting that people are classified into distinct groups with specific needs and identities. The paradox of identity politics is that accentuation of difference has only made it harder, rather than easier, to accommodate difference in wider society.

A very specific issue has now emerged as the kernel of the debate about religious freedom in Australia: the capacity of citizens in a secular liberal and multicultural democracy to dissent from the new orthodoxies about gender, human sexuality, and the family. Any democratic society comprising citizens who enjoy equal rights of participation and equality before the law will be characterised by diversity of belief, morality and ideology. The test of the health of such a society is the extent to which it can tolerate diversity and manage the conflict bound to arise between people asserting conflicting rights. As Henry Ergas warns in the essay that opens this collection, any suppression of religious belief, practice or identity is a serious matter because it concerns more than mere opinion but rather the deepest convictions constitutive of human identity. Only when a greater and more grievous harm is to be averted, is any interference with religious liberty warranted.

Needless to say, those now striving to interfere argue consistently, if somewhat erratically, that the pursuit of religious belief and practice poses the threat of just such grievous harm; whether that harm is physical or mental. Advocates for fewer restrictions on the exercise of fundamental freedoms of speech, conscience, association, and religion, for example, frequently meet the objection that the exercise of such liberties is likely to have harmful consequences for the mental health of those exposed to the very freedoms that characterise a liberal democratic society.

Therefore, the weaponisation of anti-discrimination law and the broadening scope of identity politics have combined to produce a highly combustible notion of harm which has been widely embraced and deployed. The 'harm' card might be played simply because an individual claims that their feelings have been hurt or that they have been offended; or it might be played in order to shut down further debate about an issue by raising the possibility of suicide should there be any further departure from the scripts of the new orthodoxies.

Although the focus of a number of essays in this collection is on matters of human sexuality, the spectre of suicide, especially youth suicide, is frequently raised whenever the proponents of some cause or other fear they may not get their way in the courts of public opinion. It featured in the arguments of those who opposed the 2017 postal vote on same-sex marriage; but it also features regularly in debates about issues such as gender fluidity, transgender identity, and euthanasia. This is not to minimise the tragedy of suicide nor to downplay the rising incidence of self-harming behaviour among young people; but it does draw attention to inflamed notions of vulnerability and emotional sensitivity that often serve as the pretext for avoiding rather than engaging in debates about difference.[2]

An invitation to accept, and live with, difference is often interpreted as an inverted demand for conformity to a model or form of life imposed by others. However, American political scientist Saul Kaplan has warned of the dangers posed by an outright refusal to accept the social mechanisms of restraint and responsibility in the pursuit of authentic self-expression what he describes as "expressive individualism", borrowing the phrase from the Canadian philosopher, Charles Taylor.[3] These mechanisms of restraint, which include the social institutions of family, community, and religion, contribute mightily to the social and cultural health of liberal, democratic society by instilling civic norms, duties, and virtues.[4] Yet an emphasis on the sensitivities of the individual has been accompanied by a markedly diminished civic readiness to live with difference; and a concomitant demand that threats posed by difference must be eradicated so any behaviour deemed to harm individual dignity is proscribed by law.

None of this is to suggest that living with difference is always easy. Customs and practices accepted in one religion or culture may conflict markedly with Australian law. Examples of such practices include child marriage, polygamy, and female genital mutilation. Insistence on the illegality of these practices must be unequivocal and perpetrators must not be able to succeed by appealing to religious liberty or to moral relativism.

However, it is not unlawful to hold differing opinions about human sexuality or the nature of marriage even when the law of the land has been amended and the issue resolved in law. Nor is it unlawful to differ in opinions about the role of women in the family and the community — even though Australia affords tremendous opportunities for women that were unavailable to women of earlier generations.

In a country with a very high proportion of citizens who are either immigrants or descended from immigrants, and who come from many diverse religious and cultural backgrounds, it should hardly be surprising that people disagree about matters of belief. Yet as Augusto Zimmerman argues in his essay, we are rapidly losing sight of the fundamental principles of tolerance advanced by John Locke; tolerance has evolved to become a signifier of acceptance and affirmation. Those who fail to affirm are deemed intolerant; and those who express 'intolerant' opinions are condemned for engaging in 'hate speech'. Denunciation, condemnation, and public humiliation are the tactics used increasingly by the defenders of new orthodoxies.

This is hardly the kind of society in which most Australians wish to live. Australia enjoys some of the highest indicators of social cohesion of any secular liberal democracy; and those who come to this country to make their home here do so for the quality of life it offers. Commitment to the social and cultural well-being of this country is what unites Australians; but the intransigence of the warriors of identity politics, who sow seeds of division, does greater harm to our culture than ever they imagine. The essays in this book serve as a call to remember that Australia is united by far more than that which divides it; but this fundamental tenet of our common life needs to be guarded with vigilance.

Notes

INTRODUCTION

1   Paul Carp "Greens promise to end religious exemptions." *The Guardian Australia* 17 May 2016 and David Crowe "Greens under pressure on religion reforms" *The Australian* 24 May 2016.

2   For example, the Labor administration in the Northern Territory in 2017 "Building Safe, Vibrant and Inclusive Communities: Modernising the Anti-Discrimination Act" Media Release by Natasha Fyles Attorney-General and Minister for Justice Northern Territory 3 September 2017 and since then Amos Aikman "Northern Territory Denies Radical Push to Curb Freedoms" *The Australian* 11 July 2019

3   Recommendation 8. Marriage Equality Submission to the Expert Panel 14 February 2018.

4   Lyle Shelton on Paul Murray Live Sky News 26 July 2016 reposted at https://www.acl.org.au/what_is_the_no_case_for_same_sex_marriage

5   Paul Karp "Marriage equality bill expected to pass Senate after amendments fail *The Guardian Australia* 29 November 2017.

6   Malcolm Turnbull Media Release "Protecting freedom of religion in Australia" 14 December 2017

7   Bill Shorten Second Reading Speech: Marriage Amendment (Definition and Religious Freedoms) Bill 2017 Hansard 4 December 2017.

8   Primrose Riordan "SSM religious freedom review sparks flood of submissions" *The Australian* 20 March 2018

9   *Sydney Morning Herald* print edition 9 October 2018. In the online edition it was changed to 'Religious freedom review enshrines right of schools to turn away gay children and teachers.'

10 The Sex Discrimination Amendment (Sexual Orientation, Gender Identity and Intersex Status) Act 2013 had been introduced by the Gillard Labor government in 2013.

11 Patrick Parkinson 'Courting religious voters in the 2019 federal election' ABC Religion and Ethics Online 3 April 2019.

12 Religious Freedom Review 1.437.

13 Harrison, J., and Parkinson, P., "Freedom beyond the Commons: Managing the Tension between Faith and Equality in a Multicultural Society" (*Monash University Law Review* 19).

14 Religious Freedom Review 1.435.

15 Religious Freedom Review 1.420.

16 Australian Government response to the Religious Freedom Review December 2018.

17 Mark Dreyfus ABC Radio National Drive 14 December 2018.

18 Rodney Croome "Why 2019 was not a religious freedom election." ABC Religion and Ethics Online 22 May 2019.

19 Patrick Parkinson "What role did religious faith play in the 2019 federal election?" ABC Religion and Ethics Online 20 May 2019, and Andrew West "How religious voters lost faith in Labor: Lessons from the 2019 federal election" ABC Religion and Ethics Online 24 May 2019

20 Greg Brown "Anthony Albanese's team in warning on religious freedom" *The Australian* 1 June 2019

21 There was some indications of the early politicisation of the religious freedom issue Anna Patty "Christian leaders say religious freedom was among issues that influenced voters" *The Australian* 20 May 2019

22 Peter Kurti, *The Tyranny of Tolerance: Threats to Religious Liberty in Australia,* (Brisbane: Connor Court 2017). .179

23 Rodney Croome "How the Ruddock Review Has Harmed The LGBTI Community" Queer News December 2019.

24 Stephen D Smith, *Pagans and Christians in the City: Culture Wars from the Tiber to the Potomac* (Emory University Studies in Law and Religion) Eerdmans 2018 Kindle loc 7530.

25 See Harrison, J., and Parkinson, P., "Freedom beyond the Commons: Managing the Tension between Faith and Equality in a Multicultural Society" (*Monash University Law Review* 19).

26 For example, Denis Dragovic draws attention even to the economic growth impact of religious freedom when he writes that "Research has found that religious freedom positively contributes to prosperity above and beyond its contribution to buttressing other freedoms." Denis Dragovic "Freedom of religion serves us all, so let's protect it" *The Australian* 19 June 2019.

27 For example, see Chapter 11 "Religion is a Team Sport' in Jonathan Haight *The Righteous Mind* (2012) and more recently in Australia the Deloitte's report for the Study of the Economic Impact of Religion on Society Deloitte Access Economics "Donating and volunteering behaviour associated with religiosity: Report for Study of Economy Impact of Religiosity on Society" May 2018 and Angela Shanahan "What do religious people do for Australia? Ask the charities" *The Australian* 9 June 2018.

28 For the roots of Australian religious pluralism in the nineteenth century, see John Hirst, *Australia's Democracy: A Short History*, p.233-43.

29 Freedom for Faith Submission to the Expert Panel "Protecting Diversity: Towards a Better Legal Framework for Religious Freedom in Australia" 15 January 2018.

30 https://www.ag.gov.au/Consultations/Documents/religious-freedom-bills/summary-document-religious-freedom-reforms.pdf

31 https://www.theguardian.com/world/2019/jul/08/religious-discrimination-bill-will-safeguard-people-of-faith-says-attorney-general

32 https://www.theaustralian.com.au/nation/politics/churches-mount-revolt-on-draft-laws/news-story/e798d46133b4d1fe418e56ebbd437352

33 https://www.theguardian.com/world/2019/jul/08/religious-discrimination-bill-will-safeguard-people-of-faith-says-attorney-general

34 https://www.theaustralian.com.au/nation/christian-porter-unveils-laws-to-protect-from-discrimination-on-basis-of-religious-belief/news-story/9b096129b

5f4ddee09beda3f89ea0532

35 https://www.theguardian.com/australia-news/2019/aug/29/religious-discrimina-tion-bill-coalition-accused-of-weakening-state-human-rights-law

36 https://qnews.com.au/big-problem-with-morrison-governments-new-reli-gion-laws/

CHAPTER 2

FROM LIBERAL TOLERANCE TO POSTMODERN (IN)TOLERANCE

1   Perez Zagorin, *How the Idea of Religious Toleration Came to the West* (Princeton University Press, 2003), p 247.

2   *Ibid*, p 247.

3   *Ibid*, p 260-1.'

4   John Locke, *A Letter Concerning Toleration* [1689] (London: John Horton and Susan Mendus, 1991), p 41.

5   *Ibid*, p 42-3.

6   *Ibid*, p 19.

7   *Ibid*, p 32.

8   Jeremy Waldron, *Liberal Rights: Collected Papers 1981-1991* (Cambridge/UK: Cambridge, 1993), p 98.

9   Thomas G. West, 'The Transformation of Protestant Theology as a Condition of the American Revolution', in Thomas S. Engeman and Michael P. Zuckert (eds.), *Protestantism and the American Founding* (University of Notre Dame Press, 2004), p 88.

10 Alejandro Chafuen. 'John Locke: A Religious Champion of Freedom', *American Conservative Union*, 30 July 2010, at http://www.chafuen.com/home/locke-and-christianity-2

11 John Locke, *The Conduct of the Understanding* [1697] (London/UK: M. Jones, 1802), p 73

12 Locke, above n.4, p 41.

13 Matthew J. Franck, 'Christianity and Freedom in the American Founding', *in* Timothy Samuel Shah and Allen D. Hertzke, *Christianity and Freedom – Volume I: Historical Perspectives* (Cambridge University Press, 2016), pp 269-70.

14 Samuel Cooper, 'A Sermon on the Day of the Commencement of the [Massachu-setts] Constitution' (Boston, 1780), at https://www.consource.org/document/a-sermon-on-the-day-of-the-commencement-of-the-constitution-by-samuel-coo-per-1780-10-25/

15 Ibid, p 42-3.

16 William Molyneux, *Case of Ireland's Being Bound by Acts of Parliament in En-gland Stated* (first published 1689), p 100, at https://oll.libertyfund.org/titles/molyneux-the-case-of-ireland-being-bound-by-acts-of-parliament-in-england-stated

17 John Eidsmoe, 'Operation Josiah: Rediscovering the Biblical Roots', *in* H Wayne

201

House (ed), *The Christian and American Law: Christianity's Impact on America's Founding Documents and Future Direction* (Grand Rapids/MI: Kregel Publications, 1998), p 91.

18 Harold Berman, *Faith and Order: The Reconciliation of Law and Religion*, Scholars Press, Atlanta/GA, 1993, p 210.

19 *Ibid,* p 42-3.

20 Referring to the Preamble of the Commonwealth Constitution, which recites that the people of the colonies who were about to form Federation, were 'humbly relying on the blessings of Almighty God, have agreed to unite in one indissoluble Commonwealth', 'it was stated by Mr Higgins that, although the preamble to the Constitution of the United States contained no such words as these, it had been decided by the courts in the year 1892 that the people of the United States were a Christian people; and although the Constitution gave no power to Congress to make laws relating to Sunday observance, that decision was shortly afterwards followed by a Federal enactment declaring that the Chicago Exhibition should be closed on Sundays. This law, he said, was passed simply on the ground that among Christian nations Christian observances should be enforced (Convention Debates, Melb., p 1734)'. – Quick and Garran, above n.87, p 952.

21 John Quick and Robert Randolph Garran, *The Annotated Constitution of the Australian Commonwealth* (Angus & Robertson, 1901), pp 283–84.

22 *Ibid,* p 287.

23 *Ibid.,* p 952.

24 *Ibid.*

25 Mark Powell, 'Evangelicals Unchained: Evangelical Christians Profoundly Influenced Australia: Stuart Piggin Talks to Mark Powell', *Australian Presbyterian*, Spring 2018, p 4. Stuart Piggin has hold several academic positions, including Director of the 'Centre for the History of Christian Thought and Experience' at Macquarie University and Head of the 'Department of Christian Thought' at the Australian College of Theology. He is presently a Fellow of the Royal Historical Society and of the Religious History Association of Australia.

26 Cited in Nicholas Tonti-Fillipini, 'Religion in a Secular Society' (2008) 52(9) *Quadrant Magazine* 82, pp 83-84. For a comparative analysis of church and state relations in Australia and the United States, see: Gabriël A. Moens, 'Church and State Relations in Australia and the United States: The Purpose and Effect Approaches and the Neutrality Principle' (1996) 4 *Brigham Young University Law Review* pp 787-813; see also: Gabriël A Moens, 'The Action-Belief Dichotomy and Freedom of Religion' (1989) (12) *Sydney Law Review*, pp 195-217.

27 D.A. Carson, *The Intolerance of Tolerance* (Grand Rapids/MI: William B. Eerdmans Publishing Co., 2012), p 12.

28 *Ibid.,* p 11. As Jesus says in John 14.6

29 Frank Furedi, 'On Tolerance' (2012) 28 *Policy* 30, p 32.

30 *Ibid.*

31 *Ibid.,* p 32.

32 *Ibid.* p 31.

Notes

33 Robert Forsyth, 'Dangerous Protections: How Some Ways of Protecting the Freedom of Religion May Actually Diminish Religious Freedom', Address at the Third Action Lecture on Religion and Freedom (Sep. 24, 2001),

34 Section 9 (1) of the Racial and Religious Tolerance Act 2001 (Vic) states: "In determining whether a person has contravened section 7 or 8, the person's motive in engaging in any conduct is irrelevant".

35 Racial and Religious Tolerance Act 2001 (Vic), Section 9(1) and Section 10

36 Tauati Ahdar, 'Religious Vilification: Confused Policy, Unsound Principle and Unfortunate Law' (2007) 26 *The University of Queensland Law Journal* 293, 301.301.

37 Joel Harrison, 'Truth, Civility, and Religious Battlegrounds: The Context Between Religious Vilification Laws and Freedom of Expression' (2006) 12 *Auckland University Law Review* 71, p 88.

38 Stanley Fish, *There's No Such Thing as Free Speech* (New York/NY: Oxford University Press, 1994). Fish comments: "When one speaks to another person, it is usually for an instrumental purpose: you are trying to get someone to do something, you are trying to urge an idea and, down the road, a course of action. There are reasons for which speech exists and it is in that sense that I say that there is no such thing as "free speech", that is, speech that has its rationale nothing more than its own production". – p 104.

39 Carl H. Esbeck, 'The Application of RFRA to Override Employment Nondiscrimination Clauses Embedded in Federal Social Services Programs (2008) 9(2) *Engage* 1, 9.

40 Derrida was more cryptic about his atheism. Speaking before a convention of the American Academy of Religion in 2002, Derrida stated: 'I rightly pass for an atheist.' However, when asked why he would not say more plainly 'I am an atheist,' he replied, 'Maybe I'm not an atheist.' How can Derrida claim to be and not be an atheist? Both the existence and nonexistence of God requires a universal statement about reality, but Derrida is unwilling to make such an absolute claim. In this regard Derrida's theology is consistent with his postmodern inclination for ambiguity. Likewise, Richard Rorty admitted at one time that he was an atheist, but in a subsequent work, *The Future of Religion*, he said that he now agreed with Gianni Vattimo that 'atheism (objective evidence for the nonexistence of God) is just as untenable as theism (objective evidence for the existence of God).' Thus, Rorty insists that atheism, too, must be abandoned in favour of something he labelled 'anti-clericalism.' Ecclesiastical institutions are dangerous, but not necessarily the local congregation of believers. 'Religion,' he says, 'is unobjectionable as long as it privatized.' See David Noebel, *Understanding the Times: The Collision of Today's Competing Worldviews* (2nd ed., Manitou Springs/CO: Summit Press, 2006), 80.

41 *Ibid*, p 97.

42 *Ibid*, p 78.

43 Kevin J Vanhoozer, *Postmodern Theology* (Cambridge/UK: Cambridge University Press, 2005) 12.

44 Alister McGrath, *The Twilight of Atheism* (New York/NY: Doubleday, 2004) 227.

45 Noebel, above n 41, p 97.

46 *Ibid,* 78.

47 Mark Lilla, *The Reckless Mind: Intellectuals in Politics* (New York/NY: New York Review Books, 2001) 150.

48 Robert Eaglestone (ed), *Routledge Critical Things* (New York/NY: Routledge, 2003), p 15.

49 Lilla, above n.47, 142.

50 Richard Wolin, *The Seduction of Unreason* (Princeton/NJ: Princeton University Press, 2004), p 6.

51 Michel Foucault, 'Nietzsche, Genealogy, History', *in* Paul Rabinow (ed.), *The Foucault Reader* (New York/NY: Pantheon, 1987), p 95.

52 Janet Afary and Kevin B Anderson, *Foucault and the Iranian Revolution: Gender and the Seductions of Islamism* (Chicago/IL: University of Chicago Press, 2005).

53 Mervyn F Bendle, '9/11 and the Intelligentsia, Ten Years On' (2011) 55(9) *Quadrant* 46, pp 47-8.

54 Pascal Bruckner, *The Tyranny of Guilt: An Essay on Western Masochism* (Princeton University Press, 2012), p 25.

55 *Ibid*, pp 25-6.

56 American jurisprudence professor Charles Rice commented: 'One who says we can never be certain of anything contradicts himself because he is certain of that proposition. If he says instead that he is not sure he can be sure of anything, he admits at least that he is sure he is not sure. Or some will say that all propositions are meaningless unless they can be empirically verified. But that statement itself cannot be empirically verified.' See Charles E. Rice, *50 Questions on the Natural Law: What it is and Why We Need It* (San Francisco/CA: Ignatius Press, 1999), p 132.

57 Upheld by government and enforced by law, the doctrine of hard multiculturalism proposes ethnic, religious and cultural diversity as an essential attribute of a fair society. It presupposes a certain kind of policy which needs to be supported by an entire bureaucratic framework designed to manage such a state-sponsored ethnic and cultural diversity. By contrast, in its soft or adjectival sense, writes Peter Kurti, 'multiculturalism ... describes what had always been Australia's social reality: that significant numbers of people from different backgrounds were assimilating into Australian society in their own way and at their own pace'. In this soft sense, 'multiculturalism is unexceptional, although terms like 'multiracial' and 'multi-ethnic' would probably be more accurate'. – Peter Kurti, 'The Fetish of Diversity' (2007) 33 (3) *Policy* 45, p 46.

58 Inquiry into Migration and Multiculturalism in Australia (Canberra/ACT: Commonwealth of Australia, 213), para. 4.27.

59 Peter Kurti, *The Tyranny of Tolerance: Threats to Religious Liberty in Australia* (Connor Court, 2017), p 96.

60 *Ibid.,* p 97.

61 This provision creates an extremely broad prohibition that represents an extraordinary limitation of freedom of speech. Such *'hurt feelings'* test is far below the

defamation threshold which applies when a person has been brought into *'hatred, ridicule or contempt'*. In our book 'No Offence Intended: Why 18C is Wrong', Joshua Forrester, Lorraine and myself provide a couple of reasons as to why section 18C, without a doubt, must be declared constitutionally invalid. Not only the language and emotions of such a provision – offence, insult and humiliation – go far beyond what is actually required in the international treaty most directly supporting the Act, but this section also infringes the implied freedom of political communication which, as repeatedly stated by the High Court, is a freedom implied in the Australian Constitution as a document which prescribes an authentic system of representative government. – See: Joshua Forrester, Lorraine Finlay, and Augusto Zimmermann, *No Offence Intended: Why 18C is Wrong* (Redland Bay/Qld: Connor Court, 2016).

62 Chris Merritt, 'Move for Blasphemy Law Could 'Turn Us Into Saudi Arabia'', *The Australian*, March 28, 2017. See also: See also: Augusto Zimmermann, 'The Push to Protect Muslims from Free Speech', *Quadrant Magazine*, March 2019, No.554, Volume LXIII, No.3, pp 34-7. See also: Augusto Zimmermann, 'Sharia By Stealth', *Quadrant Magazine*, June 28th, 2018, at https://quadrant.org.au/opinion/qed/2018/06/sharia-stealth/. See also: Augusto Zimmermann, 'Labor Move for Extending 18C Could Impose Islamic Blasphemy Law', *The Spectator Australia*, 3 April 2017, at https://www.spectator.com.au/2017/04/labor-mov22, e-for-extending-18c-could-impose-islamic-blasphemy-law/

63 *Ibid.*

64 *Ibid.*

65 *Ibid.*

66 *Ibid.*

67 On 14 December 2017, the Commonwealth Government released broad terms of reference for its Religious Freedom Review. Headed by former Attorney General Phillip Ruddock, the Expert Panel was instructed to consider the intersections between the enjoyment of the freedom of religion and other human rights. The panel was consisted of the Hon Ruddock (chair), Professor Nicholas Aroney, Professor Rosalind Croucher AM (President of the Australian Human Rights Commission), the Hon. Dr Annabelle Bennett AO SC, and Father Frank Brennan SJ AO. Although the scope of the Freedom of Religion Review was manifestly broad, this Review was a direct outcome of the recent debate about marriage, in which arguments were made that the Bill passed through the Parliament to amend the Marriage Act did not afford adequate safeguards for freedom of religion and conscience. Prime Minister Scott Morrison and Attorney-General Christian Porter released, on 13 December 2018, both the Ruddock Religious Freedom Review and the government's response. – 'Government Response to Religious Freedom Review', Media Release by Prime Minister and Attorney General, December 13, 2018, at https://www.pm.gov.au/media/government-response-religious-freedom-review.

68 Report of the Expert Panel, 'Religious Freedom Review', Commonwealth of Australia, 18 May 2018, p 4.

69 Neil Foster, 'Religious Free Speech After Ruddock: Implications for Blasphemy and Religious Vilification Law', Paper presented at 'Religious Freedom After Ruddock', the University of Queensland, St Lucia, April 6, 2019, p 50,

at   file:///C:/Users/user/Downloads/foster-full-paper-for-rf-after-ruddock-confer-
ence.pdf

70 *Ibid.*

71 Hugo Grotius, *The Truth of the Christian Religion* [1627] (Indianapolis/IN:
Liberty Fund, 2012), pp 86-87.

CHAPTER 3

A WATERSHED MOMENT

1   The survey returned 7,817,247 or 61.6% "Yes" responses and 4,873,987 or 38.4%
"No" responses. The total turnout was 12,727,920 which comprised 79.5% of
those who are actually eligible to vote, which is roughly 16,000,000.

2   https://www.childabuseroyalcommission.gov.au/final-report

3   "Faith No More: Parishioners Lose Trust in Church', *Sydney Morning Herald,* 11
February 2018.

4   Religious Freedom Review Report of the Expert Panel 1.84

5   Rebecca Urban, "Churches, schools fear anti-discrimination changes", *The
Australian*, 10 October, 2017,

6   Emily Baker, "ACT Education Minister Yvette Berry cautions Schools on same
sex marriage" *The Age*, September 21 2017.

7   Madeleine Teahan, "Government Integration advisor: Catholic schools cannot
oppose gay marriage", *The Catholic Herald*, 11 January 2017.

8   Rachael Pells, "Private Jewish schools fails third Ofsted inspection for not
teaching LGBT issues", *The Independent*, 26 June 2017.

9   https://consult.education.gov.uk/school-frameworks/operating-the-
independent-school-regulatory-system/supporting_documents/180214%20%20
ISSAdvice%20v13.0draftforCS.pdf

10   "Chardi father claims human rights violation over children's sex education",
Jewish News, 3 January 2019.

11   Deborah Gyapong, "Hamilton Dad loses appeal over parental rights on sex
education", *The Catholic Register*, November 22, 2017,.

12   Derek Ross, "A New Canada Summer Jobs Attestation for 2019: the Good, the
(Potentially) Bad, and the Unknown", December 20, 2018.

13   Amanda Connelly, "Liberals changing Canada Summer Jobs attestation after
reproductive rights controversy", *Global News*, December 6 2018.

14   "Catholic Care loses its gay adoption fight", BBC News, 2 November 2012.

15   "Family First stripped of charity status", *New Zealand Herald*, 21 August 2017.

16   Ellen Coyne, "Catholic counsellors to help gay couples", *The Times,* July 18
2018.

17   "Christian Youth Camps loses appeal against gay discrimination ruling", *ABC
News*, 17 April 2014.

18   Joe Kelly, "Same-sex marriage scandal: job lost over No vote", *The Australian*,

September 20, 2017.

19 Alle McMahon, "White magazine shuts down after refusing to feature same-sex weddings", *ABC News*, 18 November 2018.

20 Joe Kelly, "Religious freedom lost as White magazine shuts", *The Australian*, November 17, 2018.

21 Camilla Turner and Tony Diver, "Oxford College bans 'harmful' Christian Union from freshers' fair", *The Telegraph*, 10 October 2017.

22 'Marriage equality campaign seeks abolition of religious rights to discriminate', *Guardian Australia*, 14 February 2018.

CHAPTER 4

FREEDOM OF RELIGION AND EDUCATION

1 Servais Pinckaers, *Sources of Christian Ethics*, trans. Sr Mary Thomas Noble O.P (Washington DC: Catholic University of America, 1995), 328.

2 See Roger Scruton's discussion of Jean Paul Satre's *Cahiers pour une morale*, in *Fools, Frauds and Firebrands: Thinkers of the New Left*, (London: Bloomsbury, 2107), 82.

3 Patrick J. Deneen, *Why Liberalism Failed*, (New Haven: Yale University Press, 2018), 31.

4 This exaltation of freedom was exemplified by the Supreme Court of the United States: "At the heart of liberty is the right to define one's own concept of existence, of meaning, of the universe, and of the mystery of human life." *Planned Parenthood v. Casey*, 505 U.S. 833, 851 (1992).

5 Samuel Gregg, "Tocqueville and the fall of Democracy in America," *The Public Discourse*, (January 19, 2017)

6 John Henry Newman, *Idea of a University*, (Indiana: UNDA, 1982), 76.

7 Deneen, *Why Liberalism Failed*, 110, 111.

8 The other 4 mission statement are:

1. Every student benefits from innovative and effective learning experiences taught by skilled and dedicated teachers.

2. Every student enjoys a safe and secure learning environment wherein they feel connected and affirmed.

3. Every student contributes to a culture of respect, dignity, care and concern for others.

4. Every student has access to excellent learning resources and is taught in the best learning facilities we can provide. Taken for St Phillip's website: https://www.spcc.nsw.edu.au/newcastle/our-story/vision-and-values_

9 Sydney Catholic Schools website: https://sydcatholicschools.nsw.edu.au/about-us/vision-and-mission/

10 https://www.campion.edu.au/about-campion/

11 Joint Statement from Australian Catholic Bishops Conference, October 18, 2018 www.catholic.org.au/acbc-media/media-centre/media-releases-new/2153-

archbishops-call-for-deeper-reflection-on-religious-freedom/file

12 Greg Craven, "Taking a Legal Leap of Faith," *The Australian*, Jan 4 2019.

There was a similar case as this in Perth when a relief teacher had his employment ended with a Baptist school after revealing that he was in a same-sex relationship https://www.abc.net.au/news/2018-10-12/gay-teacher-attacks-push-for-religious-school-discrimination/10365816

CHAPTER 5

PROTECTING RELIGIOUS FREEDOM IN AN AGE OF MILITANT
SECULARISM

1   See further, Joint Standing Committee on Foreign Affairs, Defence and Trade, Interim Report, *Legal Foundations of Religious Freedom in Australia* (2017) (hereafter, 'the Andrews Committee'), Chapter 5.

2   Australian Law Reform Commission, Report no 129, *Traditional Rights and Freedoms—Encroachments by Commonwealth Laws* (2016), p.134, at 5.26.

3   *Grace Bible Church Inc v Reedman* (1984) 36 SASR 376.

4   *Constitution Act 1934 (Tas.)* s.46.

5   *Coco v The Queen* (1994) 179 CLR 4; *Canterbury Municipal Council v Moslem Alawy Society Ltd* (1985) 1 NSWLR 525.

6   Australian Law Reform Commission, Report no 129, *Traditional Rights and Freedoms—Encroachments by Commonwealth Laws* (2016).

7   Report of the Religious Freedom Review at: https://www.pmc.gov.au/domestic-policy/religious-freedom-review.

8   *Anti-Discrimination Act 1998 (Tas)* s. 16.

9   See the Abortion Law Reform Act 2008 (Vic.), discussed in Frank Brennan, 'The place of the religious viewpoint in shaping law and policy in a pluralistic democratic society: a case study on rights and conscience'. Paper given at Values and Public Policy Conference: Fairness, Diversity and Social Change, Centre for Public Policy, University of Melbourne, 26 February 2009. See also the account by Dr Mark Hobart of the complaint against him: available at: https://www.parliament.qld.gov.au/documents/committees/HCDSDFVPC/2016/18-HealthAbortion/submissions/885.pdf. Dr Hobart, a GP, was requested by a couple to refer them to an abortion practitioner. The woman was 19 weeks' pregnant at the time. The reason for the request was that during a routine ultrasound, they had discovered that the baby was a girl. As Dr Hobart understood it, the requested abortion was purely for sex selection purposes.

10 See e.g. *Public Health and Wellbeing Act* 2008 (Vic) s.185D. A constitutional challenge has been heard in the High Court. See *Clubb v Edwards & Anor; Preston v Avery & Anor* [2018] HCATrans 210.

11 Mark Powell, '18C weaponised', *The Spectator Australia*, 18th October 2017.

12 Patrick Billings, 'Anti-Discrimination Commission to hear complaint over Hobart preacher Campbell Markham's blogs' *The Mercury*, August 7th 2017.

13 Equality Australia, https://equalityaustralia.org.au/news: 'Australia Needs to

Legislate for Equality not Religious Exceptionalism'.

14 Stanley Fish, 'Almost Pragmatism: Richard Posner's Jurisprudence' (1990) 57 *U Chicago Law Review* 1447 at 1466.

15 JD Heydon, 'Religious 'Toleration' In Modern Australia: The Tyranny of Relativism'. Inaugural PM Glynn Lecture on Religion, Law and Public Life, Australian Catholic University, Adelaide, October 2017, pp. 8-9.

16 Denis Shanahan, 'GetUp!-backed petition seeks to deregister doctor from No-case ad,' *The Australian*, September 4th 2017.

17 B. Lee, 'Christian Lobby Academic Heads Law School', The Saturday Paper, July 21st 2018.

18 P. Parkinson, *For Kids' Sake* (2011) at https://www.acl.org.au/for_kids_sake.

19 Above n,2 at p.147, 5.97.

20 For a discussion see Rex Ahdar & Ian Leigh, *Religious Freedom in the Liberal State* (Oxford University Press, 2nd ed, 2013), chapter 10.

21 This is discussed in Patrick Parkinson, 'Christian Concerns about an Australian Charter of Rights' (2010) 15 *Australian Journal of Human Rights* 83.

22 Jewel Topsfield, 'Religious Freedom Review Enshrines Right of Schools to Turn Away Gay Children and Teachers' *The Age*, 9th October 2018, p.1.

23 *Discrimination Free Schools Bill 2018,* introduced by Senator Di Natale (Greens), 16 October 2018.

24 Andrews Committee at 2.33.

25 *Constitution Alteration (Rights and Freedoms) 1988.* It received support from only 31% of voters and did not receive majority support from voters in any State.

26 National Human Rights Consultation Committee, *Report on the National Human Rights Consultation* (2009).

27 It did enact the establishment of a joint parliamentary committee by the *Human Rights (Parliamentary Scrutiny) Act 2011.*

28 See generally, Patrick Parkinson, 'Christian Concerns about an Australian Charter of Rights' (2010) 15 *Australian Journal of Human Rights* 83.

29 (2011) 245 *CLR* 1.

30 Will Bateman and James Stellios, 'Chapter III of The *Constitution,* Federal Jurisdiction and Dialogue Charters Of Human Rights' (2012) 36 *Melbourne University Law Review* 1. See also Helen Irving, 'The Dilemmas in Dialogue: A Constitutional Analysis of the NHRC's Proposed Human Rights Act' (2010) 33 *University of New South Wales Law Journal* 60.

31 Patrick Parkinson and Nicholas Aroney, Submission to Attorney-General's Department, *Consolidation of Commonwealth Anti-Discrimination Laws,* January 2012.

32 See for example, Christian Schools Australia, 'ALRC provides further support for CSA approach to discrimination law' (2016) at https://csa.edu.au; George Pell, 'Religious Freedom in an Age of Militant Secularism' (2013) 57 *Quadrant* 28 (October 2013).

33 Australian Law Reform Commission, Report no 129, *Traditional Rights and Freedoms—Encroachments by Commonwealth Laws* (2016) at [5.111].

34 National Council of Churches in Australia, Submission, 17 January 2018, p.4.

35 *Christian Education South Africa v. Minister of Education*, [2000] ZACC 11, 2000 (10) B. Const. L.R. 1051 at [36].

CHAPTER 6

MATCHING WORDS WITH ACTION: WHAT THE GOVERNMENT SHOULD DO TO STRENGTHEN RELIGIOUS FREEDOM

1 Joe Kelly, "Morrison's stand on freedom of religion", *The Australian*, 13 December 2018.

2 Commonwealth, *Parliamentary Debates,* House of Representatives, 4 December 2017, 12323 (Bill Shorten).

3 Joint Standing Committee on Foreign Affairs, Defence and Trade, *Legal Foundations of Religious Freedom in Australia (Interim Report)*, Canberra, November 2017, vii.

4 Expert Panel, *Religious Freedom Review: Report of the Expert Panel* (18 May 2018), [1.13].

5 'Marriage legislation puts religious freedom in doubt', *The Australian*, 8 December 2017.

6 Expert Panel, *Religious Freedom Review: Report of the Expert Panel* (18 May 2018), iii.

7 Ibid, [1.56].

8 Australian Government, *Australian Government Response to the Religious Freedom Review* (December 2018), 4.

9 See, for example, Nick Evershed, 'Was Julia Gillard the most productive Prime Minister in Australia's history?', *The Guardian,* 28 June 2013.

10 Expert Panel, *Religious Freedom Review: Report of the Expert Panel* (18 May 2018), 5 (Recommendation 15).

11 Australian Government, *Australian Government Response to the Religious Freedom Review* (December 2018), 4.

12 Prime Minister and Attorney General, *Transcript of Press Conference with Attorney General (Religious Freedom, Commonwealth Integrity Commission)*, 13 December 2018.

13 See, for example, Lorraine Finlay, "Religious Freedom Act should be opposed as a back-door Bill of Rights", *Online Opinion*, 6 August 2018. Lorraine Finlay, Joshua Forrester and Dr Augusto Zimmermann, *Submission to the Expert Panel on Religious Freedom* (Submission No. 14792), 12 February 2018.

14 The case that best exemplifies the narrow approach taken by the High Court of Australia to s. 116 is *Kruger v Commonwealth* (1997) 190 CLR 1. See also Australian Law Reform Commission, *Traditional Rights and Freedoms — Encroachments by Commonwealth Laws* (ALRC Report 129), 2 March 2015,

[4.21]; Alex Deagon, 'Liberal Assumptions in Section 116 Cases and Implications for Religious Freedom' (2017) *Federal Law Review* 113.

15 See, for example, submissions made to the Expert Panel by Freedom For Faith (Submission Number 2520); Neville Rochow SC (Submission Number 2539); the Victorian Christian Legal Society Inc (Submission Number 9984); the Wilberforce Foundation (Submission Number 6435); Associate Professor Neil Foster (Submission Number 14570); Associate Professor Keith Thompson (Submission Number 14157); Professor Greg Craven (Submission Number 14665); Australian Catholic Bishops Conference (Submission Number 11901); Catholic Archdiocese of Hobart (Submission Number 15057); the Church of Jesus Christ of the Latter-Day Saints (Submission Number 9913); Anglican Church Diocese of Sydney (Submission Number 7482); Presbyterian Church of Australia (Submission Number 4008); Uniting Church in Australia Assembly (Submission Number 3428); Australian Christian Lobby (in conjunction with the Human Rights Law Alliance) (Submission Number 14932); Australian Baha'i Community (Submission Number 14836); and the Australian Federation of Islamic Councils (Submission Number 2832 All submissions can be accessed at: <https://www.pmc.gov.au/domestic-policy/religious-freedom-review/review-submissions>.

16 Expert Panel, *Religious Freedom Review: Report of the Expert Panel* (18 May 2018), [1.122].

17 Freedom for Faith, Submission to the Expert Panel Religious Freedom Review (Submission Number 2520) (29 January 2018), 82. See also Catholic Archdiocese of Hobart, Submission to the Expert Panel Religious Freedom Review — Attachment Two (Submission Number 15057) (13 February 2018), 9.

18 U.S. Department of State, *Secretary of State's Determination Under the International Religious Freedom Act of 1998 and Frank R. Wolf International Religious Freedom Act of 2016,* 21 December 2018.

19 The ten countries designated as countries of particular concern were China, Eritrea, Iran, Myanmar, North Korea, Pakistan, Saudi Arabia, Sudan, Tajikistan, Turkmenistan. The relevant constitutional provisions providing some form of protection for religious freedom can be found in the constitutions of China (Article 36, *The Constitution of the People's Republic of China,* 1982); Eritrea (Article 19, *Constitution of Eritrea,* 1997); Myanmar (Article 34, *The Constitution of the Republic of the Union of Myanmar,* 2008), North Korea (Article 68, *Socialist Constitution of the Democratic People's Republic of Korea,* 1972 rev. 1998); Pakistan (Article 20, *Constitution of the Islamic Republic of Pakistan,* 1973); Sudan (Article 6, *Interim National Constitution of the Republic of Sudan,* 2005); Tajikistan (Article 26, *Constitution of Tajikistan,* 1994); and Turkmenistan (Articles 18 & 41, *Constitution of Turkmenistan,* 2008 rev. 2016).

20 Judge Learned Hand, *The Spirit of Liberty* (Speech given at 'I Am an American Day' ceremony in Central Park, New York City, 31 May 1944).

21 Carolyn Evans, *Legal Protection of Religious Freedom in Australia* (Federation Press, 2012), 107.

22 Joint Standing Committee on Foreign Affairs, Defence and Trade, *Legal Foundations of Religious Freedom in Australia (Interim Report),* Canberra,

November 2017, viii.

23 The key anti-discrimination statutes at the Commonwealth level are the *Age Discrimination Act 2004* (Cth), *Disability Discrimination Act 1992* (Cth), *Racial Discrimination Act 1975* (Cth) and *Sex Discrimination Act 1984* (Cth). At a State and Territories level see *Discrimination Act 1991* (ACT); *Anti-Discrimination Act 1977* (NSW); *Anti-Discrimination Act* (NT); *Anti-Discrimination Act 1991* (Qld); *Equal Opportunity Act 1984* (SA); *Anti-Discrimination Act 1998* (Tas); *Equal Opportunity Act 2010* (Vic), *Equal Opportunity Act 1984* (WA).

24 Australian Human Rights Commission, *Religious Freedom Review: Australian Human Rights Commission Submission to the Expert Panel*, February 2018, [92].

25 Although notably this is not the case in every jurisdiction, with New South Wales and South Australia providing more limited protections and religion not being a protected attribute at the Commonwealth level. See Expert Panel, *Religious Freedom Review: Report of the Expert Panel* (18 May 2018), [1.98].

26 Lorraine Finlay, Joshua Forrester and Dr Augusto Zimmermann, *Submission to the Expert Panel on Religious Freedom* (Submission No. 14792), 12 February 2018.

27 Jeremy Waldron, *The Harm in Hate Speech* (Cambridge, MA: Harvard University Press, 2012), 127.

28 *Equal Opportunity Act 1984* (WA), s. 3. Similar language is used in the objects clause of other anti-discrimination laws at both the federal and state levels.

29 See Patrick Parkinson, 'Protecting religious freedom in an age of militant secularism'; Australian Law Reform Commission, *Traditional Rights and Freedoms — Encroachments by Commonwealth Laws* (ALRC Report 129), 2 March 2016, [5.111].

30 Helen Andrews, *The Limits of Australian Anti-discrimination Law* (The Centre for Independent Studies, Research Report, August 2016), 11.

31 Expert Panel, *Religious Freedom Review: Report of the Expert Panel* (18 May 2018), iii.

32 Angela Shanahan, 'Same-sex lobby threatens Catholic Archbishop over Christian booklet', *The Australian,* 4 July 2015. Accessed at: < https://www.theaustralian.com.au/national-affairs/samesex-lobby-threatens-catholic-archbishop-over-christian-booklet/news-story/61d790b105b5ab3b4b2ce8813dfcf728>

33 Angela Shanahan, 'Yes Side in Marriage Debate Ignores the Implications for Freedoms', *The Australian,* 3 September 2017.

34 Frank Chung, 'It's not okay to be homophobic': Canberra contractor sacked for 'vote no' Facebook post, *News.com.au,* 19 September 2017.

35 Jackie Trad, 19 March 2018. Accessed at https://twitter.com/jackietrad.

36 Greg Craven, 'Taking a legal leap of faith', *The Australian,* 4 January 2019

37 See James Spigelman, 'Free Speech Tripped up by Offensive Line', *The Australian,* 11 December 2002, 12, quoting Jeremy Waldron, *The Harm in Hate Speech* (Harvard University Press, 2012), 106.

38 Expert Panel, *Religious Freedom Review: Report of the Expert Panel* (18 May 2018), [1.409]

39 Expert Panel, *Religious Freedom Review: Report of the Expert Panel* (18 May 2018), 6 (Recommendations 17 & 18).

40 Expert Panel, *Religious Freedom Review: Report of the Expert Panel* (18 May 2018), 7 (Recommendation 19).

41 Unfortunately only an inaugural meeting was ever held, with future meetings being cancelled following the resignation of Tim Wilson as the Human Rights Commissioner in February 2016. For further information about the project see: <https://www.humanrights.gov.au/our-work/rights-and-freedoms/projects/religious-freedom-roundtable>.

42 Nathan Hondros, "Canning MP Andrew Hastie hits back over Coopers controversy", *Mandurah Mail*, 14 March 2017.

43 Change.org petition, *Boycott Coopers Brewery until they support Marriage Equality in Australia.*

44 Rachel Baxendale, 'Coopers loses bottle after Bible Society row', *The Australian*, 15 March 2017.

45 Helen Andrews, *The Limits of Australian Anti-discrimination Law* (The Centre for Independent Studies, Research Report, August 2016), 11.

46 Expert Panel, *Religious Freedom Review: Report of the Expert Panel* (18 May 2018), [1.6].

CHAPTER 7

A HUMEAN TAKE ON RELIGIOUS FREEDOM

1 Letter from Adam Smith to William Strachan, 26 August 1776.

2 John Rawls, *Political Liberalism* (Columbia University Press, 1993) 190—191.

3 John Rawls, *A Theory of Justice* (Harvard University Press, 1971) 11—12, 16, 137.

4 Rawls, *Political Liberalism* (n 2) 223.

5 Ibid 191—194.

6 Ibid 215, 217.

7 See, *inter alia*, James Allan, *Democracy in Decline* (2014, McGill-Queen's University Press, republished in Australia by Connor Court).

8 Or even, in Australia, vote for a party I thought I liked but whose elected representatives, partway through their mandate, opted to overhaul by defenestrating a leader who had won a massive majority and replacing him with one keen to take it in a noticeably different direction.

9 I have criticised bills of rights at length and in a host of contexts. For a selected few instances see e.g., James Allan, 'Bills of Rights and Judicial Power — A Liberal's Quandary?' (1996) 16 *Oxford Journal of Legal Studies* 337; 'Rights, Paternalism, Constitutions and Judges' in *Litigating Rights: Perspectives from Domestic and International Law* 29 (Grant Huscroft and Paul Rishworth, eds., 2002); 'Oh That I Were Made Judge in the Land' (2002) 30 *Federal Law Review* 561; 'A Modest Proposal' (2003) 23 *Oxford Journal of Legal Studies* 197; 'An Unashamed Majoritarian' (2004) 27 *Dalhousie Law Journal* 537; James Allan and Grant Huscroft, 'Rights Internationalism Coming Home to Roost?' (2006) 43

San Diego Law Review 1; 'Portia, Bassanio or Dick the Butcher? Constraining Judges in the Twenty-First Century' (2006) 17 King's College Law Journal 1; 'Jeremy Waldron and the Philosopher's Stone' (2008) 45 San Diego Law Review 133; 'Meagher's Mischaracterisations of Majoritarianism' (2009) 20 King's Law Journal 115; and Democracy in Decline (McGill-Queen's University Press, 2014).

10 Anti-Discrimination Act 1998 (Tas) ss 17, 19.

11 Anti-Discrimination Act 1991 (Qld) s 109(2); Equal Opportunity Act 1984 (WA) ss 72—73; Equal Opportunity Act 2010 (Vic) ss 82—84; Discrimination Act 1991 (ACT) ss 32—33; Equal Opportunity Act 1984 (SA) ss 34(3), 50; Anti-Discrimination Act 1992 (NT) ss 30(2), 37A, 51; Anti-Discrimination Act 1998 (Tas) ss 51—52; Anti-Discrimination Act 1977 (NSW) s 56; Sex Discrimination Act 1984 (Cth) ss 37—38.

12 Racial Discrimination Act 1975 (Cth) s 18C.

13 Ibrahim Abu Mohamed, Submission No 140 to Parliamentary Joint Committee on Human Rights, Parliament of Australia, Inquiry into Freedom of Speech in Australia (21 December 2016).

14 Equal Opportunity Act 2010 (Vic) ss 27, 66A, 74; Anti-Discrimination Act 1991 (Qld) ss 25, 102; Discrimination Act 1991 (ACT) s 45; Equal Opportunity Act 1984 (WA) s 66; Anti-Discrimination Act 1988 (Tas) s 53.

CHAPTER 8

ON RELIGIOUS FREEDOM AND ITS CULTURAL DESPISERS: AN ANGLICAN PERSPECTIVE

1 "Cardinal Nichols and Archbishop Welby call on Government to address persecution of Christians and promote freedom of religion." Catholic News 17 April 2019 http://www.catholicnews.org.uk/Home/News/Religious-Freedom.

2 Courtney Lee, "Prince Claims to Be Defender of All Faiths, not 'The' Faith." Christian Today. 5 June 2006.

3 James Macintyre, "Religious Freedom 'Is a Litmus Test of Overall Freedom' Says EU Special Envoy," World 27 Oct 2016.

4 Rex Ahdar and Ian Leigh, Religious Freedom in the Liberal State (2nd ed.; Oxford: OUP, 2013), 1.

5 Martin R. Castro et al. Peaceful Coexistence: Reconciling Nondiscrimination Principles with Civil Liberties. US Commission on Civil Rights., p. 29.

6 I owe this sentiment to Simon Smart of the Centre for Public Christianity.

7 Pew-Templeton Global Religious Futures Project. Restrictions on Religion 2016

8 According to Patrick Parkinson: "The recommendations of the Ruddock expert panel were flawed in that they failed to grapple adequately with the most important religious freedom issue put to the panel: the right of faith-based organisations to maintain their religious identity and values particularly in relation to the selection of staff. " Patrick Parkinson, "Religious Freedom After Ruddock," Freedom for Faith. 3 April 2019.

9 Ahdar and Leigh, Religious Freedom in the Liberal, 17-20.

10 Stephen Macedo, *Diversity and Distrust: Civic Education in a Multicultural Democracy* (Cambridge, MA: Harvard University Press, 2003).

11 William A. Galston, *Practice of Liberal Pluralism* (Cambridge: CUP, 2005), 23-40.

12 Macedo, *Diversity and Distrust*, 139-45.

13 Macedo, *Diversity and Conflict*, 142.

14 Macedo, *Diversity and Distrust*, 43.

15 Jürgen Habermas, "Intolerance and Discrimination," *International Journal of Constitutional Law* 1.1 (2003): 2, 6 (2-12).

16 Carolyn Evans and Beth Gaze, "Between Religious freedom and Equality: Complexity and Context," *Harvard International Law Journal* 49 (2008): 41 (40-49).

17 Twitchy Video, "Hillary Clinton – Religious beliefs have to be changed," 24 April 2015.

18 See https://www.sydneycatholic.org/pdf/dmm-booklet_web.pdf.

19 *Walsh v St Vincent de Paul Society of Queensland (No.2)* [2008] QADT 32.

20 Michael Rectenwald, Rochelle Almeida, and George Levine (eds.), *Global Secularisms in a Post-Secular Age* (Berlin: Walter de Gruyter, 2015).

21 From George Washington to the Hebrew Congregation in Newport, Rhode Island, 18 August 1790.

CHAPTER 9

RELIGIOUS FREEDOM IN AUSTRALIA TODAY: A JEWISH PERSPECTIVE

1 https://www.theguardian.com/world/2018/jan/14/jewish-service-calls-for-removal-of-london-coroner-over-burial-delay

CHAPTER 10

MUSLIM PERSPECTIVES ON RELIGIOUS FREEDOM

1 The White House. Remarks by the President at Cairo University, 6-04-09

2 (Bukhari, *Sahih*, 9, 84, hadith 57)

3 "Grand Mufti seeks Racial Discrimination Act cover for Muslims" *The Australian* 18 January 2017

CHAPTER 11

TAKING THE RIGHT WAY BACK

1 3 John: 3-4 (NJB)

2 Some of those challenges include: exclusion zones around facilities where terminations of pregnancy occur which, among more legitimate purposes, prevent public prayer and offers of Christian charity to pregnant women and their partners (see, eg, the *Reproductive Health (Access to Terminations) Act 2013* (Tas) s9; *Health Act 1993* (ACT); *Public Health Amendment (Safe Access to Reproductive Health Clinics) Act 2018* (NSW); *Termination of Pregnancy Law Reform Act 2017* (NT); *Public Health and Wellbeing Amendment (Safe Access Zones) Act*

2015 (Vic);*Termination of Pregnancy Act 2018* (Qld)), requirements for medical professionals with a conscientious objection to abortion to provide referrals or directions to pregnant women seeking that procedure (see, eg, *Abortion Law Reform Act 2008* (Vic) s 8, *Termination of Pregnancy Law Reform Act 2017* (NT), *Termination of Pregnancy Act 2018* (Qld),NSW Ministry of Health, Policy Directive: NSW Health Policy Directives And Other Policy Documents, (May 17, 2016), legislation which seeks to override the confidentiality of religious confessions and legislation which leaves unclear the rights of religious persons to provide religious instructions on moral matters such as the meaning of marriage (see Editor, "Complaint against Catholic anti-equality booklet, "Don't Mess with Marriage", to be lodged today" *Tasmanian Times* (Web Page, 28 September 2015)

3   Australian Bureau of Statistics, 2016: Census Religion 2016 Census data reveals 'no religion' is rising fast (Media Release 074/2017, 27 June 2017)

4   A detailed examination of the influence of Christianity is beyond this short paper but good surveys can be found in Roy Williams, *Post God Nation?* (ABC Books, 2015) 1-141; Augusto Zimmermann, *Christian Foundations of the Common Law, Volume I: England* (Connor Court, 2018).

5   Robert S Pasley, "The Position of the Law school in the University" (1966) 51 *Catholic University Law Review* 34, 50-51; Roger Trigg, *Equality, Freedom & Religion* (Oxford University Press, 2012) 27-29.

6   The Christian roots of the duty of care to one's neighbour are referred to directly in the seminal case of *Donoghue v Stevenson* [1932] AC 562; [1932] All ER 1.

7   Williams (n 4) 92.

8   Luke 10:29-37.

9   Alex Deagon, *From Violence to Peace* (Bloomsbury, 2017) 189.

10   Michael Quinlan, "The Law Ethics And Religion" *Parish Connections* (Web Page, April/May 2018)

11   As recognised in international law by Article 18(3) of the *International Covenant on Civil and Political Rights* (ICCPR) to which Australia is a signatory provides that

> [f]reedom to manifest one's religion or beliefs may be subject only to such limitations as are prescribed by law and are necessary to protect public safety, order, health, or morals or the fundamental rights and freedoms of others': *International Covenant on Civil and Political Rights,* opened for signature 16 December 1966, 999 UNTS 171 (entered into force 23 March 1976) art 18(3).

12   Michael Quinlan, "The chimera of freedom of religion in Australia," *News Weekly* (Web Page, 9 February 2019) 14-17.

13   Greg Sheridan, *God is Good For You* (Allen & Unwin, 2018) 172.

14   Andrew Markus, "Mapping Social Cohesion The Scanlon Foundation Surveys 2018" (Report, Faculty of Arts, Monash University) 17 McCrindle, 'Faith, Belief & Churchgoing in Australia' *Social Analysis* (Blog Post, 24 March 2016)

15   Mark 7:6.

16   Francis S Collins, *The Language of God* (Free Press, 2006) 41.

17 *ibid* 40.

18 Roy Williams (n 4) 75.

19 Anthony Percy, *The Theology of the Body made Simple* (Pauline Books and Media, 2005) 12.

20 Percy (n 14).

21 *ibid*; Allan Carlson, "Family And Society The End of Liberalism" *News Weekly* (Web Page, 23 February 2019)

22 Carlson (n 21).

23 Percy (n 14).

24 Carlson (n 21).

25 *ibid.*

26 *ibid.*

27 David Indermaur, "Contemporary Attitudes to the Death Penalty: An Australian Perspective" (2006) 17(3) *Current Issues in Criminal Justice* 444, 446.

28 *Church of the New Faith v Commissioner of Pay-Roll Tax* (Vic) (1983) 154 CLR 120, 136.

29 Candace S Alcorta and Richard Sosis, "Ritual, Emotion and Sacred Symbols. The Evolution of Religion as an Adaptive Complex" (2005) 16(4) *Human Nature* 323, 325.

30 *ibid* 325.

31 *ibid.*

32 *ibid* 348

33 *ibid.*

34 Carlson (n 21).

35 St Justin Martyr, "First Apology' *New Advent"* (Web Page) <http://www.newadvent.org/fathers/0126.htm>; Ephesians 5:19; 1 Corinthians 14:26-40

36 1 Corinthians 1.23-24.

37 Alcorta and Sosis (n 29) 328.

38 *ibid* 340.

39 *ibid* 344.

40 *ibid* 340.

41 St Justin Martyr (n 29); Williams (n 14) 74.

42 Carlson (n 21); Williams (n 4) 80.

43 Williams (n 4) 75.

44 See, eg, Ecclesiasticus 2:1; Luke 9:22-25.

45 Luke 13:2-3.

46 *Catechism of the Catholic Church*, (St Pauls, 1994) [2271]: "Since the first century the Church has affirmed the moral evil of every procured abortion. This teaching has not changed and remains unchangeable. Direct abortion, that is to say, abortion willed either as an end or a means, is gravely contrary to the moral law: "You shall not kill the embryo by abortion and shall not cause the newborn

to perish."; *Didache* 2,2:ÆCh 248,148; cf. *Ep. Bárnabae* 19,5:PG 2 777; *Ad Dognetum* 5,6:PG 2,1173; Tertullian, *Apol* 9:PL 1,319-320.

47 See, eg, Genesis 1:28; Psalm 127:3-5; Psalm 127:3; Proverbs 22:6; John 16:21; Isaiah 54:13; Matthew 18:1-3; James 1:17; Proverbs 17:6; 3 John 1:4; Matthew 18:10; Mark 10:14; Numbers 6:24-26; Jeremiah 29:11; Ephesians 6:4; Psalm 127:1-5.

48 As quoted in: Williams (n 4) 75.

49 Carlson (n 21).

50 *ibid.*

51 Robert Dixon et al, "Research Project on Catholics who have stopped attending mass Final Report" (Conference Paper, Pastoral Projects Office Australian Catholic Bishops Conference, Feb 2007) 3.

52 Ying Chen and Tyler J VanderWeele, "Association of religious Upbringing With Subsequent Health and Well-Being From Adolescence to Young Adulthood: An Outcome-Wide Analysis" (2018) 187(11) *American Journal of Epidemiology* 2363.

53 Paul R Amato, "Marriage, cohabitation and mental health" (2015) 96 *Family Matters* 5-6; Linda J Waite and Maggie Gallagher, *The Case For Marriage* (Broadway Books, 2000) 124-140; American Psychological Association, Kentucky Psychological Association, Ohio Psychological Association, American Psychiatric Association, American Academy of Pediatrics, American Association for Marriage and Family Therapy, Michigan Association for Marriage and Family Therapy, National Association of Social Workers, National Association of Social Workers Tennessee Chapter, National Association of Social Workers Michigan Chapter, National Association of Social Workers Kentucky Chapter, national Association of Social Works Ohio Chapter, American Psychoanalytic Association, American Academy of Family Physicians and American Medical Association, Submission in *Obergefell et al. v Hodges, Director, Ohio Department of Health, et al.*, 6 March 2015, 15; Richard G Wight, Allen J Leblanc and M V Lee Badgett, "Same Sex Legal Marriage and Psychological Well-Being: Findings From The California Health Interview Survey" (2013) 103(2) *American Journal of Public Health* 339, 339.

54 Elizabeth Abbott, *A History of Marriage* (Seven Stories Press, 2015) 171-177; Linda J Waite and Maggie Gallagher, *The Case For Marriage* (Broadway Books, 2000) 124-140; Sherif Girgis, Robert P George and Ryan T Anderson, 'What is Marriage?' (2010) 34 *Harvard Journal of Law and Public Policy*, 257-259; Kristin Anderson Moore, Susan Jekielek and Carol Emig, "Marriage from a Child's Perspective: How does Family Structure Affect Children and What Can We do about It?" (Research Brief, Child Trends, June 2002) 1- 2; Andrew J Cherlin, *The Marriage-Go-Round* (Vintage Books, 2009) 100-101; Stephanie Coontz, *Marriage, a History: How Love* and *Conquered Marriage* (Penguin, 2005) 293; D Paul Sullins, "Emotional Problems among Children with Same-Sex parents: Difference by Definition" (2015) 7(2) *British Journal of Education, Society & Behvaioural Science* 99, 114; The Witherspoon Institute, "Marriage and the Public Good: Ten Principles" (Report, The Witherspoon Institute, August 2008); American College of Paediatricians et al, "Brief of Amici Curiae American

College of Paediatricians, Family Watch International," Loren D. Marks, Mark D. Regnerus and Donald Paul Sullin in Support of Respondents' Submission in *Obergefell et al. v Hodges, Director, Ohio Department of Health, et al.*, 3 April 2013; Deborah Dempsey *"Same-sex parented families in Australia"* (Working Paper No. 18, Australian Institute of Family Studies, December 2013); Mark Regnerus "How different are the adult children of parents who have same-sex relationships? Findings from the New Family Structures Study" (2012) 41 *Social Science Research* 752, 766; D Paul Sullins, "Child Attention-Deficit Hyperactivity Disorder (ADHD) in Same-Sex Parent Families in the United States: Prevalence and Comorbidities" (2015) 6(10) *British Journal of Medicine and Medical Research* 987, 988; Wendy D Manning and Kathleen A Lamb, "Adolescent Well-Being in Cohabiting, Married, and Single-Parent Families" (2003) 65(4) *Journal of Marriage and Family* 876, 890; Wendy D Manning, "Cohabitation and Child Wellbeing" (2015) 25(2) *The Future of Children* 54, 58-59.

55 D R Evans and J Kelly, *Australian Economy and Society 2002: Religion, Morality and Public Policy in Perspective 1984-2002* (Federation Press, 2004) 44.

56 Chen and VanderWeele (n 52) 2355, Hongtu Chen et al, "Religious Participation as a predictor of mental health status and treatment outcomes in older persons" (2007) 22 *International Journal of Geriatric Psychiatry* 144, 150-152; Izet Pajevic, Osman Sinanovic and Mevludin Hasanovic, "Religiosity and Mental Health" (2005) 17(1-2) *Psychiatria Damubina* 84, 86; Nick Spencer et al, "Religion and Well-being: Assessing the evidence" (Report, Theos, 2016) 10, 15.

57 Andrew Newberg and Mark Robert Waldman, *How God Changes Your Brain* (Ballantine Books, 2010) 60.

58 Chen and VenderWeele (n 52) 2357; See also Alcorta and Sosis (n 29) 324; Thomas J Bouchard et al, "Intrinsic and extrinsic religiousness: genetic and environmental influences and personal correlates" (1999) 2 *Twin Research* 88, 97; Alexander Moreira-Almeida, Francisco Lotufo Neto and Harold G Koenig, "Religiousness and mental health: a review" (2006) 28(3) *Rev Bras Psiquiatr* 242, 244-245; Andrew Newberg and Mark Robert Waldman, *Born To Believe* (Free Press, 2006) 127; Justin L Barrett, *Born Believers* (Free Press, 2012), 225, 233-235; Brian J Grim and Melissa E Grim, "The Socio-economic Contribution of Religion to American Society: An Empirical Analysis" (2016) 12(3) *Interdisciplinary Journal of Research on Religion* 1, 3; Greg Walsh, "Same Sex Marriage and Religious Liberty" (2016) 35 *University of Tasmania Law Review* 2, 106.

59 Chen and VenderWeele (n 52) 2355.

60 Newberg and Waldman, *How God Changes Your Brain* above n 55, 61,174, 149; Newberg and Waldman (n 57) 127. One long-term longitudinal US study found that those attending church at least once a month had a thirty to thirty-five per cent reduced risk of dying.

61 Adam Possamai et al, "Muslim Students' Religious and Cultural Experiences in the Micro-publics of University Campuses in NSW, Australia" (2016) 47 *Australian Geographer* 313; Cydney J Van Dyke and Maurice J Elias, 'How forgiveness, purpose and religiosity are related to the mental health and well-being of youth: a review of the literature' (2007) 10(4) *Mental Health, Religion & Culture* 395, 409.

62 Newberg and Waldman (n 54) 140; Van Dyke and Elias (n 50) 410.

63 Chen and VenderWeele (n 52) 2357; See Spencer et al, (n 56) 11.

64 Anthony Lester, *Five Ideas to Fight For* (One World , 2016) 57, John Norberg, Progress (OneWorld, 2016) 188

65 *Catechism of the Catholic Church* (n46) [2270]-[2272]

66 Fr. Donald Kloster, "Traditional Latin Mass National Survey" *Liturgy Guy* (Web Page, 24 February 2019) In a study of 291 women who had terminations in Buffalo in the US in 1993 45% were Catholic and 44% Protestant: Catherine Cozzarelli and Brenda Major, "The Effects of Anti-Abortion Demonstrators and Pro-Choice Escorts on Women's Psychological Responses to Abortion" (1994) 13 *Journal of Social and Clinical Psychology* 4, 404, 409.

67 Kloster ibid.

68 *ibid.*

69 *ibid*

70 *ibid*

71 *Catechism of the Catholic Church* (n 46) [1601].

72 *Catechism of the Catholic Church* (n 46) [2180].

73 Ibid [1457] (references omitted)

74 Kloster (n68)

75 *ibid.*

76 American Samoa, Australia, Cook Islands, Fiji, Guam, Kiribati, Marshall Islands, Micronesia, Northern Mariana Islands, Nauru, New Caledonia, New Zealand, Niue, Palau, Papua New Guinea, Polynesia, Samoa, Solomon Islands, Tokelau, Tonga, Vanuatu, Wallis and Fortuna Islands

77 Center for Applied Research in the Apostolate, "Global Catholicism: Trends & Forecasts" (Report, 4 June 2015) 42

78 Philip Lewis and Richard Abel (eds), *Lawyers in Society* (Beard Books, 2005) 271.

79 R Powell and M Pepper 'Local Churches in Australia: Research Findings From NCLS Research' (NCLS Research, 2016)

80 *ibid.*

81 *ibid.*

82 Center for Applied Research in the Apostolate (n 70) 41.

83 Dixon et al (n 51) 3.

84 *Catechism of the Catholic Church* above (n 46) [1250] (references omitted): The Catholic Church teaches that "[t]he Church and the parents would deny a child the priceless grace of becoming a child of God were they not to confer Baptism shortly after birth."

85 Dixon et al (n 51) 46.

86 *Catechism of the Catholic Church* (n 46) [1307] (references omitted).

87 Alcorta and Sosis (n 29) 325.

88 Australian Bureau of Statistics, '2071.0 Census of Population and Housing:

Notes

reflecting Australia- Stories from the Census, 2016, RELIGION IN AUSTRALIA' (Web Page, 28 June 2017)

89 Mary Eberstadt, *How the West Really Lost God: A New Theory of Secularization* (Templeton, 2014) 165; Alexandra DeSanctis, "The Indefensible Morality of Andrew Cuomo" *National Review* (Web Page. 26 January 2019) Deacon Keith Fournier, 'Nancy Pelosi, Boasting of her Devout Catholic faith, is a Heretic' *Catholic On Line* (Web Page, July 17 2017)

90 Michael Koziol, "Legalise same-sex marriage for the 'common good', says Catholic priest Fran Brennan" *The Sydney Morning Herald* (1 September 2017), Archbishop Anthony Fisher OP "Archbishop Fisher: Does Pope Francis support same-sex marriage?" *Catholic Weekly* (31 August, 2017)

91 Renee Viellaris, "Arrival of Barnaby Joyce and Vikki Campion's baby an unwelcome distraction for Malcolm Turnbull" *The Courier-Mail* (online, 16 April 2018)

92 Royal Commission into Institutional Responses to Child Sexual Abuse, Final Report (Web Page 2019) <https://www.childabuseroyalcommission.gov.au/final-report>.

93 McCrindle, "Faith And Belief in Australia" (Report, May 2017) 35.

94 Markus (n 14) 17, 62.

95 *ibid* 62

96 *ibid* 163-164.

97 Laurence R Iannaccone,"'Why Strict Churches Are Strong" (1994) 99(5) *American Journal of Sociology* 1180-1211.

98 *ibid.*

99 *ibid* 1190,1194,1197,1205.

100 *ibid* 1182.

101 *ibid* 1183.

102 Congregation for Divine Worship to the Presidents of Episcopal Conferences, "*Quattuor Abhinc Annos Indult* for Use of Roman Missal of 1962" (Web Page, 3 October 1984) See also Saint John Paul II, 'Ecclesia Dei' (Web Page, 2 July 1988)

103 Pope Benedict XVI, 'Summorum Pontificum' *Vatican* (Web Page, 17 July 2007)

104 Kloster above (n68)

105 *ibid.*

106 *ibid.*

107 Anon, "The Growth of the Latin Mass" *The Saint's Pub* (Web Page, 7 November 2016) AP, 'The current situation for the TLM in Italy' (Blog Post, 23 February 2010)

108 Collins (n 16) 40.

109 As quoted in Williams (n 4) 75.

CODA

1 Much of this work was subsequently published in Peter Kurti, *The Tyranny of*

Tolerance: Threats to Religious Liberty in Australia, (Connor Court: Redland Bay, QLD, 2017).

2   For a detailed examination of some of these matters, see Greg Lukianoff and Jonathan Haidt, *The Coddling of the American Mind: How Good Intentions and Bad Ideas are Setting up a Generation for Failure*, (Penguin: New York, 2018).

3   Saul D. Kaplan, "Social Sources and Perils of the Trump Presidency", *The American Interest*, (Volume 14, No. 4, 2018).

4   Saul D. Kaplan, as above. See also, Peter Kurti, *Cracking Up? Culture and the Displacement of Virtue*, (Centre for Independent Studies: Sydney NSW, 2019).

www.ingramcontent.com/pod-product-compliance
Lightning Source LLC
Chambersburg PA
CBHW061248220326
41599CB00028B/5567